POVERTY

IN THE SAME SERIES

1. RELIGIOUS SISTERS
2. VOCATION
3. OBEDIENCE
5. CHASTITY

RELIGIOUS LIFE
IV

POVERTY

Being the English Version of
La Pauvreté in *Problèmes de la Religieuse d'aujourd'hui*
Translated by Lancelot C. Sheppard

THE NEWMAN PRESS
WESTMINSTER, MARYLAND

First Published 1954

Printed in *Great Britain by*
Arthurs Press Ltd., Woodchester, Glos.

FOREWORD

As with the other volumes in this series the following pages comprise the papers read at the, by now, regular annual conference held in Paris to consider the needs of the modern French nuns. Despite the apparent limitation of nationality the proceedings of these conferences, made up for the most part of priests, secular and religious, concerned with the direction and support of religious sisters, have been found instructive and useful in translation for English speaking religious. The present essays on Religious Poverty will be found equally applicable, or at least instructive. Only one essay by an eminent French economist has been omitted from the present translation as being of interest more exclusively to France ; this is the first chapter of the third part of the original *La Pauvreté—Notes sur le statut économique des communautés religieuses dans la vie économique de la France contemporaine*, by François Perroux. Some of the papers that appear here in English may at first sight appear to be equally confined to France, as for example Part I chapter 6 by Père Duval, O.P., who begins by declaring that he is writing only of his own country. But a glance at this or any of the other papers that begin on a French theme will show their interest and utility for English speaking sisters. For this reason the volume appears in its entirety with the one exception. The authors themselves have generously co-operated in the translation and have here and there revised or amended a phrase or two. But substantially the papers are as they were read in 1951.

The original volume is entitled *La Pauvreté* in the series *Problèmes de la Religieuse d'aujourd'hui* published by Les Editions du Cerf, Paris, in 1952.

C.P.

Nihil Obstat : Georgius Smith, S.T.D., Ph.D.
Censor Deputatus

Imprimatur : E. Morragh Bernard
Vic. Gen.

Westmonasterii, die 8a Maii, 1954

CONTENTS

PART III : Modern Problems

PREFACE TO THE FRENCH EDITION

The number and difficulty of the problems raised by the vow of poverty for nuns and religious sisters at the present day are increased by the fact that it is more closely connected than the two other vows with conditions of time and social class.

Solution of these problems is not to be found, as with the vow of obedience for example,[1] by merely returning to the quickening spirit of the Gospel ever threatened with suffocation under the weight of the letter. Nor is it to be found merely by studying those changes in customs and psychology which have made the pedagogical practice of last century obsolete and urge us to a judicious effort of adaptation in order to preserve the spiritual fertility of the vows and evangelical virtues.

The vow of poverty raises all these problems, and aggravates them with a further difficulty : however poor we may desire to be we cannot entirely disregard our bodies and the need of food, clothing and shelter. The vow of poverty has not the absolute character of the vow of chastity.[2] It must be accommodated to a minimum of material possessions ; it is its function to gauge their use according to country, period and economic and financial custom.

The vast implications of the economic system in the world to-day, and the speed with which it appears to be evolving— whatever the future of Marxism—beyond capitalism, sets comparatively new and serious problems for the practice of the vow of poverty.

For this reason the chapters in this book have not been confined to a mere reminder of the teaching on religious poverty by holy Scripture, Church history, theology, canon law and psychology. The economic and financial factor had also to be given a place. After recalling its importance in secular life— from the differing viewpoints of an economist and a working

[1] Cf. the last volume published in this series : *Obedience*.

[2] The next volume in this series will deal with the vow of chastity.

class Catholic actionist—an endeavour is made to state its precise role in the religious life itself, bearing in mind especially the recent Apostolic constitution *Sponsa Christi* by which work is imposed on contemplatives as an obligation in conscience.

Consequently it seemed profitable to put forward suggestions on accountancy[1] and the scientific organization of work. In spite of the material nature of these methods they will prove useful to superiors concerned for an improved return not only financial but spiritual, of the work and activities of their religious. In this way they will be able more accurately to adapt the means to the end of the religious life and prove themselves faithful to the spirit of their founders. Concern for such material details is to be found in fact in all the great poor of Christ, as is shown for example in this injunction of St Teresa of Avila on the subject of the visitation of convents : 'Examine the work carried out, calculate what each nun has earned by the work of her hands ; there is a double advantage in this : it is an encouragement and a token of gratitude to those who have done much, and it provokes emulation in the other monasteries for, in addition to the material benefit, in every way there is great advantage in paying particular attention to the work of the nuns'.

To make use of the world and to be as if not using it is an invitation to detachment but not to anarchy or an ignoring of the laws and human requirements of work. If these are recognized and adapted to the religious state they will enable nuns and religious sisters to draw from the vow of poverty its whole potential of liberation from the servitude of the world, its whole strength of evangelical witness in the face of Mammon and its power to anticipate eternal blessedness.

ALBERT PLÉ, O.P.

---

[1] This chapter has been omitted from the English version as the methods and conditions envisaged appeared to be peculiarly French in setting.—*Editor*.

CHRIST'S CALL TO POVERTY

By Louis Bouyer, Cong. Orat.

Christ's call to poverty contains an obvious element of paradox. The Beatitudes, which form the beginning of the Sermon on the Mount, run systematically counter to what is generally considered a self-evident truth : instead of 'Blessed are the rich, unhappy the poor,' Christ lays down 'Blessed are the poor, unhappy the rich'. This paradox is intended to strike us forcibly, to stir up a wholesome reaction, to awaken us from the unhealthy dream that we were mistaking for reality. Yet, like all paradoxes, there is a danger of its being misunderstood ; its precise application must be grasped, for if it is not the most accurate of explanations will achieve no more than the foundation of a system on an inadmissible absurdity or the voiding of the Christian message of its fundamentally incisive character. In this case, as always in exegesis, logical reasoning, since it is abstract, helps us but little and historical research alone will throw some light on the complex reality of our problem. Otherwise we shall fall into what has been called Ebionism, namely an uncompromising defence of poverty leading inevitably to the condemnation both of all God's creation and of human achievement, or else the Gospel message will be watered down to such an extent that there remains only a 'spiritualized' poverty with nothing poor about it. In the course of this study it will emerge clearly enough how the first error, which is the most ancient, can and must be avoided but it will be useful to begin by emphasizing the importance of a relentless destruction of the second for there is none more likely utterly to vitiate religious life. It has to be acknowledged, too, that the harshest, and frequently justified, criticisms of this life by our contemporaries are in reference to poverty as they see it practised by us.

I

The Gospel paradox can be understood only historically, but that does not mean that it should be interpreted as if history would enable us so to enlarge the eye of the needle and so to shrink the camel that no paradox at all remains. The contrary, indeed, is true. In the Jewish context and the general religious setting of Israel adopted by our Lord at the beginning of the Sermon on the Mount his statement at the outset had a more scandalous ring about it than it has for us. And that was true not merely in connexion with a degenerate religion, if indeed Judaism at the time of Christ was in that state, as we seem on occasion somewhat too ready to assert, but also if it is confronted with the firmest, deep-rooted tenets of the religion of Israel. We should first recall the Exodus, that important memory which furnished the principal reason for Jewish hope and its significance from our point of view. It meant that God had given proof of his loving kindness towards his people by snatching them from slavery in which they were stripped of everything and by leading them to the promised land, that is to the land of plenty, the land flowing with milk and honey which was given to them in ownership.

All the promises, forming the counterpart of the ten Commandments, bore a similar meaning. They amounted to the same thing as the blessings of the patriarchs which speak always in terms of fruitful herds, fat pastures, fertile fields : material property, the security attaching to the fruitful, guaranteed, firm possession of all earthly goods represented for ancient Israel the sign of God's blessing, if indeed it was not its substance.

This characteristic note, which certainly goes back to the very beginnings, was to endure. The eschatological ideal of the promised restoration after the defeat and exile of Israel was depicted by Ezechiel in the shape of a definitive sharing out, among the reconstituted tribes, of a Palestine miraculously enriched in some sort by Yahweh's tangible presence. Put in simpler terms, was not the devout Israelite's ideal of that blessed peace for which he longed after all his tribulations, just to sit quietly beneath his fig tree in his own garden, gathering the plentiful crops of his fields and surrounded by his wife and numerous offspring ? That is what is depicted by Psalm 127 : 'Blessed are they that fear the Lord . . . Thy wife as a fruitful vine, on the sides of thy house, thy children as live plants, round about thy table . . .' It is a constantly recurring theme in the Psalter and, indeed, in the whole Bible. It is worth pointing out that the only instance of contrary teaching believed to occur in a Psalm turns out to be a mistranslation. The end of Psalm 143 has been seen as a contrast between the mistaken happiness of those for whom it means riches and permanent possession and that completely spiritual happiness of the people whose God is Yahweh. But the real meaning of the text, on the contrary, is that the happiness of fidelity to Yahweh is precisely the happiness that comes from the promise of that material security which he procures for his people.

That is true of the Old Testament. But notice what point is given to the paradox in the Gospel. In the New Testament, as in the last of the prophets, like Ezechiel for example, if a new trend seems to be introduced the underlying principle of ancient Semitic religious thought is by no means obscured. On the contrary, it may be asserted that the great prophets, followed by the Christian apocalypse, bring it out still more clearly. The hope of the New Testament is the expectation of the resurrection of the body in a world transformed, henceforth in consonance with man's needs and capable of procuring for him even a material enjoyment on a scale and to a degree of enduring security far surpassing Israel's ancient hopes. Periodically, of course, the Church was compelled to react against the tendency to an excessive materialization of this picture, as in the case of the Millenarians, but she reacted no less against the tendency to an exaggerated spiritualization of it, even when one of the greatest spiritual leaders like Origen was concerned.

Yet if this note, which can be heard at the beginning of biblical revelation, echoes with increasing clarity and undiminished quality until the end, another also was soon to be heard which finally became the dominant.

II

What happened when the establishment of the people in Palestine was eventually completed and instead of nomads with neither hearth nor abode they had achieved a more comfortable position as settled tillers of the earth in the land promised them of old which they now held in undisputed possession ? It began to appear that the riches of this land, the riches of creation which the work of man, blessed by God, was to cause to increase and multiply, were under the control of strange intermediaries. The earth and its life-giving riches seemed to Israel, once they were established there, to belong to gods, to Baalim to whom they must devote themselves if they were to obtain the fruits of the earth. Chananite agricultural methods appeared to be closely linked with the practice of idolatry towards the powers controlling the crops. In fact, Israel gathered in the fruits of its labour, in this land which was indeed Yahweh's, only by adoring 'on every high hill and under every green tree', or, in other words, by transferring to a series of golden calves the worship which it should have given to Yahweh.

That does not mean that this extraordinary experience lessened in any wise the strong convictions already referred to : Yahweh, the creator of all good things, remained the one who shared them out as he liked and as a token, even, of his favour. Nevertheless, though Israel began to see this as a truth, perhaps as the fundamental truth, it did not take it for the whole of the truth. In other words although the fruits of the earth created by Yahweh were good, even very good, that did not prevent events being so arranged that in practice these fruits became a trap in the hands of Yahweh's enemies which operated for their sole benefit. Consequently the better these fruits the greater the essential sacredness of the reward in obtaining them and, also, under these conditions, the greater the tragedy, the more inescapable the misapprehension which, founded on the very goodness shown by Yahweh, only worked as a subtle means of turning away from him those who were absorbed by the mirage of material greed. Here was the cause of the prophets' initial revulsion : Israel, established in the land where flowed milk and honey, instead of giving thanks to

Yahweh seized the opportunity of demonstrating an infidelity which seemed almost endemic. Faithful in the destitution of the exodus and the pilgrimage through the desert, regularly it became unfaithful—experience was there to prove it—once plenty was acquired. Osee's line of reasoning appears as the direct conclusion of this assertion :

'(Israel said) : "I will go after my lovers, that give me my bread, and my water, my wool, and my flax, my oil, and my drink". Wherefore behold I will hedge up thy way with thorns, and I will stop it up with a wall, and she shall not find her paths. And she shall follow after her lovers, and shall not overtake them : and she shall seek them and shall not find them : and she shall say : "I will go, and return to my first husband, because it was better with me then than now". And she did not know that I gave her corn and wine, and oil, and multiplied her silver, and gold, which they have used in the service of Baal. Therefore will I return, and take away my corn in its season, and my wine in its season . . . And I will destroy her vines and her fig trees, of which she said : "These are my rewards, which my lovers have given me" : and I will make her as a forest, and the beasts of the field shall devour her . . . Therefore, behold I will allure her, and will lead her into the wilderness : and I will speak to her heart. And I will give her vine-dressers out of the same place, and the valley of Achor for an opening of hope : and she shall sing there according to the days of her youth, and according to the days of her coming up out of the land of Egypt. And it shall be in that day, saith the Lord, that she shall call me : "My husband," and she shall call me no more "Baali". And I will take away the names of Baalim out of her mouth, and she shall no more remember their name.' (*Osee* 2, 5-17)

In this way the idea is introduced that deprivation of goods, which are still recognized as gifts of God, can be the necessary means to the rediscovery of God. Without this deprivation, which is to a certain extent remedial, it seems that man is irresistibly drawn to the adoration of God's gifts, the natural powers of life and nature, in the place of their giver.

In these early origins of a religious eulogy of poverty it is important to notice what precisely is commended. *It is*

dependence on God. When man sees his earthly goods increase
and become firmly established it is in them and in their natural
origins that he puts his confidence. At once the fruits of the
earth, or what enables him to obtain them, act as a screen in
front of the one true God and tend to occupy his place.

Thus it will be understood that, in the Old Testament, at
the outset it was not the poor who were blessed but the rich
who were cursed (which is the opposite order of the beatitudes).
In Isaias formal condemnation of riches goes hand in hand
with denunciation of the chosen people's entirely earthly,
fleshly hope which they had substituted for faith in God. The
prophet sees it as an ineluctable sequence of events : Israel
seeks to establish itself, to be certain of a place in the sun and
promptly God is forgotten, it is forgotten that he is the Almighty
and the Master : no longer is reliance placed on him, nor is
there any wish to depend on him ; whence, finally, arises
injustice towards men and idolatry in place of God's service.

'Woe to you that join house to house, and lay field to field,
even to the end of the place : shall you alone dwell in the midst
of the earth ? . . . And the work of the Lord you regard not,
nor do you consider the works of his hands . . . Woe to you that
call evil good, and good evil : that put darkness for light and
light for darkness : that put bitter for sweet, and sweet for
bitter. Woe to you that are wise in your own eyes, and prudent
in your own conceits . . . that justify the wicked for gifts, and
take away the justice of the just from him. Therefore as the
tongue of the fire devoureth the stubble, and the heat of the
flame consumeth it : so shall their root be as ashes, and their
bud shall go up as dust : for they have cast away the law of the
Lord of hosts, and have blasphemed the word of the holy one
of Israel.' (*Isaias* 5, 8 et seq.)

For Isaias, the man accursed of God is typified by the upstart
Sobnah who built for his own use not only extremely luxurious
houses but also a princely tomb. Yet neither were to be his
resting place and his corpse was thrown upon a dung heap
after all these properties on which he had set his heart were
taken from him.

It is with Jeremias, however, that the complementary,
opposite notion takes shape : the man who is destitute, the

outlaw, is the blessed one of God. For divine inspiration obliged Jeremias to live in this state among his people even before the time of plunder and ruin. And when his destitution had reached its extreme point he discovered that God was still with him and that this presence was worth all the earthly goods that it had caused him to lose. Ezechiel was to give this teaching its full significance : he showed the divine presence abandoning the sanctuary in Jerusalem, which had been profaned by idolatry, and invisibly accompanying into exile the people deprived of their dwellings, their goods and even their Temple.

Towards the end of the exile Israel came to recognize the type of their new-found hope in the servant of Yahweh whose canticles are scattered throughout the second part of the book of Isaias. It is striking that this ideal servant was poor and probably suffering from disease, misunderstood into the bargain and unjustly punished just like Job. Consequently, it is not to be wondered at that so many of the later Psalms seem to equate the poor with the righteous man and to see the cause of the poor as identical with Yahweh's.

Duguet, a French spiritual writer of the end of the seventeenth century, following the same line of thought as St Augustine in his *Enarrationes in Psalmos*, has summed up the spiritual teaching of these *anawin* so admirably that his own words are well worth reproducing here.

'Princes have been held to scorn and the poor man has been enlightened. This poor man is a beggar who ascribes nothing to his own efforts and awaits all from the mercy of God, who daily clamours at his master's door, who knocks that it may be opened to him, who is naked and shivering with cold, who asks for clothing, who keeps his eyes cast down to the ground, who beats his breast. It is this beggar, this poor man, this humble heart that God sustains with his powerful help. This poor man is many families, a whole host of peoples, a multitude of churches. He is also one only Church, one people, one family. What magnificent teaching is hidden beneath these types, and what depths! Indeed it is a great mystery that the whole Church is but a poor man, that all the saints together make up but one poor man whose prayer alone is heard.'[1]

[1] *Traité sur la prière publique*, 7th ed., Paris, 1713. Pp. 142 *et seq.*

III

At the coming of the Gospel Israel, aware since the exile that without bitter disappointment it could no longer base its hopes on this earth, knew already that the kingdom of God is not 'of this world', and does not belong to the historical order, to the present aeon. With the Apocalypse the best of God's people expect the 'consolation of Israel' of the coming aeon, of the divine Kingdom which will come down from on high with the Son of Man appearing on the clouds of heaven.

The old earth-bound messianism was by no means entirely eradicated. The Psalmists, and not a few Jews with them, looked forward to another David as Messias who here on earth would crush the earthly forces which were oppressing Israel and bring to pass the almost entirely material hope of a kingdom of God on earth in a Palestine physically made free. Jesus refused to be hailed as this Messias, but he gave himself out to be the supernatural Son of man of the Apocalypse, though not without merging the description with the suffering servant of the second part of Isaias. 'The Son of man came not to be served but to serve and to give his life as a ransom for many.' Thus there could be no possibility of mistake concerning the entirely supernatural, transcendent character of his glory as the Son of man, and it was by way of the Cross that he was to enter into it.

His call to poverty is to be understood in the light of this messianic consciousness as it was interpreted by all his acts. Like John the Baptist he saw the axe already laid to the root of the tree, that is the 'world', the present aeon already brought to nought. To go forward on the way to the heavenly aeon, the coming aeon, means going with him to the cross, to his cross. It means the deliberate giving up of all possessions which make a man fixed and secured in *this* world. It means so far as possible, making oneself able to confront this same world without a heart divided, without claiming to be a follower of the Master in whom the kingdom comes while giving allegiance to the prince of this world. It means, especially, freedom, but freedom to welcome the King and the Kingdom, and by the same token freedom for the struggle against the enemy.

All that the enemy has and now uses to bind us in chains still belongs to the King of the world to come. He will give it back to us, increased a hundredfold, but not unless we have first given it up for his sake. The cross, the cross freely accepted for his sake, in union with him, is the sure way to the resurrection, to the eternal Kingdom, but it is the only way. 'For wide is the gate, and broad is the way that leadeth to destruction, and many there are who go in thereat. How narrow is the gate and strait is the way that leadeth to life : and few there are who find it !'

PART ONE

History of Religious Poverty

CHAPTER I

EVANGELICAL POVERTY IN PRIMITIVE MONASTICISM

By M. OLPHE-GAILLARD, S.J.

I

Two New Testament themes predominate in the history of poverty in primitive monasticism : Christ's invitation to the rich young man (*Matthew* 19, 21 ; *Luke* 18, 22), and the fraternal community of the Church in its beginnings (*Acts* 2, 44 and 4, 32-35).

The invitation to the rich young man is no chance isolated episode in the Gospel. Although it was addressed to a specific person it recalls and emphasizes the great rule of self-denial which is required of all who would be followers of Christ. It adds to his other recommendations the suggestion of a counsel which, taken literally, is not of universal application : 'If thou wilt be perfect, go sell what thou hast, and give to the poor . . .'

This act of effective and total renunciation, in obedience to a general precept but in consequence of a special invitation, earned for the first generation of monks the generic name of 'renouncers', *apotactites*. This name, which is encountered as early as the fourth century, is an express allusion to *Luke* 14, 33 : 'Every one of you that doth not renounce (*apotassetai*) all that he possesseth, cannot be my disciple'. To be effective the invitation to the rich young man requires more than a mere interior disposition. By a real separation from the world it designates the engagement of a whole life : 'Come, follow me'.

When this invitation resounded in Antony's ears in his village church in Egypt it turned his whole life upside down to such an extent that there and then he made up his mind to start on the adventure that was to make him into the father of monasticism in his country.[1] The form of asceticism which he began was characterized primarily by the distribution of his goods to the poor. This unequivocal answer to Christ's invitation distinguishes him from those ascetics before him whose renunciation was confined to virginity or continence as its sole specific element. Yet, before Antony's appearance, the Gospel counsel was not neglected. The documents which describe the life of the ascetics in connexion with the Christian communities in which they dwelt either in their families or in still loosely organized groups shows us their ideal as abstinence from sexual relationship joined to a certain poverty; but there is nothing to lead us to suppose that they had made a public and complete renunciation of their hereditary possessions.[2]

Christ's example and teaching were too categoric for fervent Christians to evade his counsels endowing detachment and fraternal charity with a reciprocal value as a means of perfection. The primitive community, as we shall see, was to pass on this ideal in a very pure form, and the growing Church looked back to it somewhat wistfully.

The missionaries whom the Didache introduces to us are apostles and itinerant prophets, professing poverty and refusing any reward for their services save their keep.[3]

The second century apologists contrast especially the depravity of the pagans with the virginity of the Christian ascetics. Although St Justin mentions the custom, which still prevailed in his time, of the faithful possessing all things in common and helping the needy, his words show us clearly that this renunciation was merely relative since the individual kept the social position that he occupied beforehand.

The African Church could boast of its many virgins. St Cyprian considered them 'the choicest part of Christ's flock'.[4] The counsels which he lavishes on them bring out the advantages of poverty as the logical consequence of renunciation

---

[1] The *Vita Antonii* is to be found in Migne *P.G.*, 26, 835 *et seq.*

[2] Cf. F. Martinez, *L'Ascétisme chrétien pendant les trois premiers siècles de l'Eglise*, Paris 1933, *passim.*

[3] *Didache*, 11, 6.

[4] *I Apol.*, 14, 2.

of the world. Not merely does it avert temptation and scandal
but gives sanction to contempt of the ostentation and pleasures
incompatible with the pursuit of divine good. St Cyprian is
speaking to virgins who have kept their position in the world ;
he enjoins on them a proper use of wealth rather than its
complete abandonment. He writes to them : 'Let the poor
think you rich, let the needy think you wealthy ; lend to God
of your patrimony ; give to Christ wherewith to eat'.[1]

Clement of Alexandria and Origen reserve a special place to
poverty among the 'Gnostic' virtues. Their preaching was
addressed to a mixed audience which did not require special
teaching on this point. But they did not forbear to point out
that the perfect Christian cannot entirely set aside the Gospel
counsel. Origen reminds priests of it especially, and recommends
it to them in view of their ideal of holiness and their ministry.[2]

Neither of the two Alexandrians alludes to an absolute
renunciation as an imperative obligation for one category of
Christians. Clement emphasizes the necessity of interior
detachment. His teaching on this point portrays much prudence
and common-sense. Just once, in passing, he contemplates the
possibility of an effective renunciation of wealth ;[3] generally
he merely preaches contempt of earthly goods. Origen discloses
that the practice of actual renunciation was not unknown in
Alexandria,[4] but the absence of monasteries prevented the
practice becoming general. In any case it seems to have been
by no means a regular custom. Nevertheless certain disadvantages of poverty alienated from its purpose were already being
made clear. Through Origen we have knowledge of accusations
of idleness and laziness against certain monks for an improper
use of begging.[5]

The two *Epistolae ad Virgines*, wrongly attributed to St
Clement, portray the state of asceticism as it was practised,
probably in Syria, in the third century. They give the impression
that the improvised methods of earlier days could not endure ;

[1] *De hab. Virg.*, XI, *P.L.*, 4, 169.
[2] Cf. F. Martinez *op. cit.*, p. 158.
[3] *Str.*, 4, 4. *P.G.*, 8, 1229.
[4] *Hom.* XVII, *in Jes. Nav. P.G.*, 11, 152.
[5] *Hom.* III, in Ex., *P.G.*, 9, 30.

the need for regulation was beginning to emerge. By that time virginity was already a recognized state of life : it enjoyed, in some sort, an established position, but abuses were severely condemned. Poverty, as it is advocated in the *Letters*, seems to be based on philosophical grounds rather than fidelity to the Christ of the Gospels : 'We consider that it is better to hate the things of this world which do not endure and are prone to corruption and to love the others which are incorruptible'.[1] That is still some way from the 'Come, follow me' which swept Antony off into the desert.

The history of monastic poverty begins to show real progress on the day when the recently orphaned young Egyptian gave up the 'three hundred measures of very fertile and pleasant land' inherited from his ancestors, sold all his furniture and gave the price to the poor save for a portion which he at first kept for his sister and then distributed like the rest.[2] Or rather it should be stated that the progress was effective when Antony's gesture found numerous imitators who became his disciples. Not all gave up such considerable fortunes, many were poor, illiterate peasants, possibly without resources. Yet there were some whose abandonment of property was impressive. Arsenius, who held a position of importance in the world, has remained famous for having scorned the ostentation of his palace and for giving up his thousand slaves and the costly carpets of his apartments.[3]

According to Cassian[4] renunciation of all the goods and riches of this world is the first step in desert spirituality, indispensable and allowing of no reserve. Woe to the unfaithful aspirant who did not give all : 'A certain monk had renounced the world, he had distributed his goods to the poor but had kept some money for himself. He came to Antony who, on discovering the hidden reserve, said to him : "Go into the town, buy meat, cut it up into small pieces and set it out on your naked body". The brother carried out his order and the birds and dogs to obtain the meat tore his limbs with beaks

---

[1] Quoted by F. Martinez, *op. cit.*, p. 181.
[2] *Vita*, c. 1 and 2.
[3] *Apoph.*, n. 36, *P.G.*, 65, 104.
[4] *Conferences* (Col.), 3, 6 : *P.L.*, 49, 564.

and teeth and claws. When he returned to Antony and showed him his torn wounded body the saint said : "Those who give up the world and keep back money are thus torn by devils".[1]

Antony himself had experienced the bitterness of such a renunciation and overcome the temptations that it involved. The first struggle that he had to undergo in the desert had brought him to grips with the memory of the goods that he had given up.[2] Vivid mental pictures, inciting him to covetousness, beset him for some time. One day he noticed in his path a large platter of silver which disappeared in a cloud of smoke when he recognized it for a work of the devil. 'Keep your money,' he shouted scornfully, 'and may it perish with you'.[3] On another occasion he was bemused by the sight of a great heap of gold. Coming to himself Antony stepped over it 'as if he were walking over a furnace' and ran off in haste. 'How often has the devil shown me gold so that I should touch it and look at it,' he exclaimed. 'But instead of that I sang psalms and treated him with scorn.'[4]

External poverty formed part of the ordinary circumstances of a monk's life in the desert. It was related of Arsenius that his clothes, after his conversion, were as poor as they had been gorgeous when he was in the world.[5] Antony's last words testify to his fidelity to the act of renunciation made when he was twenty. His entire clothing consisted of two tunics and a worn out cloak. He bequeathed one of these tunics and the cloak to the bishop Athanasius who had given him the latter ; the other tunic he left to the bishop Serapion.[6]

The furniture of these holy men was rudimentary : a rush mat with a small pillow made of reeds as a support for the head during sleep and as a stool by day.[7] In connexion with their daily fare and crockery the meal described by Cassian occurs at once to the mind : 'But on that day the aged and holy Serenus had treated himself to a somewhat choicer pickle

[1] Rufinus, 67, 68, *P.L.*, 73, 772 ; *P.G.*, 65, 81, n. 20.
[2] *Vita*, c. 3.
[3] *Ibid.*, c. 6.
[4] *Ibid.*, c. 13.
[5] *Apoph.*, n. 4, *P.G.*, 65, 88.
[6] *Vita*, c. 32.
[7] *Col.*, 1, c. 23, cf. J. and H. Bremond, *Les Pères du Dèsert*, c. V and VI.

than usual, seasoned with a little more oil, three olives cooked in salt and a few boiled chick-peas'.[1]

Evangelical poverty as a means of perfection ('if thou wilt be perfect') although expressed in a public act of renunciation loses thereby none of its fundamentally spiritual character. The spirit by which it is animated endows the act, which is given material expression by distributing goods to the poor, with a power of detachment far different from that enjoined by the Stoics. Fr André Bremond once sketched a striking parallel between the monk and the pagan philosopher, the first won by the love of Christ, the other disillusioned by the world and life.[2] 'Become a sphere rounded and at rest,' says Marcus Aurelius, showing resentment for the disappointments of a life of which he has grown weary.[3] His seeming humility, patience, indifference and piety is in his case entirely a matter of restraint, more or less an exhibitionist attitude. The cynic's threadbare cloak has nothing in common with Arsenius's or Antony's worn out one. These monks did not leave the world under an impulse of despair. In their case everything bears witness to a good-natured and attractive optimism. Their purpose has none of the harsh inflexibility of the grave and serious-minded Stoics ; their equanimity comes from their spirit of faith, their charitable concern for their neighbour, their spiritual joy which in their prayer, prudence and humility, knows no bounds.

The spiritual joy with which the poverty of the desert is resplendent is not yet endowed perhaps with the irrepressible and whimsical character that it had in St Francis, but from the very first sentences addressed by Antony to his monks it is well in evidence : 'We have fought on earth but we shall not inherit it ; we shall inherit heaven and having left this mortal body we shall put it on again clothed in immortality . . . Let no one among you imagine that he has left much by leaving all that he possessed. For if the whole earth compared with the vast expanse of the heavens appears as a mere dot even if we

---

[1] *Col.*, 8, c. 1.

[2] *Le Moine et le stoicien* in *Revue d'Ascétique et de Mystique*, 1927, pp. 26-40.

[3] *The Meditations of the Emperor Marcus Antoninus*, ed. with trans. and commentary by A. S. L. Farquharson. Vol. I. p. 161 (Oxford, 1944).

had possessed it all and given it up what should we have done
to merit obtaining the kingdom of heaven ?'[1]

Spiritual joy made radiant by the hope of heaven is the
incentive to fidelity, the stimulus of constant endeavour. It
also accounts for the heart's aversion to the goods of this earth
which is one of the fruits of conversion to the 'perfect life'.
No need to seek elsewhere the origin of the equanimity of these
monks in the face of the discomforts of this life. A thief breaks
into their cells and they are full of forbearance towards him
for giving them the opportunity to merit the kingdom of
heaven.[2]

The two motives which perhaps govern their complete
improvidence about the future are their trust in divine
Providence and their love of work. These monks are no beggars.
For one Arsenius, who takes the opportunity of humbling himself
by accepting an alms given for the love of God,[3] we can find
a great number who refuse the money offered to them.[4] To a
disciple who desired to keep for himself two crowns out of the
money earned by his work one of them made answer : 'Is
your hope based only on these two crowns which you might
lose ; doesn't God take care of you ? Put your trust in him and
he will not forsake you.'[5]

Rightly or wrongly certain monks were blamed for making
their poverty an excuse for living on alms in idleness.[6] That
is a reproach which the true spirit of the monks of the Desert
runs no risk of incurring. Idleness was entirely foreign to their
whole existence as the following scene (an excerpt from M.
Draguet's book) well shows ; its picturesque character is no
bar to its accuracy. 'If we would keep to the truth we must
take care not to portray our monks kneeling lost in prayer,
their arms held crosswise and their eyes lifted to heaven, on
the excuse that they were great contemplatives—which in fact
they were. They should be depicted seated busy in their cells,

[1] *Vita*, cap. 8.

[2] *Vitae Patrum*, nn. 73, 74 ; *P.L.* 73, 773.

[3] *Apoph.*, n. 20 ; *P.G.* 65, 92.

[4] *P.L.* 73, 871 and 891 ; cf. J. and H. Bremond, *op. cit.*, pp. 138 *et seq.*

[5] *P.L.* 73, 892.

[6] Cf. Julian the Apostate, *Oratio* VII quoted in *Dictionnaire d'Archéologie
chrétienne et de Liturgie*. (Hereinafter referred to as DACL) I, col. 2607.

a box of rushes or palm leaves by their side, plaiting their rough material and sewing it in concentric circles to make baskets or weaving it to form rush mats ; in a corner the hermit's disciple was set to steep the rushes in an earthenware pot ; in another corner jumbled together stood their domestic pots and pans ; lastly, if we could use the convenient device of the ancient portrait engravers, on a scroll issuing from the monk's mouth would appear some verse of the Psalms, for instance "O God come to my assistance", for while they were at work the recitation of Scripture raised up their souls to God.'[1]

The place occupied by manual labour in desert asceticism is considerable. It is regarded as a weapon to overcome sloth and to ward off temptations of the flesh. It appears as a guarantee of freedom. Cassian, who is not without humour, shows that monks are freer than kings : 'for the latter,' he says, 'live on alms whereas the monk provides for himself'.[2] Agatho's gesture in refusing the coins offered to him must have been imitated very frequently by his followers who could have answered as he did : 'The work of my hands is sufficient to feed me'.[3]

All idea of profit was foreign to this work. Cassian maintains that the Egyptian solitaries chose for preference a barren soil in order to avoid the temptation of making an unnecessary profit. From other sources we learn of the abbot Paul's great love of keeping to his cell : he would not allow his work to furnish him with an excuse for going out. Consequently he reduced his diet to a minimum so that he could provide for his needs with unremunerative work ; he continually made and unmade the same rush mat and so obviated having to move about.[4]

Manual labour and poverty thus went hand in hand, the one sustaining the other as a means of spiritual perfection which includes detachment as well as personal effort.

The economic problem remained nonetheless a stumbling block for these monks as long as social life was not so organized that it fostered their renunciation. St Antony and his disciples

[1] R. Draguet, Les Pères du Désert, p. XXXVIII.
[2] Col. 24, 12 ; cf. Dictionnaire de Spiritualité, II, 251.
[3] P.L. 73, 871.
[4] P.L. 73, 773, n. 73.

appear to us to have been tolerably nomadic. They possessed neither tools nor a plot of ground to cultivate. How, in practice, could their work help them to feed themselves ? It seems that they hired themselves out at harvest or sowing time, earned a little money and then went back to their solitude.[1] Later on, when the hermits lived more closely together and formed colonies around the cell of the 'senior' they replenished their stores on the occasion of the Sunday meeting for worship. There was a kind of bursary from which provisions for the week were distributed to the hermits scattered in the desert or on the mountain. That was the situation encountered by Pachomius in the Upper Thebaid when he became a hermit under the direction of the aged Palaemon.[2]

Christ's advice to the rich young man, therefore, did not remain unanswered. The eremiticism which expanded so rapidly and in so short a time is a consequence of the Gospel of which the Church may well be proud. Cenobiticism, which followed, by no means exhausted the movement set on foot by a renunciation in accordance with the Gospel summons. Monks and religious of all observances were afterwards to take their inspiration from the incident which made Antony the Father of monks. The obligation they contracted was their personal response to the 'Come, follow me' which is the justification for the renunciation of their temporal inheritance.

A further stage began, however, a decisive stage, initiated under the inspiration of St Pachomius. It was an organization on a strictly community basis which, by achieving a stable solution of the economic problem, was to enable the ideal of the counsel given by Jesus to the young man in search of perfection to become more widespread and to be carried out more completely. Cenobiticism was soon to open before its followers still newer perspectives. Without eclipsing the initial gesture of a personal renunciation it was to seek in poverty a virtue appertaining to the community and no longer a merely individual one. A nostalgic memory of the Church of Jerusalem has ever been a characteristic of fervent Christians. Antony was turning over his ideas on the subject as he wended

---

[1] DACL, art. *Cénobitisme*, col. 3087.

[2] Cf. Mgr Ladeuze, *Étude sur le cénobitisme pakhomien*, pp. 156 and 162.

his way to the village church on the very day when Christ's
summons was made clear to him.[1] Cassian has handed down to
us the echo of a tradition according to which the honour of
instituting monasticism is to be ascribed to certain fervent
christians who had remained faithful to the customs mentioned
in the Acts.[2]

In any case cenobiticism was ever afterwards to exemplify
remembrance of the Church of the apostles at Jerusalem. In
this sense it was the inauguration of an early form of 'apostolic
life'.

II

In reality St Basil was the first to model himself explicitly
and unswervingly on the primitive ideal, though it cannot be
denied that this ideal is more or less consciously implied by
the *Vita communis* which was the purpose of the Pachomian
foundation.

K. Heussi wrongly considered this foundation to be a
brilliant achievement of economic organisation and nothing
more.[3] Such a view is a perversion of the contribution made
to the common life by the rules of St Pachomius. In them the
economic aspect is, in fact, quite secondary and the concern
for poverty appears so far subordinated to obedience that the
word is not even mentioned in the legislation emanating from
Tabennesi. The prescriptions concerning it derive from the
necessity of establishing uniformity of system to ensure the
stability of common life. The genius of Pachomius is to be
seen in the wall encircling the cells, already grouped round the
church, and in the spiritual father, though as yet a hierarchical
organisation was lacking. Henceforward everything in the
cenobitic community was under the superior's control. This
novel conception of monastic life is primarily a reaction against
the more or less anarchic vagaries to be found among the
hermits. Poverty was stamped with the by no means novel
but strongly emphasized characteristic of dependence.[4]

[1] *Vita*, cap. 1.
[2] *Der Ursprung des Mönchtums*. 1936, pp. 126-8.
[3] *Ibid.*
[4] Cf. H. Bacht, *L'importance de l'idéal monastique chez saint Pacôme pour
l'histoire du monachisme chrétien*, in *Revue d'Ascétique et de Mystique*, 1950,
pp. 308-27.

The Coptic *Vita* informs us that Pachomius did not at the beginning devise the rigid discipline of poverty which he finally imposed on his followers. A first essay, somewhat wider in scope on this point, met with failure : 'When he saw that the brethren were forming a group round him he gave them the following rule : each should maintain himself and provide for his own needs, but deliver up to Pachomius a share equal to their own for all that concerned material needs . . . For they ate in common.' And the author of the *Vita* adds : 'And that was the way in which he acted because he saw that they were not yet ready to bind themselves mutually in a perfect community after the pattern of what is written in the Acts about believers. But Pachomius quickly perceived that it was not successful. The more in all humility he spent on behalf of others the more he became the object of insult and derision. Rupture was inevitable.'[1] The sequel is known : Pachomius armed with a bar from the door, expelled all his monks who desired to injure him.

He thereupon re-formed his community on a stronger basis. There is no question of 'vows' in the Rule and no mention of a 'promise' but 'renouncing the world' comprises separation from relations and giving up all wealth (*contemnere facultatem*, as St Jerome translates it).[2] The detailed legislation which must be accepted by the monk submits him in all things to obedience : when he returns from the fields tools and clogs are to be given back to the superior. Nothing may be taken or given without permission ;[3] the monk is to be content with what the monastery furnishes to each one, and as it is laid down in meticulous detail.[4] This pooling of the resources necessary for subsistence, this state of belonging to the community, and through the community to Christ, is a vivid reminder of the unity which reigned when the first Christians of Jerusalem laid their goods at the feet of the apostles and none called his own what belonged to him. The community structure restored by the Pachomian rule solved an initial problem : it provided an effective remedy

[1] *Ibid*, p. 320.
[2] *Praecepta*, 49. ed. Boon, p. 25.
[3] *Ibid*, 73.
[4] *Ibid*, 72.

to the arbitrary nature and a certain tendency to anarchy evinced by the previous eremiticism. But the somewhat military discipline required by so considerable an agglomeration as the first Pachomian monastery was difficult to blend with the spirit of brotherhood demanded by the evangelical ideal and recalled by the primitive community in Jerusalem. Pachomius sought particularly to combat self-will among his disciples. But a true family atmosphere had still to be created among the cenobites so that their common life might be imbued with the charity desired by Christ for his followers.

It was precisely this gap that St Basil filled. Sustained by his experience as a hermit and his knowledge of Pachomian cenobiticism he concentrated his attention on the ideal of brotherhood and family spirit which was to become the characteristic of his foundations. He censured eremiticism because it made impossible the practice of those specifically Christian virtues which social life requires;[1] he noticed that in the Pachomian foundation the relationship of abbot and monks, who were too numerous effectively to know each other, could not be actuated by the spirit of love. Dom David Amand, referring to Basil, is right in speaking of a feeling of nostalgia for the infant Church to be discerned in his writings, especially in his Rules which quote frequently from the Acts of the Apostles.[2] In them poverty is given an emphasis which goes beyond anything to be found in Pachomian legislation. Dom Amand employs the expression 'integral communism' which, though unfortunate as a term, brings out clearly the fundamental feature of the Basilian community. The two elements that it comprises are based directly on the primitive Christian community.

In the first place community of goods is prescribed, implying an effective formal renunciation on the part of the individual, and poverty which consists in being satisfied with what the monastery provides. On the other hand it requires watchfulness on the part of superiors that members of the community lack nothing that is necessary to them. This is a precise application

[1] *P.G.* 31, 928, 933.

[2] Dom David Amand, monk of Maredsous, *L'ascése monastique de saint Basile*, pp. 128-144.

of *Acts* 4, 34-5 : 'For neither was there any one needy among
them. For as many as were owners of lands or houses sold them,
and brought the price of the things they sold, and laid it down
before the feet of the apostles. And distribution was made to
every one according as he had need.'

It is true, of course, that the Pachomian monk gave up all
his possessions when he entered the monastery. His intention
of doing so was signified by putting off his secular clothes.
The *facultatem contemnere* of the *Praecepta* (n.49) says no more
than this. St Basil requires a public renunciation and a
distribution to the poor safeguarded by precise legal precautions.
In his view riches that are given up are henceforth consecrated
in the same manner as the person of the monk who gives them
up. They belong to God and are not to be foolishly squandered.
If the person concerned is unable to make a sensible distribution
he is to entrust it to capable persons who have given proof of
their honesty and prudence. Neglect of these precautions
would mean committing a kind of sacrilege since these goods
belong to God.[1] Once this renunciation has been effected the
monk can no longer receive anything by way of either inheritance
or gift. In imitation of the first Christians in Jerusalem Basil
desires that whatever the monk might receive after his entry
to the monastery should be made over to the bishops for them
to dispose of as they wish.[2]

Basil owes much to his predecessors regarding the practice
of poverty, though he somewhat increases its severity. Pachomius
allowed two tunics ; Basil grants one only as well as a single
pair of sandals and a belt, not to make the garment more elegant
but to facilitate manual labour. The food is to be the same for
all ; on this point dispensations should not be granted without
serious reasons.[3] The tools, strictly necessary for work, take
on the character of consecrated articles ; to damage them or
lose them by negligence is a sort of sacrilege.[4]

Just as in the Church of Jerusalem no one called his own
what belonged to him so Basil forbade a monk to say that

[1] *The Greater Monastic Rules*, 9 ; *P.G.* 31, 941.
[2] *The Lesser Rules*, 187 ; *P.G.* 31, 1208.
[3] Cf. *Dom Amand, op. cit.*, p. 323.
[4] *The Lesser Rules*, 143 and 144 ; *P.G.* 31, 1177.

anything was his own. To do so, he declared, was to cut oneself off from the Church of God and the charity of the Lord.[1]

It will be seen how clearly poverty stands out in Basilian monasticism. It is one of the chief virtues of a cenobite because it is a characteristic element of a consecrated community formed in the likeness of the primitive Church which originated in Jerusalem. It no longer merely complies with the necessity of overcoming the monk's selfish desires nor even with the need of establishing uniformity among those who share a common life. It is enhanced by a highly expressive mystical note whereby it becomes as it were the outward sign of that state of belonging to God, already ratified by virginity, and made concrete by the worship of God effectually recognized as the Lord and Master of the monastery.

This idea corresponds also with that solicitude which Basil desires to prevail among the authorities of the community towards its members. The attentive kindness, patience and charity of the Superior, and of those holding office, is to be based on the love shown by God to his creatures but more especially it is to draw its inspiration from the attitude of the apostles providing for the needs of the first Christians. The community should act like a Providence which frees the monks from anxiety over temporal matters. St Basil recalls that needs differ. Those in authority ought, therefore, to grant reasonable alleviations avoiding at the same time all favouritism which is prejudicial to harmony.

The appeal to the infant Church recalled by this communal conception of poverty in no way lessens the attraction of personal perfection brought to mind by the summons to the rich young man. Basil frequently takes his inspiration from it. But the history of primitive monastic poverty, which we are summarizing here, notes particularly what was done by the future bishop of Caesarea to consolidate the social character of poverty with reference to the ideal picture depicted by the Acts in the life of the first Christians.[2]

We are not yet at the time when the question arose of poverty as an obligation of the community itself. A long period of

---

[1] *Ibid.* 85; P.G., 31, 1144.

[2] Cf. *Dom Amand, op. cit.,* pp. 321 *seq.*

preparation was still required before a new Pentecost should give rise to a novel conception of evangelical poverty. It is beyond the scope of this paper to mention Benedictine poverty which is a prolongation of the stage just dealt with. But mention must be made of St Caesarius, whose conception of poverty went farther than St Basil's in this sense, that his own legislation bears the stamp of an intensification of community life.

This intensification, suggested to the disciple of St Honoratus by his experience at Lérins, can be found in two important innovations : stability and the abolition of separate cells.[1] Continual and definitive subjection to a very strict discipline and absolute proximity at every instant give obvious importance to the practice of poverty. Its essential prominence becomes clear at the time of the monk's entry when a legal precaution is made to emphasize the meaning of the public act in the form that this initial renunciation now assumes. Caesarius desires that the alienation of inherited possessions recorded in legal form should add to the mere verbal renunciation the sanction of a written and official document : *venditionis chartam faciat.*[2]

The rules for nuns, in which the personal experience and acute psychology of Caesarius are shown to greater advantage— although the influence of St Augustine and Cassian may be perceived in them—inculcate emphatically the spirit of poverty. Two of his prescriptions appear to me especially remarkable on this score : on the one hand the enclosure—Caesarius is possibly its originator—which effectively prevents the infiltration of worldly vanities into monastic life and imposes an attitude of aloofness towards relations and friends outside ; on the other, the restraint required throughout the establishment from which all that is superfluous is excluded, since even devotional pictures or carvings are forbidden.[3]

In practice, however, Caesarius counselled discretion. He required of superiors much kindness and understanding,

---

[1] Cf. A. Malnory, *Saint Cesaire*, Paris, 1894, pp. 245-82.

[2] *Regula ad Monachos*, cap. I, *P.L.* 67, 1099, and *Statuta virginum*, n. 5 (Dom Morin's edn. p. 6). Under n. 6 (p. 7) will be noticed the allusion to Ananias and Saphira whose example is to be a lesson to nuns tempted to keep some possession for themselves.

[3] *Statuta* 21 (p. 9), 45 (pp. 16 *seq.*).

especially in relation to the sick.[1] These are characteristics
which were profoundly to influence later tradition, continually
tending increasingly to humanize the attitude of authority
while maintaining on the part of subordinates the strictest
requirements of the spirit of the Gospels.

The period that we have just examined cursorily, so rich in
bold endeavour, so faithful to the teaching of the apostles,
propounds very clearly the principle of an effective and total
poverty. The desire for the highest perfection : the longing to
establish on earth an ideal society which should be actuated by
the purest form of fraternal charity and show itself already as
the reflexion or anticipation of heaven : such are the essential
considerations which uphold and foster the inspiration given
by the Word made flesh, the friend of the poor and himself
poor in the eyes of the world. The future will contribute new
motives, provoke new trends, which will enrich still further
the conception and practice of evangelical poverty. A beginning
has been made. Antony, Pachomius, Basil, Caesarius gave
wonderful guidance in laying the foundations with never a
deviation from the original plan which is religious in the whole
etymological force of the word.

[1] *Ibid.* 42 (p. 15).

CHAPTER II

POVERTY IN THE RULE OF ST BENEDICT

By DOM O. ROUSSEAU

The renouncing of one's possessions counselled in the Gospel early became—in the form it assumed in the Benedictine rule—the recognized conception of religious poverty in the West. On the one hand it is a faithful reflexion of the Gospel, and on the other it represents and is a continuation of the ideal of the first Christian community and of the further development of this ideal in traditional desert spirituality. But to the latter it contributed an element of sobriety and restraint which, though not depriving it of its basic immutable severity in essentials, stabilized them to some extent by clearly defining their limits. In this conception of religious poverty—apart, perhaps, from Franciscan tradition—the principles underlying the whole body of later teaching and legislation may be said to have found their expression.

Nevertheless, since its practice was a matter of some delicacy, there was often a danger of relaxation. The safeguarding of poverty was in nearly every case the object of the numerous reforms which the monastic order was obliged to undergo ; to it refer, directly or indirectly, the regulations of the Decretals ; a whole theology of evangelical poverty was developed in the Middle Ages to make it better understood. Moreover, the Mendicant Orders became an imperative necessity in the Church in the thirteenth century chiefly by reason of the decline in the practice of poverty in the monasteries in which havoc had been wrought by the interference of the outside world and by the appetite for private possessions. But in these Orders also several reforms had to be introduced in the course of centuries since attachment to the goods of this earth ever remains a great temptation for man, and it is difficult for him to free himself from it completely. After all is it not on the question of attachment to earthly goods that the great social crisis which we are now undergoing is dividing mankind ? The religious life merely clothes the teaching of Christ in tangible and uncompromising forms.

We shall examine successively how the Benedictine Rule expresses evangelical renunciation, how it purposes to reproduce the gesture of the first christians, coming to lay the price of their possessions, in order to be detached from them, *ad pedes apostolorum*, and how it is a development and a continuation of the detachment practised by the early Fathers of monasticism.

At the beginning of this account it should be noticed that the threefold division of the vows of religion, poverty, chastity and obedience, has no place, and was destined to have scarcely any, in the obligations the monks undertook at their profession. It is true, of course, that the notion of a threefold renunciation is to be found in early Benedictine authors, and even in the Rule, but the idea of including it in the actual formula of what is promised to God never occurred to the monks of old, so obvious did it seem to them.[1]

The term 'poverty', understood as a virtue, does not occur in the Rule. In it there is much about obedience, which the monk promises solemnly when he enters, together with stability and *conversatio morum*; the term 'chastity' may also be found in several places; but 'poverty' and 'poor' occur only in connexion with the poverty of the site, and the abnormal position of a monastery without resources (cap. 48), or in dealing with the poor themselves to whom alms must be given (cap. 4). That is why, for the time being, the word here used is renunciation, which is a more accurate interpretation for us, in modern times, of the idea of the holy Patriarch.

Moreover, it is curious to note that although in the monastic and canonical world the influence of the theology of a threefold oblation—the three vows of the future—is already marked in the twelfth century, long before scholasticism found the need to formulate it, the corresponding terms appear in the customaries in the form of *castitas, obedientia, communio*. Such was the case, for example, at St Geneviève in Paris. A letter of Odo of St Victor, prior of St Geneviève in 1140, uses this

---

[1] Papal decrees, however, thought it worthwhile to equate this formula with the vows. Cf. Innocent III : *Abdicatio proprietatis sicut et custodia castitatis adeo annexa est Regulae monachali, ut contra eam nec summus Pontifex possit licentiam indulgere* (cap. 6 *de statu monachorum*, P.L., 66, 624 B.).

formula and comments at length upon it.[1] It is hardly necessary to say that here *communio* means *vita communis*, the common life, having all things in common, that is the idea denoted later by the term 'poverty'.

It was not the mendicant Orders which made this term popular, for it already existed previously in the teaching of the Fathers : in early times St John Chrysostom,[2] St Ephrem,[3] St Jerome[4] especially had extolled the poverty of Christ and encouraged the monks to imitate it. Sulpicius Severus says of St Martin : *pauper et modicus, caelum dives ingreditur,*[5] repeating an idea in the Gospel. Similarly Cassiodorus spoke of the poor of Christ, deprived of this world's goods but rich in God.[6] In the Middle Ages in St Bernard and many others may be found the invitation to poverty—*paupertas*—as a religious virtue.[7] But it is quite probable that, side by side with the charismatic exaltation of soul found in Franciscan poverty, reaction against the lack of discipline in the common life, which had become one of the key points in the legislation of the new orders, counted for much in the introduction of the word 'poverty' into the formularies of profession from this period onwards.

Nevertheless if the word as such does not occur in the Rule, the idea is certainly to be found there as we shall now see.

I. EVANGELICAL RENUNCIATION IN THE RULE

Christ came to exalt poverty which until then had been generally disparaged. The *pauperes* were proclaimed by him to

[1] *Epist. I. P.L.* 196, 1399.—Cf. on this subject L. Hertling, *Die Professio der Kleriker und die Enstehung der drei Gelübde* in *Zeitschr. f. Kath. Theologie,* 1932, p. 148 *seq.* Dom Martène, in his commentary on the Rule, quotes a form of profession from the Abbey of St Denis which before the formula of the Rule inserted an explicit statement of the three vows, *P.L.* 66, 820.

[2] *Hom.* 18 *in Epist. ad Hebr.* 2 and 3 ; *P.G.* 63, 236.

[3] 'Apply thyself to the poverty of Christ so as to enrich thyself with his divinity in the heavenly home.' (*De Jejunio,* vol. III, p. 22.)

[4] In the commentary on the verse *Beatus qui intelligit super egenum et pauperem.* (Brev., in ps. 40 ; *P.L.* 26, 946.)

[5] *Ep.* 3 *ad Bassulum, P.L.* 20, 184 C.

[6] *Introd. in ps.* 101 ; *P.L.* 70, 705.

[7] *Ditior est Christi paupertas cunctis opibus, cunctis thesauris, Serm.* 4 in *Vig. Nat.,* 6 ; *P.L.* 183, 102.—Cf. also the commentary on the first beatitude in the *Serm.* I *in fest. Omn. Sanctorum,* 7 and 8, *P.L.* 183, 456.

be blessed (*Luke* 6, 20) ; St Paul teaches us that Christ made himself poor to make us rich and that, in very truth, it is through his poverty that we have so become (2 *Cor.* 8, 9). Nevertheless, save for these phrases 'poverty' in the Gospel is mentioned, using that term, as a state in which a man may find himself— and he is to be treated with kindness for Christ is to be encountered in him—but not as a state that is to be embraced. Christ alone, rich as he was in a transcendent manner from all eternity, made himself poor and humble by giving himself to us. Yet the aspect of voluntary destitution is to be found in the invitations to renunciation scattered throughout the Gospel. All must be left if one is to find God, to follow Christ. Notice, however, that it does not say 'become poor' but 'give to the poor' : 'If thou wilt be perfect, go, sell what thou hast, and give to the poor . . . and come, follow me' (*Matt.* 19, 21). One does not make oneself poor for the mere pleasure of being poor, in order to be destitute of all things, but in order at the same time to give away all one's possessions. And if, once all has been given away, one renounces all further possibility of possessing for the future, one does so in order to prolong this initial donation not of what one has, but of what one is. This is renunciation of earthly goods and this is what is meant by giving up one's personal property.

This statement is extremely important for an accurate understanding of the different kinds of religious poverty in the Church. It is to be noted, moreover, that all those who have loved poverty for itself have begun by loving it in their neighbour in whose person they discerned Christ. In the last resort love of the poor was the incentive to poverty.

In his life of St Benedict, St Gregory the Great says of the holy Patriarch that 'he had left all his possessions with the desire of pleasing God alone', *relicta domo rebusque patris, soli Deo placere desiderans.*[1] His disciples also who, like him, were to have no other end but to seek God alone—*Si revera Deum quaerit* (cap. 58) : *nihil sibi a Christo carius existimant* (cap. 5)— were likewise to give away all they possess. Directly he has chanted the solemn *Suscipe* of his oblation, asking God to accept him in sacrifice and to receive him as completely his,

[1] *Prolog.* 1.

the newly professed monk must at once, according to the Rule, strip himself of all his possessions, keeping back for himself nothing in this world (cap. 58). That is the first step in the way of renunciation for him who desires to give up all to follow Christ—*abnegare semetipsum ut sequatur Christum* (cap. 4)— and who 'will no longer be allowed to have either his body or his will at his own disposal' (cap. 33).

Thus the renunciation is to be absolute. Continuing this initial gesture of abnegation the monk will begin the great struggle to follow Christ in his lowliness, in his nakedness, even to giving his life, *Imitans Dominum de quo dicit Apostolus* : *factus obediens usque ad mortem* (cap. 7).

To ensure this advance in virtue, following in Christ's footsteps, the monk must be protected from all personal attachment and all possibility of turning back. He can no longer possess anything : 'It is this spirit of individual renunciation,' wrote Dom Morin in his well-known work *The Monastic Ideal*, 'which vitalizes poverty as it was understood and prescribed by St Benedict'.[1] The question occurs quite clearly in chapter 33 of the Rule : 'If monks ought to have anything of their own'. The answer is categoric : 'This vice of ownership particularly must be utterly rooted out of the monastery'. There must be no personal possessions : 'whatever it is, whether book, tablets, or pen, in a word, absolutely nothing,' *nihil omnino*. It could not be put more clearly.

It is important to emphasize this severity in order to refute a certain legend which has grown up regarding Benedictine tradition. Moderation, which is a characteristic of the rule, is by no means tacit acceptance of indulgent condescension towards natural inclinations. A publicist wrote in 1945 : 'We might easily be scandalized at a certain leniency in the Rule' which provides for 'time to be allowed for the lazy to come to Office', and 'gives the impression that the membership was, in some respects, of very mediocre quality' and which, in consequence, 'avoids teaching of too elevated a mystical doctrine'.[2]

[1] Chapter IX.

[2] E. Delaruelle, *Saint Benoît* in *Le Christianisme et l'Occident barbare*, Paris, 1945, p. 408. The author provides, however, the necessary correction to the remarks quoted above.

This incorrect and superficial idea of the religious thought of St Benedict is bound to come to grief in face of his uncompromising attitude with regard to renunciation of possessions and obedience. The truth is that on fundamental principles St Benedict shows the most rigorous severity and his commentators have never deviated from his spirit. The sanctions in the Rule against offenders in the matter of ownership are extremely severe : 'If anyone takes pleasure in this detestable vice (of ownership) he shall be admonished once or twice ; if he does not mend his ways he is to be punished' (cap. 33). 'Let no one have the temerity to give or receive anything without the abbot's permission' (cap. 33). 'On no account shall a monk be allowed to receive letters, devout tokens, or any small gifts whatsoever, from his parents or other people or his brethren, or to give the same without the abbot's permission. And if he has been sent anything even by his parents, let him not presume to take it before it has been shown to the abbot. If the abbot allow it to be received, it shall be his to decide to whom it is to be given' (cap. 54).

St Benedict tried one or two unfortunate experiments—he makes no secret of them—in allowing children, who entered very young, to retain the capacity of ownership. His definitive legislation, finally, blocked up every loophole. 'And in this way let every opening be stopped so that the boy may have no expectations whereby (which God forbid) he might be deceived and ruined, as we have learned by experience' (cap. 59).

In the Benedictine Rule, then, there was the greatest possible severity as regards the renunciation of personal possessions, but this severity would appear to be less where the monastery itself is concerned. On this point cavillers might perhaps find themselves on firmer ground. Nevertheless, St Gregory shows us with numerous examples how St Benedict was uncompromising on the subject of the second part of the precept : *Da pauperibus.* 'He would give to the poor,' he tells us, 'all the goods of the monastery, having decided to give in this way everything on earth in order to lay up everything in heaven,' *qui cuncta decreverat in terra tribuere, ut in coelo omnia servaret* (cap. 28). Yet, when the novice was professed, the Rule lays down 'if he possess any property, let him either give it beforehand to the poor, or make a formal donation bestowing it on the monastery' (cap. 58).

To the modern mind this alternative may provoke a comparison between Franciscan poverty and the Benedictine tradition to the detriment of the latter. The monk can possess nothing but the monastery may do so. *Faciat donationem monasterio.* There is some risk, consequently, of conventionalizing this prescription of the Rule in a manner out of all proportion to its meaning, as human nature does so easily with many pious maxims inscribed on monastic walls, and so imperceptibly of endowing collective egoism, the enrichment of the community, with the appearance of a virtue. St Benedict certainly understood this for he counselled the abbot above all not to have greater solicitude for fleeting, earthly and perishable things than for the souls in his charge (cap. 2) ; not to be excessively anxious about a possible lack of material means, reminding him that it is written : 'Seek ye first the kingdom of God and his justice, and all these things shall be added unto you' (ibid) ; to sell the produce of the monastery 'a little cheaper than it is sold by people in the world, *ut in omnibus glorificetur Deus*' (cap. 57), etc.

Yet it would be an anachronism to desire to compare the condition of Benedictine monasteries in the past with the state of the mendicant Orders. St Francis of Assisi appears in the history of religious orders as a charismatic of an entirely new kind, destined to propagate in the Church the practice of a Gospel maxim which had not, so far, been brought out clearly in all its implications. St Benedict, though himself a charismatic and a wonder-worker, made no innovations in spiritual matters ; he simply adapted the old monasticism to the countries of the west. In this way he is closely connected with another charismatic, the great St Antony of the Desert, the father of monks who, under divine inspiration and altogether unwittingly, brought into being the whole of the Church's monastic life. St Antony's vocation and that of St Francis are, moreover, strangely alike. Both, going into a church, heard at the Gospel a saying of Christ's which struck them. In one case the result was flight from the world and in the other absolute poverty and preaching. 'If thou wilt be perfect, go, sell what thou hast . . . and come, follow me.' Antony obeyed at once, sold his possessions and sought the desert. 'Do not possess gold, nor silver, nor money in your purses : nor scrip for your journey, nor two coats, nor shoes, nor a staff . . .' Francis discarded his staff, took off his shoes, put on a cord instead of a belt, gave away his purse and began his apostolic life.

St Benedict, the Roman successor of Antony and Pachomius, had in no wise received the gift of a mendicant life. This latter, in various forms, had not been unknown in primitive monasticism, but as an eremitical peculiarity and not as a form of common life. St Benedict renounces his possessions in accordance with the recommendations of the early fathers, clearly seeing how the advantages of the cenobitical life could help to perfect and continue this renunciation. To prevent the monk's possessing anything as his own he desires him to give up all, either to the poor or to the monastery. Francis would have none of this gift to the monastery. We know his answer to the bishop of Assisi who recommended him to keep something so as to avoid being left entirely without resources : 'If we have possessions arms will be required to defend them from thieves, bailiffs and lawyers to uphold our rights against the cunning of usurpers, men and women as servants to exploit our farms'. The facts of monastic decadence were there to support his apprehensions. But St Benedict, in allowing his monasteries to have possessions, had different ends in view, and ends, it should be noted, no less apostolic than Francis's. This is the second point that I should like to make in connexion with the Benedictine idea of what the Gospel means by renunciation of property, namely that it is an effective continuation of what was done by the primitive Christian community.

II. The Ideal of the Primitive Christian Community and the Benedictine Rule

The life of the first Christian community has always formed an ideal for those who have sought after the perfection of the Gospel. It was the origin of Antony's vocation since, according to St Athanasius's account, on his way to church on the day of his conversion to the monastic life he was meditating on how the first Christians, 'as it is written in the Acts sold their goods and laid the price at the feet of the apostles to be distributed to those who had need, and on how great was the reward which awaited them in heaven'.[1] The Rule of the Holy Fathers lays down likewise that no one in the monastery should 'consider anything his own, but that, as it is written in the Acts of the Apostles, all should possess everything in common'.[2] Again St Basil says: 'Those who are at the head (of communities) shall take as their rule this saying: "distribution was made to every one according as he had need"'.[3]

St Benedict had meditated on this teaching and made it his own. Submission, from a spirit of faith in the word of the apostles, to the kind of life described in the Acts, became for him a holy rule. A man gave up his possessions and bestowed them on the community which had need of them and they were shared round or distributed. 'And all they that believed were together, and had all things in common. Their possessions and goods they sold, and divided them to all, according as every one had need' (*Acts* 2, 44-5). 'For as many as were owners of land or houses sold them, and brought the price of the things they sold, and laid it down before the feet of the apostles. And distribution was made to every one according as he had need' (*Ibid*. 4, 34-5). Gifts are to be made to the community not that it should grow rich, therefore, or amass wealth, but so that those who have given all, or who are in want, may obtain relief. In a certain sense, then, the community is the dispenser of alms. Gifts are made to the community only in order to achieve greater detachment from earthly possessions and to ensure through it the continuance of the gesture of helping the needy. Clearly that is St Benedict's idea. And if those, who in this way practise the poverty of the Gospel, should happen to receive what the Gospel promises—*omnia adjicientur vobis*—after all it is only strict justice that they should. But there is a further principle to be emphasized: all superfluity is to be rigorously avoided, *quod superfluum est amputari debet*. We can now examine how St Benedict applied these principles.

[1] *Vita Antonii*, cap. I.
[2] *Reg. SS. Patrum*, I, 12, *P.L.* 103, 441 D.
[3] *Interr.* 94. *Vers. Rufini*; *P.L.* 103, 524 AB.

It has been pointed out very rightly that St Basil chose cenobitism instead of eremitism not for social or economic reasons, but on account of Christianity itself. 'Whose feet does a hermit wash ?' he asks, 'whom does he help ? Eremitism cannot possibly provide a complete ideal of Christian living.'[1] After the ideal proper to Pachomian cenobitism of a number of separate individuals and under close regimentation which, once the period of first fervour had passed, tended to degenerate into an association of more or less devout workers, Basil effected a real restoration. Under him in the monastery the Christian community was reconstituted in all its fullness. In this spirit St Benedict was in the strictest sense his disciple. Monks are to practise the Christian virtues, and particularly fraternal charity. But the especial place, the workshop—*officina*—of this charitable activity is to be for them the *claustra monasterii* (cap. 4) wherein, firstly among themselves and then in the neighbourhood, they will serve Christ in their brethren. Stability in the monastery will be for them a pledge of perseverance until death—*usque ad mortem in monasterio perseverantes* (Prol.)—in the exercise of these virtues.

They have given all to God but from him, in the person of the abbot, they expect what they need. They can possess nothing but their hope bestows on them what is absolutely necessary : *omnia vero necessaria a patre sperare monasterii* (cap. 33). The scene in the Acts is here recalled : *Omnia omnibus sint communia, ut scriptum est, nec quisquam suum aliquid dicat vel praesumat* (ibid). The needs and necessities of each one can be different, in accordance with that same text : *Sicut scriptum est* : *Dividebatur singulis prout cuique opus erat* ; one will receive more, another less, according as each one has need—*infirmitatum consideratio*. He that needs more should be humble for his infirmity ; he who needs less should not be discontented, but thank God (cap. 34).

There is great emulation of charity in the Rule and it is always in the shape of almsgiving, its classical form in primitive christianity, that it appears. It is poverty which always attracts it, poverty which is in need and on behalf of which self-denial must be practised. The guest is one without shelter who is to

---

[1] Reg. fus. tr., Interr. 7, *P.G.* 933 B.

be received like Christ because he said 'I was a stranger and you took me in' (cap. 53). Especial care is to be taken of the sick, 'before all things and above all things, *ante omnia et super omnia, sicut revera Christo* for he said : "I was sick and ye visited me" and "what ye did to these least ones, ye did unto me" ' (cap. 36).

St Benedict feared avarice in his monks. How, it may be asked, could those who have given up everything be tainted with this vice ? Experience proves, unfortunately, that if egoism is present in a soul it quickly plays havoc in that direction and a man, who in the world might have learnt to be generous, in the cloister may find himself one day infected by a veritable mania for possessions. The holy Patriarch reminds his disciples of the example of Ananias and Saphira and fears for his monks the temptation to dishonesty, *ne subripiat avaritiae malum* (cap. 57). Also, the abbot is frequently to examine the beds of the monks to forestall the instinct for concealment, *propter opus peculiare, ne inveniatur* (cap. 55).

It should be noted at once, however, that to prevent legitimate claims arising on this score St Benedict lays down that the monks should receive for their use what is necessary and he goes so far as to enumerate what he considers to be so : a cowl (thick and woolly in winter, but thin or worn in summer), a tunic (two of these for the same reason and that one may be washed while the other is in use, for St Benedict makes a point of cleanliness), shoes, stockings, girdle, knife, pen, needle, handkerchief and tablets. In this way all pretext of need is taken away (cap. 55).

St Benedict is strict about superfluities : he forbids them absolutely. But he does not consider it superfluous to have two cooked dishes at table to allow him 'who cannot eat of the one to make his meal of the other'. In the same way he allows the use of wine in moderation. He evinces discretion in his cenobitism : *nihil asperum nihil grave* (Prologue). But without entirely excluding certain amenities in daily life he does not desire monks to be allowed luxuries—what would be called nowadays 'little comforts'. He requires his monks to be un-affected by the worldly spirit which fosters the endeavour to rise in the social scale, and encourages them to make progress

in perfection to the point of being content with the meanest
and worst of everything (cap. 7). In addition, should it happen
that through poverty the monks are obliged to the heavy work
of the fields, like gathering the harvest, 'let them not be discontented,' says St Benedict, 'for then they are truly monks,
when they live by the labour of their hands like our fathers
and the apostles. Yet let all things be done in moderation on
account of the faint-hearted' (cap. 48). The holy legislator
anticipated, therefore, that even heavy work would be done by
the labour of the monks ; he encouraged them, but not un-
reservedly and seemed to think that such work would remain
an exception. He gave evidence of a prudence and wisdom
that it is well to remember at the present day. Monastic life,
properly practised, with its regular hours of work, already is
of its nature hard enough, and penitential enough, for the
human constitution.

The poor are the especial object of his attention. *Pauperes
recreare*, he says in listing the tools of good works (cap. 4) ;
the porter is to exercise particular care in receiving them (cap.
66) ; anything that is worn out is to be returned to the clothes
room at once for their use (cap. 55) ; the guest-master particularly will have them in his care : 'In the reception of poor men
and pilgrims special attention should be shown, because in
them is Christ more truly welcomed' (cap. 53). The cellarer is
to carry out his office in their regard with the greatest care, as
indeed in the case of all who are needy : the sick, children,
guests, the poor, 'knowing without doubt that he will have to
render an account for all these on the day of judgement' (cap. 31).

It may well be urged, however, that St Benedict's recommendation to be particularly attentive to the relief of distress
shows clearly that he allowed wealth because, in short, it is
the rich who are able to give to the poor. On the other hand,
the saint's life depicts him frequently bestowing alms, giving
away all the substance of the monastery, to the great annoyance
of the brethren, and working miracles to relieve their want.
The general effect of all this demonstrates how far removed
from the holy Patriarch's spirit are those who believe in wealthy
monasteries. What use are riches to those who have renounced
all ? If they have them it is only in order to give them away.

We shall have something to say later about monastic wealth.

If it is true, as has been said, that 'St Benedict fixed no limits to the material expansion of the monastery'[1] all the same he did not say—and it would have been of little importance in the mentality of those days if he had done so—that this expansion was without limit. He did not fix an age limit for the office of abbot, but at the same time he did not lay down that the abbot must at all costs keep his charge until death.

III. PRIMITIVE MONASTICISM AND BENEDICTINE TRADITION

St Benedict was no innovator, therefore, concerning renunciation of property. As we have said, he merely repeated the precepts of earlier legislators, and codified them with prudence and moderation, and it is revealing to examine in some detail how he preserved in all essentials the evangelical renunciation of the goods of this world as it was practised in the desert.

St Benedict puts the candidate for monastic life to the test. But with him there are none of those provoking demands, running counter to all reason which, in the *Vitae Patrum*, were sometimes used to estimate the detachment of newcomers. He desires merely to ascertain if they are sincerely seeking God. Only at profession is the monk stripped of his goods, but then of all of them. The *Verba seniorum* tells the story of a postulant who, to overcome his repugnance, gave to the poor even his clothes and came naked to the monastery.[2] This action was understood and he was at once clothed with the habit. Substantially that is what St Benedict requires at profession : the candidate is stripped of his own clothes, says the Ritual, and at once dressed in the clothes of the monastery. And that takes place during the ceremony. *Mox ergo in oratorio exuatur rebus propriis quibus vestitus est, et induatur rebus monasterii* (cap. 58).

Nowadays such a practice would give offence and be held to be wanting in decency. Yet it is of deep significance. At the present time in Benedictine abbeys postulants generally bring

---

[1] Dom G. Morin (op. cit., p. 159).

[2] Lib. III, 67 ; *P.L.* 73, 772 B.

with them a complete outfit marked with their initials and it is left for their use as long as it lasts. No change in this is made at profession : often, indeed, in a broad-minded way they are allowed to keep a certain number of books, small personal possessions, toilet articles, a razor, watch, fountain pen. I know many a novice who has been saddened by this toleration ; they would have preferred the contrary practice. Is there any gain in not allowing, at such a moment, the realisation of an act of complete generosity ? Is it not capital to be laid out to advantage, not parcelled up in small portions ?

In the East the ancient custom has been kept in the ceremonial of profession. The monk, and even the nun, comes before the altar bare-headed and unshod, clad only in a shift. The monastic habit is put straight on to the body thus stripped of its clothing. It is by no means a bad thing to leave old rules unchanged on this point. Most true vocations to some extent unconsciously seek the desert and the desert is a place where there is nothing. Why, then, fill it up and so create illusions ?

The unconditional assignment of property has already been mentioned. Nothing, absolutely nothing, can be kept back for any reason whatever. St Benedict on this point enjoyed the advantages of cenobitism ; for that alone he intended to legislate. Cenobites are certainly the category of monks the most favoured in regard to detachment. Of the four kinds enumerated at the beginning of the Rule two are proscribed, the Sarabaites and the Gyrovagi because they in no wise renounce the world and are given up to their own desires. St Benedict has hard words to say about them (cap. 1). St Jerome had already lashed these counterfeit forms of monasticism with his sarcasm. He censures the cunning employed by certain monks who amass riches by imposing on well-endowed widows *marsupium suffocantes, matronarum opes venantur obsequiis*.[1] This vice was so widespread that the Emperor Valentinian issued a law forbidding monks and clerics to visit the houses of widows, and asked Pope Damasus to have its terms read in the churches. The hermit was certainly obliged to make an act of absolute renunciation of all his possessions when he retired to the desert. But gradually, on account of the necessities

[1] *Ep.* 60 *ad Heliodor.* ; *P.L.* 22, 596.

of solitary life, for the cultivation of his garden and the upkeep of his cell he had to have tools and household utensils. And so it happened that, by an unforeseen deviation, he was once more an owner. The cenobite was to have all things in common : it was a great advantage for the safeguard of his state of renunciation. St Benedict terms this category of monks the *genus fortissimum monachorum*. Indeed the cenobite is protected by the common life from many dangers, among others that of ownership.

Referring to another idea in the Acts (4, 32), passed on by the tradition of the desert, St Benedict requires the monk to refrain from calling the articles that he uses his own (cap. 33). All the ancient monastic lawgivers held to this custom which is to be encountered in Cassian,[1] St Basil,[2] St John Chrysostom,[3] in the rules of St Ferreolus,[4] St Fructuosus,[5] St Augustine.[6] It was possibly a method of little importance but was yet considered an effectual guarantee against the instinct of ownership. There is a difference, perhaps, between calling an object one's own, using a complete sentence—subject, verb, predicate —'this is mine', etc., and employing a possessive adjective that has been much weakened by usage and is nowadays tolerated. Still, in many religious houses the use of the plural possessive is maintained, or at least an effort is made to do so.

We know with what jealous constancy the heroes and giants of poverty believed themselves to be laying up riches in heaven —*habebis thesaurum in caelis*—in proportion as they went without possessions here below. This eschatological way of considering the wealth of heaven played an important part in the theology of the early monks. It even exerted an influence on the objects possessed in common by the brethren, for these objects became in this way things of God appertaining to his worship, holy things. Cassian, St Basil and the early rules all use this language,[7] and St Benedict adopts the same point of

[1] *Inst.* 4, 13 ; *P.L.* 49, 168.
[2] *Reg. fus. tr.* 32, 1 ; *P.G.* 31, 995.
[3] *Hom.* 33. *sup. Gen* ; *P.G.* 53, 309.
[4] C. 10 ; *P.L.* 66, 963 D.
[5] C. 4 ; *P.L.* 87, 1101 D.
[6] Ep. 211 ; *P.L.* 33, 960.
[7] *Interr.*, 103 *Vers. Rufini* ; *P.L.* 103, 526 D.

view. He enjoins on the cellarer the duty of considering all the belongings of the monastery as so many sacred vessels to be treated with great reverence (cap. 31). For this reason the Rule is exceedingly strict about their preservation and upkeep. A list of them must be kept, they must be treated carefully and kept clean ; severe punishments are to be undergone by those who, oblivious of the sacred character of these things, use them in a slovenly or careless manner (cap. 32, 35). The same concern for the possessions of the monastery to be regarded as God's, appears in St Benedict's care in securing that the oratory should ever remain the house of prayer ; it is not to be used for other purposes outside service time (cap. 52).

It is well known that Benedictine tradition with characteristic magnanimity has always regarded as a virtue a certain prodigality in matters connected with worship. Many of the old monasteries and monastic churches tend to make one think of the wealth of Solomon. But this was the consequence of gifts made by the mighty ones of this earth in a spirit of devotion and, it should never be forgotten, these gifts were made to God. When monks came to look on themselves as the beneficiaries it was a sign that their ideal had degenerated into a system of profit-making. The sarcasms of Rabelais and Marot may be recalled in this connexion ; caricatures they no doubt were but there was an element of truth in them :

'What more shall I add ? To live in safe quarters,
  Sleep without fear, eat and drink for nothing,
  Do nothing, learn no trade,
  Give nothing away, grasp all one can,
  Waxing fat and powerful, well fed and dressed—
  That's what they call purity and virtue.'[1]

Even before the barbed remarks of the humanists St Bernard, and others before him, had raised their voices against the sacred possessions of the monasteries thus covetously converted into a means of making money or a vulgar display of wealth. But that is a side of Benedictine history that falls outside the scope of this paper, though it has not a little to teach us.

An attempt, founded on the romanticism of the nineteenth century, was made to revive the fashion of these gifts, which

[1] Marot, quoted by Lavisse and Rambaut, *Histoire de la France*, V, I, p. 308.

were a specifically medieval institution. This 'Gothic revival',
a false imitation of the institutions of the Middle Ages, continued
perhaps to the first decades of this century. It has now come
to an end ; devout patrons are no longer to be found and
nowadays monasteries, like everyone else, are obliged to
conform to changes in the social order and earn their own
living. Pontifical instructions will be found, if need be, to
remind them of it. Our faith should be strong enough for the
omnia adjicientur to occur of itself ; it is for us to look after the
essential condition—to seek God and his justice (*Matt.* 6, 33).
And if the increase be granted may we, like our fathers in the
ages of faith, be able to carry out in some way the equivalent
of their renowned almsgiving—*dare pauperibus*.

Perhaps an objector will be found to accuse me of insufficient
respect for the thought of several recent commentators on the
Benedictine Rule who have been at pains to show its implicit
agreement with the way of life of our bourgeois society. But
is it not to evince an excessive kindness towards the things of
this world to desire thus to harmonize the Gospel and
institutions which should be its faithful reflexion with the
pattern and customs of any social system ? The Kingdom of
God is not of this world and that is why detachment from the
world is so excellent. Christianity is made not for a society of
Roman patricians, nor for such and such an empire, nor for a
feudal system, nor for a bourgeois world any more than it is
made for a proletarian world. It is made for all systems without
exception and must make shift as well as it can with every one
of them, but without ever so far coming to terms with them as
to compromise its universal character, its catholicity. That is
true also of the great religious orders which have adapted
themselves to all parts of the world. Unfortunately it happens
nowadays that these orders can frequently assimilate only a
few of those who, under the impulse of their generosity and
faith, might find a place in them, and who go away, put off by
a narrow class-conscious mentality. The requirements laid
down sometimes seem to derive from nothing more than the
virtue of prudence. In fact they lack any sort of Christian
grandeur, and yet we live in a period when such a widening
of spiritual horizons constitutes a grave obligation.

For admission to an Order, or into a particular category of religious, it is necessary to have a kind of education and up-bringing, a body of settled ideas and social prejudices which are rarely, and increasingly so, to be encountered in the same person. I ought particularly to say something of the dowry ; I do not do so because in reality the most recent Pontifical instructions seem to prepare the way for its gradual suppression, but it is obvious that the dowry of nuns corresponds with an essentially middle-class state of mind. And not only are our religious orders narrow in outlook but, we should not fear to say, in some degree our Catholicism is also. There are generous noble souls who could come in but who, for that very reason, could not possibly fit in. It is the Catholicity of the Church which is at stake and which requires us to widen the horizon of our religious mentality.

Once again St Benedict's teaching has a valuable contribution to make. Whereas the Rule of St Augustine (I mean Letter 211, the rule for nuns) clearly allowed two categories of religious with different food, clothes, bedding, etc. according to the social class from which they came,[1] St Benedict, on the contrary, insists on the absolute equality of all *non convertenti ex servitio praeponatur ingenuus . . . quia sive servus sive liber, omnes in Christo unum sumus. et sub uno Domino aequalem servitutis militiam bajulamus* (cap. 2)—a further proof that Benedictine monachism is bound intrinsically neither to the aristocracy nor to the bourgeois world. Of its nature it is independent of any class ties.

In order to extol the harmony of Benedictine monachism with bourgeois society it has often been asserted, and not without reason, that excessive poverty was harmful to the spiritual life of the monasteries. But it has not been emphasized enough that if sufficiency, with the help of prudent and christian management, was the cause of prosperity in the monasteries, wealth, in the proper sense of the word, resulted very often in

---

[1] Si eis quae venerunt ex moribus delicatioribus ad monasterium aliquid alimentorum, vestimentorum, stramentorum, operimentorum datur, quod aliis fortioribus, et ideo felicioribus non datur, cogitare debent quibus non datur quantum de sua saeculari vita illae ad istam descenderint, quamvis usque ad aliarum quae sunt corpore fortiores, frugalitatem pervenire nequiverint. *P.L.* 33, 961.—The context shows clearly that it is not only a question of health but of previous education.

worldliness and decadence. Such assertions were often only
the consequence of that over optimistic complacency for the
present which was alluded to above. 'Some of the great religious
Orders,' it has been rightly said—but why not say all ?—'in
the seventeenth century in practice identified Christianity with
the world of a rising middle class'.[1] Every Order, of course,
bears the stamp of the period of its foundation, but at the
same time, if it would continue to live, it must free itself from
all immersion in the merely human. The monastery derives
from the desert. There it acquired its authentic greatness and
magnificence. If this greatness in certain centuries was matched
by the magnificence of the most sumptuous art, it was for
God's sake and it was a gift of God, and this could only then
have been of profit when it laid on the monks, with these
wonders in charge, the duty of practising even better and
more nobly that most thorough-going evangelical renunciation
on which St Benedict had founded his Rule.

[1] J. Daniélou, *Christianisme et Histoire* in *Etudes*, 1947, p. 177.

Chapter III

MENDICANT POVERTY: ST DOMINIC

By M.-D. Chenu, O.P.

Words become quickly commonplace, and the keen perception which brought them to life under the impact of stirring reality soon seeks to redress the balance with a falsely spiritual interpretation whereby at little cost former fervour may create for itself a good conscience. The history of mendicancy as an economic system of christian religious groups on fire with the Gospel is full of lessons, yet even the mention of mendicant Orders in the twentieth century smacks of gratuitous medievalism. But, though history may lower them in our estimation, it cannot hide this enduring folly of a Christian presence in the world which, in order to love the world, began and continued by a complete break with that primary perversion which is the power of money.

The word mendicancy dates, as we know, from the end of the twelfth century when it became the distinguishing mark, both economically and spiritually, of a heterogeneous series of religious revivals in the west. Two of the more successful forms—founded by St Francis and St Dominic—took permanent shape independently of the ancient *Ordo monasticus*, which was also vowed to poverty, and served thenceforward as patterns for subsequent attempts: they formed a twofold evangelical revival, fundamentally identical but differing in inspiration and structure, though based as always on the condemnation of money. Canon law and the customs of the time may well have produced a similarity of constitutions and rule but their spirit preserved the irreductible, and salutary, difference of emphasis.

The chroniclers in their quaint narratives have managed to reproduce the authentic spirit of the original conception which governed, and continued to govern, the temporal and spiritual forms of this twofold though identical poverty. The Franciscan documents are known from the revelations of the Portiuncula down to the final Testament: Fr Leclercq, in the following paper, refers to them and interprets their meaning : the great attraction of poverty, an effective realization of love of the poor combined with imitation of Christ, which by a refusal of any kind of dwelling, of all ownership, left complete freedom for the grace of the Gospel and brotherly love. Reliance on others for one's subsistence means trusting in the charitable providence of brotherhood.

There are far fewer documentary references to St Dominic, but Pierre de Vaux-de-Cernay, the author of the *Historia Albigensis*, has preserved for us an account of the crucial episode which took place near Montpellier in the very year (1206) that St Francis began his life as a hermit. Dominic, at that time the companion of the Spanish bishop Diego, was traversing the south of France, one of the regions of Christendom where both faith and morals were contaminated by error concerning God and man, the individual, sex and the social system, and by that incoherent mixture of idealism and decadence attendant on the excessively abrupt transformation of a humanity fretting at its own weakness. Society, challenged in its purpose and its structure, was breaking up and together with it the Church, which was too closely identified with the wealthy and obsolete feudal system. For thirty years past Rome had been seeking a religious antidote to this mortal fever and, to offset clerical failings and ignorance, more than once had called into action Cistercian monks, still at that time near enough to St Bernard to benefit by his reputation and sanctity. On this occasion three of their important abbots, with a special commission from Innocent III, were in charge of operations, going from place to place in the south with a considerable retinue. Their failure was complete. They were on the point of abandoning their mission when at Montpellier, a great road junction and cultural centre, they encountered Diego and Dominic. 'Leave your retinue here and like our Lord go on foot, taking neither gold nor silver, copying in all things the way of life of the apostles (*vita apostolica*). Then devote yourselves to preaching the Gospel.' But the aforesaid legates, adds the chronicler, 'unwilling to make any innovation on their own account replied that if some favourable authority were willing to initiate this method they would gladly follow it'. There we see portrayed respect for established forms which are no longer efficacious at a time when pastoral methods are out of touch with the human conditions which formerly governed them. But it was there, in his awareness of this cleavage, that Dominic found his vocation as an itinerant preacher in evangelical poverty.

We know the sequel : the establishment of a team entirely freed from all forms of security and economic ties ; communication made possible with men at variance with ecclesiastical feudalism and its pomp ; direct preaching of the Gospel and bearing witness to it ; travelling about from town to town replacing the former monastic stability with its implied bondage to landed property ; a canonical life in which the obligation of traditional public worship was both lightened and sustained by contemplation, study and the requirements of the apostolate ; soon, the education of the young in the very heart of those university schools in which the culture of the rising generation found expression ; lastly, communities taking shape of their own accord on the pattern of the new social organizations with frequent elections as a juridical expression of their brotherhood and as a means of apostolic flexibility. As a foundation and an aid for this spiritual organization *evangelical* poverty was adopted by the renunciation of even collective ownership which had remained the economic basis of the old monasteries : the 'brethren' were to live from day to day, without revenues or benefices (see below), by the spontaneous offerings of the faithful and their associations wherever they preached the Gospel. The general chapter of Bologna, in 1220, gave definitive ratification to this new embodiment of the elements of the *vita apostolica*, renewed once more according to the pattern of the first disciples of Christ.

What then was the meaning of this 'mendicancy', the spiritual meaning which lay behind the temporal manifestation ? The romantic picture of the collector of alms in kind, going from door to door, is not entirely without truth—an austere truth— and hagiographers have not spared us their edifying accounts of this practice. But such a picture, in reality, is somewhat discarnate and unconsciously disregards the contingencies governing the fundamentals and laws of this poverty. Recognition of the real contingencies precisely by means of which this poverty became institutionalised to a degree surpassing mere individual fervour is no lessening of its evangelical quality or its mystical purity ; on the contrary, in this way its effectiveness stands revealed.

Evangelical poverty may always be regarded in the first place as a rejection, an economic rejection governed by a spiritual one ; the following of Christ means primarily breaking away from the pomp of the world and its institutions. It may thus be defined as a twofold and as a single movement : a mystical adherence to Christ and the rejection of an established abuse ; and the second movement forms the symbol, and the guarantee, of the first. This established abuse is not merely the moral relaxation of certain persons in high office whose avarice is repudiated and whose injustices are denounced ; it is the whole system of a human society which has been endowed with the rules and customs necessary for its collective life, relationships and culture. When this collective life, or these relationships, are modified, when the conditions of security are changed, or the culture is in a state of ferment, the entire system, though formerly lawful, is at once laid open to question. Ancient rights, which were the guarantees of stability and freedom become outworn privileges, institutionally productive of avarice and injustice. The impatience of the rising generation loudly asserts the decadence of the system and refuses to accept the teaching of its elders. History records such periodical transmutations in the established order. The twelfth century was the scene of an evolutionary process of this nature. For three centuries the feudal system ensured the stability, permanence and culture of society, but it could no longer satisfy the material and spiritual needs of a changed society—indeed it was incapable of doing so. New centres of population, technical and commercial development, the gradual or sudden emancipation of the serfs, the growing predominance of urban centres, the tendency towards fraternities which were unwilling to humour traditional paternalism, and to which the oath of fealty could give neither juridical nor moral status, the increased number of crowded cultural centres, were all so many factors whereby feudalism, which had formerly promoted justice and social charity, had become the enduring cause of a state of disorder inacceptable from the human and christian point of view, and degenerated into petty rivalry and the most selfish form of conservatism.

The Church, nevertheless, had accepted responsibility for the immense effort of organisation which, from the chaos of the barbarian invasions, had resulted in this feudalism. She had given a spiritual significance to the system of manorial economy in which the monastery was the religious counterpart of the baronial castle, and quite recently Cîteaux had renewed this close connection with the land. The Church had endowed with religious sanction the oath which forged the links of this society and together with fidelity had extolled the evangelical virtues of justice and charity. She blessed the arms of the knights so that under pain of perjury they should be employed in the service 'of widows and orphans, of all the servants of God, against the cruelty of the heathen'; in this way chivalry became an element in the establishment of peace; Roland and the Cid, though not perfect Christian heroes, are examples of how far a religious sense had penetrated the brutality of that warlike age. By concerning herself even with the fiscal system the Church, with the revenue provided by tithes, established a social security service, an essentially charitable undertaking, which automatically gave financial aid in the frequent disasters, and provided a quasi-legal remedy for the permanent inequalities in the distribution of property. Hospitality, by putting the evangelical counsel on the basis of customary usage, extended to the relationships, journeys and mishaps of daily life the benefits of this social privilege. Schools, which grew up under the protection of monasteries and churches, with the intellectual and financial support of the clergy, existed voluntarily under the jurisdiction of the Church; she settled their curriculum and financed them. In short, she had become the stay and guarantor of a social system from which she was the first to benefit; the temporal activities of the clergy at all levels of administration was the normal condition of its spiritual effectiveness.

Three centuries of successful operation endowed this system with every appearance of unalterable truth. Consequently the

Church looked coldly on all plans which would upset this established order and the community of interests which bound prelate and nobleman to identity of tradition, added economic interest as a further reason for her moral resistance. Content with the organised charity under her control she took little interest in the evolution taking place in the social condition of peasants and artisans; setting value on allegiance and the religious nature of the oath she did not favour the charters of emancipation which could only be obtained with some degree of violence; nor could she recognize in these instances of collective advancement an opportune application of her high regard for spiritual values and her Gospel. In the same way, at the political level, she did not understand the full significance of the communal movement which many of her prelates looked upon as the result of revolutionary agitation; 'the great majority of the bishops remained indifferent or hostile towards a trend which drew its inspiration from the desire to put an end to the despotism of the nobility that had originated in a form of selfishness that was entirely pagan' (A. Fliche). Consequently, at the very time that she was continuing to preach her Gospel of justice and charity her commitments in the temporal order closed her eyes to the reforms that were necessary.

As a result the people became imbued with a profound disaffection for a clergy so heavily burdened with routine and the temporal administration of feudal property. Even where religious fervour seemed to have freed clerics from these contingencies a certain lack of understanding constituted an obstacle that was practically insuperable: thus it was that despite papal scoldings and the good intentions and spiritual strength of Cîteaux, with its reactionary attitude in this matter, the Church could no longer touch the soul of the people of those days any more than St Bernard had been able to understand Abelard's curiosity. The apostolate no longer found a basis for action nor the word of God hearers. The episode at Montpellier is extremely significant. A serious, austere return to common life among the clergy (the 'canonical' clergy) in some places during the century had, it is true, awakened the ideal of evangelical poverty as a support for a pastoral preaching of greater efficacy ; but the followers of such reforms rapidly fell back on the ideal of personal salvation ; and the evangelisation of the population of the towns remained without provision. What seemed, in the case of the Church, to be only an accidental want of adaptation to external conditions stood revealed as a fundamental failure in the very sphere of her own message.

So it is that whenever in the eventful progress of civilisation, as social and political institutions evolve and as things are working up for a renewal of man, for a type of renewed humanity, socially speaking, the Church, which is stable, suffers from a kind of time lag which leaves her temporarily backward, yet possessing the means of imbuing with grace not only individuals, but also the new institutions and communities. But it is also precisely at that moment, by a natural instinct wherein our faith discerns the presence of the Holy Ghost, that the Church reacts, with a movement of her whole body, to acknowledge this new humanity as ideal ground for the grace of Christianity.

These resources, ranged in simple yet audacious fervour, are derived from the very condition of social ferment. Society in the twelfth and thirteenth centuries, with all its passion for commerce, liberty, progress and culture remained instinctively receptive to the religious spirit, exceedingly devout even among its élite, and not untinged with an absolutism which found expression in its spiritual impatience and urge to proselytism. Zeal for renewal turned men's thoughts to developments in the primitive Church ; on all sides there arose, spontaneously, groups which, seizing lovingly on those passages of the Gospel referring to the sending out of the disciples with neither money nor provisions (*Mark* 6, 8-10), and of the *Acts* (4, 32), concerning the common life of the first Christians, founded on this literalist interpretation their complete severance from decadent society and the conformist attitude of Christians. Such an undertaking is full of risk and we can learn from history that eminent sanctity is required if it is to succeed ; but no risk of excess, no failure can invalidate the principle of this return to the Gospel as the appropriate means to spiritual release and the necessary movement for far-reaching reforms.

Now poverty is more than the ascetic condition of this

severance, it is rather its effective symbol. No longer were
there merely individuals living as poor men but even institutions
(whereas poor individuals had been living in a rich Church)
seeking their bread from day to day and refusing that economic
stability which created, even in the Church, the vigour of their
forerunners and the power of the monasteries. It could not be
stated more explicitly. It meant taking a resolute stand against
the dangers of wealth in the development of society in its new
forms and at the same time trusting to it for a Christendom
which as a matter of course made provision for its apostles.
Consequently mendicant poverty became, if it may be so
described, the economic foundation both of an itinerant
apostolate whose preachers were wayfarers, as well as of a
community of brethren joyfully dependent on the improvisations
of Providence. Therefore they were no longer housed in stately
permanent monasteries (by the time they had begun to build,
the first youth of their apostolic fervour was over), but in poor
buildings, wherever opportunity offered, in popular or student
quarters of the towns. Obviously the new apostles could look
for lodging, food and the means of livelihood to those alone
who shared with them that sense of human fellowship which
had become the object of their Christian fraternity. The full
force of this vital protest fell directly on the 'benefices' by
which the feudal system assured the maintenance of the clergy,
and of the material side of divine worship, but the multiplication
of which—that veritable scourge of feudalism—had become a
scandal under the new economy. These poor men did away
with tithes, the system of mutual aid, hospices and charitable
institutions, which were henceforth taken over by communities
devoted to these purposes, now that grace had restored to
human nature its social resources. Their spiritual dynamism,
and that of these undertakings now restored to their natural
leaders, was thereby increased tenfold.

Such is the meaning of mendicant poverty seen in and
through these relevant factors ; such was even then its organic
constitution. Its whole inspiration and value was fundamentally
evangelical (folly to the wise !), its social interpretation lessens
in no wise its mystical content since, on the contrary, it was an
effective manifestation of that particular feature. A vow of

'mendicancy' meant, in the thirteenth century, a categoric institutional, economic rejection of the ecclesiastical feudal system, 'benefices,' levying of tithes, even when apostolic or charitable means were involved ; in this way the liberty of the word of God was set free from the trappings of the feudal system. Neither Francis nor Dominic, of course, had the slightest idea of choosing or rejecting an economic system ; nor does the Church possess either the grace or the competence to instigate, construct or oppose any such organisation of worldly goods. The Mendicants excluded feudalism even as nowadays the Mission de Paris excludes capitalism : in each there is an identical evangelical violence but entire absence of economic ideology. Inherent in the return to the Gospel is always a rejection of personal or collective abuses. Moreover it can be clearly seen that those who refused this rejection, this poverty, even if individually they were saints, remained unconsciously in sympathy with established abuses and so were rendered incapable of effectively preaching the Gospel. The rising generations perceived this, left them forthwith and went to people the houses of the Friars Minor and Preachers.

There were, as has been mentioned, two very different types of evangelical poverty brought into being by these Minors and Preachers, differing in inspiration—in accordance with the indefinable adaptability of one and the same Spirit—and in origin. For the Minors, even in their early lay condition, represented a categoric and impulsive movement carrying all before it, whereas the Preachers achieved the paradox of realising this new-born evangelism within the confines of a clerical organisation. But in spite of these differences the two Orders encountered each other in a spirit of friendly fellowship among those very circles from which they emanated and whose secular plans were turned to account in producing a novel form of religious life : they formed a cognate environment in which their social, cultural, and spiritual ferment could find, on the religious level, both its requisite satisfaction and its balance. They took the monastery from the solitary valleys to the centre of the great towns ; and this was more than a mere symbol. They threw over abbatial paternalism in order to live in a brotherhood where rights and duties were derived from the common good discerned by all in chapter meetings which were those of mature men. Their government, whether local or central, was based on the principle of frequent elections and subjected to permanent supervision ; it was the counterpart of the economic and political institutions of the period. They straightway entered the universities as students and as teachers and rapidly made their own the religious, philosophical and scientific pre-occupations of their contemporaries. These poor friars introduced Aristotle (until then prohibited) and christened the wisdom of the Greeks, at the same time fostering the revival of biblical studies by the correction of texts and the production of concordances and other works of reference. They became the counsellors of princes and, better still, the originators of the communal laws and constitutions of the free towns. They were the obvious chaplains for the corporations and confraternities which had difficulty in finding a spiritual centre in the parishes or monasteries. For the benefit of their itinerant apostolate they adopted the mobility of these business men and became the promoters of the international interests of peoples and of Christendom.

Thus Preachers and Minors were deeply committed to the new order of which they found themselves, as if by spontaneous generation, the spiritual inspiration. It may appear paradoxical that a return to the Gospel in all the severity of its purity and supernatural integrity should lead to such compromises with social structures. It is nothing of the sort. Indeed it is the constant rhythm of the Church's life, of a Church without blemish which yet dwells among busy and sinful humanity, of a Church which struggles and suffers in the building up of Christendom in successive generations whereby all mankind, in every civilisation, is assumed in grace, in the likeness of Christ in whom the whole man is assumed by the divine Person. The more faithful the Christian the deeper can he commit himself without fear of compromise or contamination. That is the paradox of the Incarnation. Poverty is always the characteristic of incarnation.

CHAPTER IV

THE POVERTY OF ST FRANCIS

By E. LECLERCQ, O.F.M.

There can be no mention of St Francis of Assisi without recalling what he loved as his Lady—Poverty. For between the religious destiny of Francis and poverty there is an essential and indissoluble bond. In his religious life poverty played a unique part; the importance that it held for him cannot be exaggerated. 'Never was a man seen,' wrote Celano, 'more greedy for gold than he was for poverty'.[1] 'For my wealth and for my Lady I have chosen poverty.'[2] One day when the brethren were met together they were wondering what virtue makes a man more especially Christ's friend. Their Father, disclosing the secrets of his heart, exclaimed: 'It is poverty, my sons. Be sure of this, it is the special way of salvation, its fruits are manifold and there are few who know it[3] . . . It is the way of perfection, the pledge of everlasting wealth[4] . . . Such is the greatness of that exalted poverty which has established you, my very dear brethren, as heirs and kings of the kingdom of God, making you poor in earthly goods, but exalted in virtue. May that poverty which leads to the land of the living be your lot.'[5]

These few quotations show clearly how poverty was the leading and characteristic feature of the religious ideal of Francis of Assisi. It may appear to some that he attributes excessive importance to poverty. We are thus led to inquire—and the question forms the subject of this study—what meaning did St Francis give to poverty? How was he led to attribute such importance to it?

[1] *Cel*. IIa ch. xxv.
[2] *Cel*. IIa, ch. li. Cf. *Legenda Antiqua* ch. lxxx.
[3] *Cel*. IIa chap. cli. Cf. *St. Bonaventure* ch. vii/l.
[4] *Cel*. IIa. ch. xxv.
[5] *Reg*. Ia, ch. vi.

The impact of St Francis on his own period

The answer to this question may perhaps be sought primarily
in St Francis's impact on his own period. His interpretation of
poverty is closely related to the needs and aspirations of his
times, and the genesis of his ideal can be explained in reference
to the trends manifested at that time in the Church. At the
end of the thirteenth century the Church was undergoing a
severe crisis. In the political sphere, through her support of
the communal revolution, she had managed to set herself free
from the protection of the Emperors and recover her spiritual
independence ; but she was still involved in the framework of
feudalism and weighed down by her luxury of ornament and
wealth which hid her religious influence. 'Who will enable me
to see God's Church as she was in her early days,' exclaimed
St Bernard, 'when the apostles let down their nets not to catch
gold and silver, but the souls of men' ? This heartfelt appeal
was soon to be echoed by Pierre Valdez : 'The prelates should
have a spade in their hands and not this sword which ill accords
with their condition'. And now Christian people were beginning
to murmur ; they had been tried to breaking point. From all
sides arose the recall to the Gospel, to poverty : Vaudois,
Humiliati, Beghards, Cathari, all were obsessed with evangelical
poverty and yearned for it as the only course leading to spiritual
release.

It is difficult, therefore, not to discern a close relationship
between what St Francis desired to achieve and the needs of
his time. His downright refusal of all property as well as of the
use of money appeared indeed to be dictated by the necessities
of the moment. Should not this radical attitude be seen as an
extreme step undertaken for reasons of public safety, urgently
demanded by a sort of 'supernatural instinct of preservation'
inherent in the heart of Christian people ? The observation
made one day by Francis to bishop Guy reveals his spontaneous
determination to escape the evil from which Christendom was
suffering : 'Your manner of life,' the prelate remarked, 'seems
too severe and impractical'. 'My Lord,' Francis replied in all
simplicity, 'if we possessed property we should require arms
to protect it'. On the spur of the moment and unintentionally

Francis, with that blunt sentence, was criticising the feudalism of the Church arising from its attitude to property. He saw clearly, and could not be unaware, that his ideal was opportune.

Yet it seems equally clear that this ideal of poverty was not the result of reflexion about his own times ; analysis of the system with a view to its reformation meant little to him. And although his ideal appeared opportune it was not born of a concern to meet a historical need. In his love of poverty any reforming or apologetic preoccupation, or indeed any thought of effective apostolic action, is to be sought in vain. So long as he pursued his ideal of poverty he appeared not to perceive the contemporary situation of the Church then struggling and at grips with heresy.

When the crucifix at San Damiano said to him : 'Francis, go and repair my house which, as you see, is falling into ruin,'[1] he never for a moment thought of the reform of the Church, but was filled with joy at having found at last what should be his ideal of perfection.[2] Rather than in historical events it is in the spiritual experience of Francis himself that we must look for the secret of his poverty. This poverty is entirely bound up with his religious conversion : it springs from it, develops with it and is revealed to him according to the depths of his experience. For a complete understanding of his poverty it must be considered as a part of this religious experience viewed as a whole.

Before the discovery of the evangelical ideal

In the first place it should be noticed that even before he discovered the evangelical ideal, poverty appears to have exercised a great attraction for Francis and to have made a deep impression on him. He understood the religious significance of the poor.

'While yet in the world,' writes Celano, 'and still concerned with secular business he began to aid the poor, offering a generously helping hand to those he observed in want, and pouring out his loving compassion on the afflicted. One day when, contrary to his usual practice, he had refused alms to a

[1] *Cel.* IIa, ch. vi.
[2] *Cel.* Ia, ch. ix.

beggar, he regretted it at once, saying to himself that it was
hateful and shameful to refuse charity to one who asked it in
the name of so great a King. Thereupon he made up his mind
henceforth always to give, so far as he could, to anyone who
held out his hand for the love of God.[1] . . . One day, he
encountered a poor and almost naked knight ; moved with pity
he gave generously, for the love of Christ, the richly embroidered
clothes he was wearing.[2] . . . It was a frequent occurrence for
him to divest himself of his clothes to cover the poor whom
he endeavoured to resemble, if not in fact, at least by his interior
attitude.'[3]

Although at this time Francis had given up his worldly life
he had not yet discovered the ideal of evangelical poverty ; it is
remarkable, in consequence, to see how his compassion for
the poor makes him spontaneously desire to share the conditions
of the poor and to experience poverty personally. 'One day,'
continues Celano, 'during a pilgrimage to Rome, out of love of
poverty he put off his fine clothes, borrowed a poor man's rags
and, in the square before St Peter's, which teemed with beggars,
took up his stand full of joy in their company'. It is surprising
that the son of a rich citizen, noted for his lordly bearing, well
known and a great favourite of all, should thus lower himself
in the social scale. It is proper matter for astonishment. What
were his reasons for this action ?

St Bonaventure, who had thought much about the experience
of St Francis, wrote as follows : 'For there was divinely planted
in his heart a certain generous compassion toward the poor
which, growing up with him from infancy, had so filled his
heart with kindliness that he was minded to give to all that
asked of him, especially if they pleaded the love of God . . .
And thereby he won abundant increase of the love and grace
of God.'[4]

Thus the origin of Francis's attraction to poverty is to be
found in an impulse of charity, of liberality, which found
expression in effective compassion for the poor. But what

[1] *Cel.* Ia, ch. vii.
[2] *Cel.* IIa, ch. ii.
[3] *Cel.* IIa, ch. iv.
[4] *St Bonaventure* ch. i, 1.

caused poverty to exercise so great a fascination on him that this compassion was soon turned to imitation ?

A decisive event occurred in the life of Francis : after he kissed the leper, when he overcame his natural repugnance, Christ crucified appeared to him. 'And from that hour,' writes Celano, 'compassion for Christ on the cross was imprinted in his holy soul'.[1] Francis thereupon felt an urgent need for self-renunciation ; his love of poverty was henceforth consonant with this overriding necessity. 'He desired,' says St Bonaventure, 'to despise worldly repute . . . He kept strict watch over the mortification of the flesh, that he might bear outwardly in his body the cross of Christ, which he already bore inwardly in his heart.'[2]

It was, then, as much a desire for self-renunciation as a feeling of compassion which caused Francis to assume an outward appearance of poverty. For the same reasons, we see him, at the same period of his life, exerting himself on behalf of the lepers. The temporary experience of poverty that he underwent at this time, like his care of the lepers, appears then as a very special epoch in his progress Godwards. But whereas the care of the lepers is simply a stage in his conversion—an important stage that Francis emphasizes in his Testament—the experience of poverty was for him the cause of a state of life, a 'form of life' ; in his eyes it became increasingly the expression of an ideal. This ideal was to be revealed to him in the Gospel as being the very form of life in accordance with the Gospel.

Revelation of the evangelical ideal

This revelation of the evangelical ideal was a decisive moment in the life of Francis of Assisi. 'No one showed me what I ought to do ; but the most high himself revealed to me that I must live according to the form of the holy Gospel.'[3] The event occurred in the little church of St Mary of the Portiuncula that St Francis had just repaired ; 'while he was devoutly hearing the Mass of the apostles, that Gospel was read aloud wherein Christ gave unto his disciples that were sent forth to

[1] *Cel.* IIa, ch. iv.
[2] *St Bonaventure* ch. I, 6.
[3] Testament V, 14-15.

preach the Gospel pattern for their life'.[1] Gradually Francis
understood the meaning of the words and directly Mass was
over hastened to ask the priest to explain the passage to him.
The priest expounded the whole passage. 'And when Francis
understood that Christ's disciples were to take with them
neither gold, nor silver, no money, purse, or wallet, no bread,
staff, shoes or a second coat, and that they were to preach the
kingdom of God, and penance, he thrilled with a divine joy :
"This is what I desire," he cried, "this is what I seek, and long
for with my whole heart".'[2] And forthwith Francis adopted
the Gospel way of life : '. . . he took off his shoes, threw away
his staff, kept only one tunic and took a rope instead of his
girdle.[3] From that moment he began to preach penance to all
and give tidings of peace.'

This evangelical ideal is the origin of the Franciscan adventure. But it should be pointed out at once that the ideal of
poverty just discovered by Francis is not the same as that of
the primitive community in Jerusalem after Pentecost. That
was a steady, established community gathered round the
Temple with its regular liturgical worship ; and in the matter
of poverty although the individual gave up his possessions it
was done for the benefit of all, the benefit of the community.
The Gospel ideal discovered by Francis is quite different ; it
is the ideal of the apostolic community gathered round the
Master, itinerant and missionary with him ; to join this travelling, floating community it was necessary to give up one's
possessions for the benefit of the poor ; and it was in this state
of radical poverty that it was possible to follow the Master
who had not 'where to lay his head'. The exacting requirements
of this evangelical ideal effectively bar any claim to personal or
collective ownership.

Directly Francis discovered this ideal poverty was no longer
for him merely a means of perfection ; it had become a state
of life, the state of the disciple of Christ. In his own words it is
'life according to the Gospel form'. It is the law by which
Christ's disciple, who bears witness to him, lives. And what in

[1] *St Bonaventure* ch. iii, 1.
[2] *Cel.* Ia, ch. ix.
[3] *Cel.* Ia, ch. ix.

his view gave it all its value was this : it had been lived and experienced by Christ himself and his apostles. His chief concern in making this law his own entirely was to imitate Christ, 'to tread in his footsteps'. Celano writes : 'His settled determination, his most ardent desire, his final aim, was always and in everything to observe the holy Gospel and, employing all his watchfulness, all his zeal, the application of his whole mind and all the fervour of his heart, to follow perfectly the teaching and footsteps of our Lord Jesus Christ'.[1]

The decision taken by Francis to live in the strictest poverty is inspired directly by Christ's example. It cannot be emphasized too strongly that the poverty of St Francis was desired and lived in imitation of Christ. 'I, brother Francis, the little, desire to follow the life and poverty of our Lord Jesus Christ and his most holy Mother, and I desire to persevere therein until the end.'[2] It is this example of Christ the poor man that continually he placed before his brethren.

'Let the brethren remember that our Lord Jesus Christ, the Son of the living and almighty God, was poor and without a dwelling, that he, the Blessed Virgin and his disciples lived on alms.'[3] 'Poverty,' he declared, 'is the queen of virtues inasmuch as she shone forth thus excellently in the King of Kings and in the Queen his Mother'.[4] 'For our sakes God became poor on earth ; for this reason and following his example and that of his most holy Mother, we have chosen the way of the sternest poverty.'[5] 'The examples of poverty given us by the Son of God should be more binding on us than on other religious.'[6]

In the light of these quotations it is clear, then, that Francis strove after poverty in imitation of Christ ; it is no less clear that he made poverty the principal point of his imitation of Christ. Does that mean he made a choice and stressed only one aspect of Christ ? It is perhaps tempting to think so but in that case there is some risk of not understanding the Franciscan

[1] *Cel.* Ia, ch. xxx.

[2] *Opusc.*

[3] Reg. Ia, ch. ix, 5-6.

[4] *St Bonaventure* ch. vii, 1.

[5] *Legenda Antiqua*, ch. iii.

[6] *Cel.* IIa, ch. xxxi.

experience and of reducing it to something rather narrow. If Francis insists so strongly on poverty it is because he considers it the foundation of an integral evangelical life.

Poverty, the foundation of an integral evangelical life

For this reason it is important to understand how the most literal interpretation of poverty, experienced as an imitation of Christ, enabled Francis to live and to discover an outlook which is entirely that of the Gospel. We shall endeavour to describe the impulse which gives Franciscan poverty this full and integral, evangelical outlook.

In the first place Francis was fully aware that evangelical poverty makes us, like Christ, 'pilgrims and strangers on the earth'.

'The brethren must own nothing, whether house, goods or anything at all. As pilgrims and strangers on earth, serving the Lord in poverty and humility, they will go begging with confidence, without embarrassment; for the Lord, for our sakes, became poor in this world.'[1]

'Let the brethren beware of accepting under any circumstances, either churches or dwellings or whatever is built for them if it is not consonant with that holy poverty which we professed in the Rule; let them dwell therein always as guests, strangers and pilgrims.'[2]

'He desired,' we read in the *Legenda Antiqua*, 'that the brethren should not be the owners of any monastery but that they should always live in them as travellers and strangers'.[3]

'Not only did this man hate any ostentation in building,' writes Celano, 'but he also held in horror any sign of wealth or elegance in their furnishing. He wished that the tables and crockery should in no way suggest worldliness; everything was to be a reminder of *pilgrimage and exile*.'[4]

'In his sermons on poverty he often quoted to the brethren this passage of the Gospel: "The foxes have holes, and the birds of the air nests; but the son of man hath not where to

[1] *Reg.* IIa, ch. vi.
[2] *Testament.*
[3] *Legenda Antiqua*, ch. xiii.
[4] *Cel.* IIa, ch. xxx.

lay his head". Wherefore he would teach the brethren that, after the fashion of the poor, they should build only poor little houses wherein they should dwell, not as their owners, but as *pilgrims and strangers* dwell in other men's houses. For he said that the rules of pilgrims were to abide under a strange roof, to thirst for their fatherland, and to pass on their way in peace.'[1]

'When one Easter day he was staying in a hermitage so distant from the dwellings of men that he could not conveniently go forth to beg, mindful of him who on that day had appeared to the disciples going into Emmaus in the guise of a pilgrim, he, as a pilgrim and beggar, asked alms from the brethren themselves. He received their alms with humility and showed them from the Scriptures that while passing through the wilderness of the world as pilgrims and strangers, and Israelites indeed, they might celebrate continually, as those poor in spirit, the Lord's Passover ; that is, his departure from this world to his Father.'[2]

We are far from a narrow conception of the following of Christ. These quotations show clearly enough how central the theme of pilgrims and strangers is in the Franciscan conception of poverty. It is of some importance to make its spiritual implications clear.

To be a pilgrim and a stranger in this world following Christ means primarily the refusal of any settled abode ; it means leaving one's home and the security it offers, to seek the great adventure of the Kingdom. It implies a state of exodus, of going forward, of continual pilgrimage. For St Francis it meant, in practice, the rejection of all comfort and all possessions whether personal or in common. But to be a pilgrim is also, as St Francis put it, 'to be received in the houses of others,' it means living on alms. Poverty should place us in a state of dependence ; it obliges us to rely on a providential generosity and liberality for our sustenance. 'The brethren will go out to beg with confidence.'[3] 'They will have recourse to the Lord's table.'[4] 'Sending out his brethren into the world Francis told

---

[1] *St Bonaventure* ch. vii.
[2] *St Bonaventure* ch. vii.
[3] *Reg.* IIa, ch. vi.
[4] *Testament.*

them : "Put your confidence in the Lord, he will take care of you".[1] Celano describes how one day Francis induced some knights to ask for alms ; he was at that time on the point of death ; the people of Assisi had sent an escort to fetch him from Nocera in order that others should not have the honour of possessing the body of the man of God. And as the knights brought him back with great veneration they arrived at Sartriano, a little mean town ; it was dinner time ; they were hungry ; in vain they searched throughout the town ; they were unable to buy anything. Whereupon the saint said to them : 'If you find nothing it is because you trust in your flies (he called coins flies) rather than in God ; but go back to the houses at which you have called and there humbly ask for alms offering in exchange the love of God. Do not blush to do this for since sin came all possessions are given to men as alms. And he who is the great Almoner gives of his bounty with kindness and mercy to worthy and unworthy alike.'[2]

We have now a clearer idea of what being a pilgrim and stranger in this world meant to Francis : poverty, in depriving man of the trust he might have in his own possessions, commits him to an experience of faith and complete confidence in God ; it leads man to look on himself as God's beggar, to turn towards God as to his one resource.

Poverty and the meaning of grace

But to understand how far poverty, according to St Francis, requires an attitude of absolute faith we must pursue our analysis further and in another direction. We must see how, beginning with his discovery of the Gospel ideal, he was led to the discovery of his own absolute poverty in the sight of God and to beg for his salvation, in faith, as for alms.

Francis began with the imitation of Christ, an imitation which he made as literal as possible. Frequently this exterior and picturesque aspect of the Franciscan experience is dwelt on exclusively, and there is a tendency to define it by what is in reality its most exterior and superficial quality. However necessary this literalism was for St Francis his solicitude for profound fidelity led him to discover other requirements in the

[1] *Cel.* Ia, ch. xii.
[2] *Cel.* IIa, ch. xlvii.

imitation of the poverty of Christ. 'There are many,' he wrote, 'who are always praying and at the offices of the Church, making a practice of much abstinence and corporal penance. But if a single word appears to them an injustice in respect of their body, or the smallest thing is taken away from them they are at once scandalised and upset. Theirs is not the spirit of poverty. The really poor in spirit is he who hates himself and is deeply attached to those who strike his cheek.'[1]

Francis understood that to be poor, following Christ's example, it was not enough to rid oneself of material possessions and go barefoot. 'For,' he said, 'in vain doth he utterly renounce the world who keeps in the secret places of his heart a shrine for his own will'.[2]

There is, then, in man a will for possession, an anxiety for ownership which goes beyond material possessions and prevents his living integrally the experience of poverty. This will for possession leads him away from the spiritual attitude which should be induced by material poverty. Freed from material possessions man continues to desire the good with the avarice of a miser, that is, as an asset coming from himself, which he draws from the good treasures of his own heart and on which he claims, as originator and owner, spiritual or other privileges. Francis, better than any, was aware of this fundamental possessiveness of man which calls in question the very meaning of material poverty. But also none better than he has applied himself to denunciation of the inherent injustice on the part of man in claiming himself as the author of good, the owner of any goods whatever. Thus throughout his writings St Francis endeavours to make us conscious of our fundamental poverty as he himself discovered it in the twofold light of his sense of sin and of God.

In the first place in the light of his sense of sin. For Francis, sin did not consist in certain exterior transitory actions from which we may easily dissociate ourselves. It is within us, like a growth : 'By our own fault we are corrupt and wretched, opposed to good, ready and willing for evil'.[3]

[1] Adm. xiv.
[2] *St Bonaventure* ch. vii.
[3] *Reg.* Ia, ch. xxii, 6.

'Wretched sinners that we all are, we are unworthy to speak thy name.'[1]

'Everyone has the enemy in his power, that is the body through which he sins.'[2]

We must recognize these emphatic sentences as something more than pious exaggeration : they are indeed a clear and profound expression of our sinfulness. St Francis's religious experience is akin to that of St Paul and St Augustine ; he belongs to the class of spiritual temperaments which, extremely conscious of our moral wretchedness, are apt in consequence for the workings of grace.

To Francis, man in his powerlessness to will what is good with a pure heart, experiences a profound consciousness of his sinful nature. 'A sinner,' he was fond of saying, 'may fast, pray, weep, mortify his flesh ; one thing he finds impossible and that is to be faithful to his Lord'.[3] We have to recognize that our will for good is only apparent or else is not derived from ourselves.

But for Francis it is the idea of God which shows definitively and clearly our essential poverty. If there is one truth with which he was imbued it was this : God alone possesses complete goodness and he alone is its cause ; he alone effects what is good and it can, in consequence, be an attribute only of him. He alone can claim it as his possession as deriving from him. We can no more boast of the good that the Lord speaks or effects through us than we can of that which he speaks or effects through another.[4] It is a sin of blasphemy to be envious of one's brother for the good which the Lord speaks or effects in him since in reality it is to be envious of the Most High who says or does everything that is good.[5]

Thus St Francis brings us back to our fundamental poverty by this twofold truth : We possess as our own only our vices and our sins ; God alone does what is good.

It is in terms of this fundamental poverty that Francis

[1] *Reg.* Ia, ch. xxiii, 9.
[2] *Adm.* X.
[3] *St Bonaventure* ch. vi, 3.
[4] *Adm.* xvii.
[5] *Adm.* vii.

endows material poverty with its entire religious and evangelical significance. His is the merit of establishing the relationship between the material state of one who is poor and our fundamental poverty, thus revealing the true meaning of evangelical poverty. For the latter cannot be reduced to a mere ascetical practice ; it is not simply a means for ensuring freedom of the spirit. Considered under this aspect alone it remains on the humanistic level. But it is the sacrament or pledge of our state as Christians ; it expresses palpably and effectively the inherent attitude of one who, having acknowledged himself poor before God in respect of all that is good, trusts in him alone for salvation through faith, and gives back to him every good thing in thanksgiving and adoration.

Material poverty, since it demands absolute dispossession, becomes in reality the foundation and the expression of the Christian experience of salvation through faith. Francis, poor before God, indigent of anything that is good, expects everything from God, and especially his salvation, as alms. It is 'God who of his sole mercy will save us ; in spite of our weakness and our wretchedness, our corruption and our shame, our ingratitude and our malice, he has, and will, do only good in our regard'.[1] Because he experienced poverty to the full Francis discovered the meaning of Agape : whosoever acknowledges himself completely poor will find that God treats him with pure generosity and absolute liberality. Thereafter even the imitation of Christ is to him something received as a gift ; it is part of salvation through grace. 'Grant to us unhappy mortals to do for thee what we know to be thy will and to desire always what pleases thee, so that interiorly purified, interiorly enlightened and kindled with the fire of the Holy Spirit we may tread in the footsteps of thy Son, our Lord Jesus Christ, and through thy grace alone attain to thee, most High . . .'[2]

From this it may be understood how Francis's religious attitude blossoms out into adoration and thanksgiving. The meaning of his renunciation of all possessions is that of restitution ; all his goods were to be given back to the one who works every good. 'In the love which is God I beseech all my

[1] *Reg.* Ia, ch. xxiii.
[2] *Letter to the General Chapter.*

brethren, preachers, speakers, workers, clerics and lay folk, to direct their efforts to be humble in all things, not to boast, not to rejoice in themselves, not to pride themselves interiorly on the good words, good works, in short on any good thing that God says, does or effects in them or through them according to our Saviour's precept: "Yet rejoice not in this, that evil spirits are subject to you".'[1]

'Let us give back all our goods to the Most High and Sovereign Lord God, acknowledging that all belongs to him; in all things let us give thanks to him from whom come all good things . . .'[2]

This impulse of gratitude is the surest way to adoration. By dint of looking on God as the source and fullness of everything that we possess our prayer becomes that of a pure heart, solely occupied in adoring him. The most delicious fruit of poverty, which makes it a form of wisdom, is surely that purity of heart which causes us to find all our pleasure in discovering that God is God and that he is 'all riches and our sufficiency'.[3]

[1] *Reg.* Ia, ch. xvii.
[2] *Reg.* Ia, ch. xvii.
[3] *Letter to Brother Leo.*

CHAPTER V

THE POVERTY OF ST IGNATIUS

By J. CREUSEN, S.J.

In order to understand the special form of poverty bestowed by St Ignatius on his Order allowance must be made for various circumstances of a personal or social nature.

The inspiration of the individual or even collective poverty of the Society is to be sought in the *Spiritual Exercises* which gave to St Ignatius and his first companions the very form of their spiritual life and, as a result, their whole concept of the apostolate.

The twofold form of poverty in the Society of Jesus—i.e., of the Residences and of the Colleges or Scholasticates—originated in a personal experience.

The rapid spread of the so-called reformation, which may be explained in part by the abuse of wealth and honours in the Church of the sixteenth century, is largely responsible for the severe form of poverty, even collective poverty, which we find laid down in the Constitutions.

The sources which must be consulted to find out the form and extent of these influences are primarily the *Spiritual Exercises*, then reports of the discussions held by St Ignatius and his first companions in Rome before laying before Paul III the first *Formula Instituti* (1540), next those which took place in 1544 when St Ignatius introduced a modification intended to make the poverty of the Residences even stricter ; the result of these discussions is to be found in the second formula submitted to Julius III (1550).

Another source to be consulted is the *Examen generale*, intended especially to instruct those who are to examine candidates for the Society and to give the latter the necessary information so that they can make up their minds with full knowledge of the facts.

Lastly, a careful study of the *Constitutions* will afford

knowledge of the principles which inspired individual poverty in the Society and the means by which it is to be realised.

Owing to lack of space I have confined myself to the study of these three sources.[1]

With the first meditation on sin the retreatant places himself in the presence of Christ crucified and having contemplated what Christ did for him 'turning his gaze upon himself he will ask what he has done for Christ, what he is doing for Christ, and what he ought to do for Christ in the future '. (1st week, 1st meditation, Colloquy.)

This idea, at this point still somewhat obscure, of a total gift of self to Christ, in response to the total gift that Christ makes us of himself, will be developed and clarified as the adorable Person of our Saviour and the mysteries of his life here below are more directly and exclusively made the subject of contemplation.

In the threefold colloquy which concludes the first repetition of the meditations on sin St Ignatius makes us ask, through Mary's intercession, for the grace of 'a knowledge of the world, in order that viewing it with horror I may put away from myself worldly and vain things'.

After the purification, which is the particular fruit of the meditations of the first week of the Spiritual Exercises, St Ignatius prepares the way for the contemplation of the mysteries of the life of our Saviour by the well-known contemplation of Christ the eternal King summoning all men to consecrate themselves with him to the conquest and establishment of his kingdom in all souls. The response to this summons may vary in generosity. Now one course open to those who desire 'to show greater affection and to distinguish themselves by entire devotion to the service of their eternal King' is the deliberate determination to imitate Christ 'in bearing all injuries, and all

[1] Critical texts of the most important sources for our purpose are to be found in the first volumes of the *Monumenta historica Societatis Jesu*, monumenta Ignatiana, T. I-III (Series tertia). In the *series secunda* will be found the text of the *Spiritual Exercises*. But one or other of the excellent, though less learned, editions will suffice. Among recent books which have succeeded in offering a satisfactory interpretation of the spirit of the Society and its Constitutions may be mentioned : M. Smits van Waesberghe, S.J., *De Geest van Sint Ignatius in zijn Orde*, Utrecht, 1940 ; De Chastonay, S.J., *Die Satzungen des Jesuitenordens*, Einsiedeln, 1938 (French trans. 1941) ; Brodrick, S.J., *The Origins of the Jesuits*, London, 1947.

reproach, and all poverty, actual as well as spiritual, if only the divine Majesty be pleased to choose and receive' the retreatant to such a state of life.

We come now to the culminating point of the Exercises in the meditation on two standards, the one of Christ our supreme Captain and Lord, the other of Lucifer, the mortal enemy of our human nature. Each calls and desires to lead all men under his standard, that is, for them to become his follower, to adopt his principles, to participate in his action. Obviously their methods are entirely opposed.

Now, according to St Ignatius, Satan endeavours in the first place to inspire men with the lust of riches 'in order that thereby they may more easily come to the vain honour of the world and afterwards to unbounded pride'. On the other hand our Lord instils into his friends and disciples quite different tactics : he charges them to draw men 'first to most perfect spiritual poverty and (if it should please his divine Majesty and he should will to choose them) not less to actual poverty'. The desire for shame or contempt is the second degree which leads to true humility.

Thereupon the retreatant begs earnestly to be received under Christ's standard by adopting, should it please God, not only spiritual, but actual poverty.

The importance of actual poverty in the saint's view appears in the meditation on three classes of men which is intended to place the retreatant in the most proper dispositions to follow solely the divine will in the choice of a state of life. And this is the example he chooses : an inordinate affection or a supernatural and perfect one for a sum of money which has been acquired not purely or solely for the love of God.

In an important note on this meditation the author of the Exercises considers only repugnance to actual poverty : 'It is to be observed that when we feel a shrinking from or repugnance to actual poverty, when in fact we are not indifferent to poverty or riches, it is a great help in order to overcome such an inordinate affection to beg in the colloquies, even though it be against the flesh, that our Lord would elect us to actual poverty ; and to protest that we desire, beg and supplicate it provided only that it may be to the service and praise of his divine goodness'.

The consideration on the three modes of humility will reveal
to us, finally, the underlying inspiration of the whole spiritual
life of St Ignatius. It is to be found entire in the Apostles'
exhortation to the Philippians : *Hoc sentite in vobis quod et in
Christo Jesu.* St Ignatius puts it this way :

'The third mode is the most perfect humility : to wit, when
the first and second modes being included, and the praise and
glory of the divine Majesty being equal in order better to
imitate Christ our Lord, and to become actually more like to
him, I desire and choose rather poverty with Christ poor, than
riches ; reproaches with Christ laden therewith, rather than
honour ; and I desire to be accounted as worthless and a fool
for Christ, who was first held to be such, rather than wise and
prudent in this world.'

Without giving a lengthy explanation of this quotation it
will be sufficient for us to notice how clearly the following
thought is given utterance : for the equal glory of God I choose
actual poverty and humiliation solely to be more like Christ.
Could there be a simpler and at the same time more profound
expression of love ? It will be understood how this disposition
is the best with which to follow in complete docility the
promptings of grace without falling victim to the illusions that
self-love may suggest.

We know how the saint practised the offering thus made in
the Spiritual Exercises : how he exchanged his officer's uniform
for a beggar's rags ; how he practised begging in the most
humiliating and often the most arduous fashion, since he would
give to others in need the best of anything he received ; he
desired the insecurity and the insults of this poverty. In a
word he practised evangelical and apostolic poverty in all its
severity.

The first companions of Ignatius were formed in the same
school and from it drew the same inspiration. In August 1534,
they desired to bind themselves more closely to God by solemn
promises. At Montmartre they gathered round the altar where
Pierre Lefevre (Fabre) celebrated Mass and committed themselves to the observance of strict poverty, to go to Jerusalem
there to work for the conversion of the Mohammedans and, if
that were impossible, to place themselves at the Pope's disposal

to carry out any apostolic works that he would be pleased to entrust to them.

We do not possess, I believe, the exact terms of these vows. The vow of obedience could scarcely bind them save in reference to the Pope for they were still far from desiring to found a new order. But their poverty already possessed the characteristics that it was later to assume in more definitive shape. But it did not bind them until their studies were over. Ignatius had already experienced the hindrance that the obligation of begging could offer to proper progress in study.

But already they committed themselves not to accept any remuneration for their ministry nor offering for the celebration of Masses. The form of their ministry was animated by their intention of living as poor men. Laynez, one of Ignatius's first companions, and his successor as Superior General, was to write words that are extremely revealing concerning the spirit which inspired that group of the first disciples. 'We consecrated ourselves to the service of God and to the salvation of souls by preaching and the care of the sick in hospitals, though it was not, originally, from the time of our sojourn in Paris until now (i.e., when they arrived in Venice) our intention to found a religious group, but rather, because we had made up our minds to live in poverty.' (J. Lainez, *Epistola de San Ignatio*. Scripta I, p. 114.)

Following in their Master's footsteps, in spirituality they too practised poverty, sometimes indeed to a degree that was heroic. Their ministry in the hospitals provided them with abundant opportunities for it. We know what the hospitals in those days frequently were. Now it was in them that often they had their lodging, and devoted themselves to the care of the sick even in the most repellant cases.

Their experiences during their life as students and then of their steps in ministering to others exerted considerable influence on the form of poverty that, under St Ignatius's direction, they imposed on the newly-formed Society.

Since they were prevented from carrying out their original plan of going to the Holy Land to labour for the conversion of the infidels Ignatius and his companions went to place themselves at Pope Paul III's disposal; he saw to it that they were provided with the necessary permissions to receive major Orders and allotted them various fields for their apostolic activity. Subsequently they met together on several occasions to draw up a rough plan of the future Institute and to submit it to the approval of the Pope.

These discussions resulted in what is known as the *Formula Instituti* which was approved by Pope Paul III on September 27, 1540. The little group received at the same time permission to draw up a Constitution. The chief responsibility in this work was entrusted to Ignatius, but the most fundamental points were the subject of long discussion between him and his companions.

The *Formula* submitted to Paul III was revised slightly and laid before Julius III who gave it his solemn approval on 21 July, 1550. Now one of the most striking points of the new *Formula* is a stricter interpretation of the collective poverty required of the Residences as opposed to the Colleges.

For a true estimation of poverty as St Ignatius and his first companions understood it, it would be necessary to reproduce here the essential parts of those discussions and the way in which the future Founder, by prayer and by the lights received from God, prepared himself for the decision to practise poverty in a truly evangelical and apostolic form.

Space is wanting here for a study of that nature. We must be content with enumerating the results of all those efforts and prayers as they appear in the two versions of the *Formula Instituti*, the *Examen generale* and the constitutions.[1]

At the time when St Ignatius started to draw up the Constitutions the chief features of the structure of poverty in the future Society were already clearly in his mind.

In the first place, in the matter of collective poverty, quite an original distinction was made between preaching, confessing, teaching children the catechism, visiting the sick, and the colleges or universities frequented by candidates for membership of the Company during the whole course of their studies. The residences could possess no fixed revenue which might be

---

[1] The *Examen generale* is a fairly detailed account of the organisation of the Society, the qualities required of those who enter it in the different categories, and the questions which the examiner should put to the candidate.

claimed as a legal right ; the colleges, however, were by their foundation to be assured of revenues on which the scholastics would live.

There was a further important innovation ; the Fathers could neither ask for nor receive for their ministrations or the celebration of Mass any sum of money which might be regarded as remuneration for the spiritual service they had rendered. Genuine alms alone could be accepted.

Obviously the Founder made no change in the essential obligations of the vow of poverty, namely the dependence on legitimate superiors in every act of ownership so that the Religious could not have the spirit of ownership (*animus domini*) in the acquisition, use, gift or loan of any object of any value in terms of money.

I. COLLECTIVE POVERTY

The section referring to this collective poverty was revised in the *Formula* of 1550. That of 1540 allowed Residences to possess fixed revenues for the maintenance of the sacristy, library and church. This exception to total poverty lay heavy on the Founder's heart. In 1544 he asked his companions to re-consider the matter. He himself celebrated many Masses, and had others celebrated as well, to obtain light on the subject. For some time he set himself to observe the spiritual reaction which was aroused when he inclined to one side or the other. It was finally decided that even in regard to this maintenance although it was of no personal advantage to the religious, all right to stable revenues should be excluded.

The following is the text of the *Formula* of 1550, as it was laid before Julius III for his approbation.

'As we have learnt by experience that a form of life removed so far as possible from the contagion of avarice and as like as possible to apostolic poverty is productive of greater joy (*jucundiorem*), is purer (more unselfish) and more likely to edify our neighbour, and knowing that our Lord Jesus Christ will give to his servants who seek only the kingdom of God the food and clothing they require, let each and all take a vow of perpetual poverty by declaring (here begins the revised text of the second formula) that neither the Professed nor their *dwelling or church* may, either individually or *in common*, acquire any legal right (*civilis*) whatever to means of support, revenues, property or any fixed possessions, with the exception of those it is proper to have for their own use and habitation, being content with what is given them by charity for the necessities of life.' (*Formula Instituti*, n. 7.)

The following is a very short explanation of the contents of the primitive text as it is amplified in the *Examen generale* and the Constitutions.

In the Residences

1. The house may be owned together with the church, a garden, a 'villa' or rest-house which may also be used for retirement to make the Spiritual Exercises in greater tranquillity.

2. A building may be accepted as an alms ; but if it is unnecessary it may be sold and the price obtained applied to some good work.

3. Even in common no fixed revenues may be owned which can be claimed as a legal right.

It was allowed to accept alms that a benefactor gave on fixed dates, but no right to them could be established ; moreover these alms could not be applied to the personal maintenance of the Fathers.

4. The Society did not accept on its own behalf the liberty granted by the Council of Trent to all Orders—except the Capuchins and Observant Franciscans—of possessing property in common and of living on their revenues while keeping the privileges of the Mendicant Orders, and also the power of acquiring property by inheritance in the name of their subjects.

(Hence, it may be mentioned in passing, the distinction between Orders which are 'mendicant in name and in fact' and those which are 'mendicant in name but not in fact'. On account of its professed houses the Society is legally an Order 'mendicant in name and in fact'.)

5. The Society cannot acquire goods by inheritance in the name of its subjects. It can only accept *specific legacies* because legally they are comparable to donations.

6. It is absolutely forbidden to ask for or to accept as *remuneration* alms or stipends for the celebration of Masses,

preaching, confessions, retreats, teaching, conferring degrees, in short for any spiritual ministrations.

Every ministration is a 'service'; God, in whose service anything is done, will provide the reward. The saint concludes Chapter XV of Part IV of the Constitutions, referring to lectures and degrees, with the following words :

'The Rector will take care not to allow Professors or any member of the Society, himself or the College to accept money or any gifts of whatsoever kind for any services rendered ; since, according to our Institute, Christ our Lord alone is to be our return, he who is our exceedingly great reward.'

The Saint went so far as to forbid alms boxes to be placed in our churches *'ut omnis avaritiae species evitetur'* (*Const*. VI, ch. II, 8).

II. THE 'COLLEGES'

Right at the beginning the Society was obliged to think of the recruitment of new members. St Ignatius had at first fixed at sixty the number of professed ; the very expansion of his Order led him to abolish this restriction. Most of the candidates had not completed their studies when they applied for reception. On the one hand St Ignatius desired for his priests, especially the solemnly professed, a really sound scientific formation, generally to be acquired in a University ; on the other, he knew by experience the obstacles that providing for one's maintenance by begging could put in the way of serious study. He solved the difficulty by imposing on the 'Scholastics' besides their simple vows a promise to enter the Society, either as Professed or as spiritual coadjutors, after the completion of their studies. He then decided that 'Colleges should be founded or should enjoy fixed revenues in proportion to the number of scholastics'.

When, later on, he allowed teaching in establishments like our colleges of humanities, or secondary or high schools, he desired at the same time that the maintenance of the teachers and other members of the staff should be provided for by foundations or fixed revenues. But the teaching was quite free.

The property of the 'Colleges' was to be administered by the Superior of the Society but he was strictly forbidden to utilize it in any way for the advantage of the residences. Only those Fathers who were necessary for the Colleges could reside and be maintained in them. It was also understood that a Father passing through might be given hospitality for a short time and an alms to continue his journey. The Saint considered that to act otherwise would be to display meanness, furnish occasion for scruples and be inconsistent with charity.

It has already been mentioned that nothing could be demanded for conferring degrees. The Constitutions contain a telling passage on the extravagances and festivities usual in Universities on the occasion of admission to the doctorate.

III. INDIVIDUAL POVERTY

1. At the outset St Ignatius desired that candidates for admission to the Society, even before entering as novices, should divest themselves entirely of their actual or future property by the well-known act of renunciation.

The Council of Trent declared invalid any renunciation made by a novice more than sixty days before (solemn) profession. As this profession made the subject incapable of acquiring property and as the religious Orders (Observant Franciscans and Capuchins excepted) could acquire and possess property in common, the monastery obtained possession, instead and in place of the professed member, of everything which he had not disposed of by his renunciation. *Quidquid religiosus acquirit, monasterium acquirit*. But the Council of Trent declared that it did not desire in any way to derogate from the Constitutions or customs of the Society.

2. If, for any reason, this renunciation could not be made before entering the Society the candidate undertook to make it when the Superior ordered him to do so and, at the latest, even for the spiritual coadjutors, before the last vows.

3. The Saint laid great insistence on the necessity of renunciation of possessions in favour of the poor and not of relations. He did so for the following motives : 'In order better to follow the evangelical counsel, to give a more telling example of renunciation of all inordinate affection for relations, to avoid the difficulties of a badly regulated distribution, to escape the danger of being able to apply subsequently to relatives or

friends and the better to make sure of one's vocation by setting aside all associations of a family nature'.

4. If there were some doubt whether it would not be better in a particular case to relinquish property to relations the matter was to be submitted to the advice of one or several arbitrators.

5. In fact the Society has increasingly conformed in practice to the prescriptions of Canon Law on this point, although its privileges in this matter have not been abrogated.

6. The professed Fathers, obliged to dwell in residences without fixed revenues, but to live on alms, were obviously in danger of wanting for the necessities of life. St Ignatius had foreseen this ; he hoped that the religious would welcome it as an opportunity of practising their self-oblation to the full.

The Saint told them that they should be ready in this case to beg for their daily bread. At the beginning Fathers and Brothers were appointed to undertake the office of begging from passers-by. But St Ignatius soon came to the conclusion that, save in special cases, it was unfitting for us to do this.

7. The general character of individual poverty was to be that of '*honesti sacerdotes*'. Given the kind of ministry undertaken it was probably the most fitting form to adopt. These '*honesti sacerdotes*' were certainly not those priests whose lives of ease called forth the bitter criticism of the 'Reformers' and even provoked good Catholics to desire a thorough-going reform of the clergy.

St Ignatius's first companions were called in some places 'the poor priests of Christ'. If it is recalled that the Founder expressed the desire to see future members of the Society imitate, and even surpass, the poverty of his first companions the appellation '*honesti sacerdotes*' cannot be seen as an inducement to lead an easy and far from apostolic life.

IV. Leading ideas and underlying inspiration

On several occasions already in the foregoing account opportunities have occurred of indicating the underlying reasons which inspired St Ignatius to choose this form of poverty. It may be useful to set them down here together in order to show the spirit which animates the prescriptions of the Formulae and the Constitutions.

The holy Founder witnessed the disturbing spectacle of many monasteries wherein the comfortable life allowed by the wealth of temporal possessions led to the decay of the religious spirit. Urged thereto by their desire for an easy life many clerics had but one thought : to obtain fat benefices with no consideration whatever of the spiritual end for which they had been founded. Simony was no rare thing and its diffusion formed a profound scandal to Christian people. In such circumstances what was to become of a genuine love of Christ, regard for his counsels, the desire of following and imitating him ?

I have already said that this love of Christ, drawn from the Spiritual Exercises, was the underlying reason which explains the entire life of the Founder after his conversion. This love caused him to desire to follow Christ as closely as possible and made the thought of being better treated than his Saviour and King quite unbearable to him.

In evangelical poverty he saw a really efficacious condition of the apostolate. It ensured to the apostle complete freedom to devote himself to the most fruitful forms of ministry even if they afforded no temporal compensation. This unselfish attitude was to extinguish in souls the scandal of a church wherein was rampant an ardent love of money and of all the advantages to be had from it.

Realizing full well that the weak point in common life is the danger of becoming second-rate through wealth of material possessions, he was convinced that the enemy of human nature would direct his most insidious attacks in this direction. On the other hand sincere, genuine poverty would be productive of noble generous souls.

Thus he said to his sons :

'Let all love poverty as a mother and, within the bounds of a holy discretion, may they on occasion feel certain effects of it ; and as it is written in the Examen let them be ready, when the first year is over, to distribute their temporal goods, if the Superior orders them to, and in the manner laid down for them in the Examen . . . Poverty must be loved as a solid bulwark of religion and kept in all its purity and to the whole extent of the inspiration of grace.'

To attain this end he obliged the Professed to promise to God never to allow a relaxation of the Constitutions on this point and to effect no change in them save to make poverty more severe. (*Const.* P. VI, ch. II.)

For ministrations of the apostolate he desired no other reward than Jesus Christ himself. It can be held for certain that he himself will take care of those whose only thought is the extension of his kingdom. Ignatius desired stable revenues in order that, as he said : 'Hope may be placed on God alone, that the Society may serve by his grace and that he will provide without any revenue all that is fitting for his greater praise and glory' (*Const.* P. VI, ch. II, n. 2).

Circumstances have obliged the Society to ask the Holy See for provisional dispensations of the Constitutions in the matter of poverty.

It must be pointed out that, with one or two exceptions, benefactors who found a college or a university are no longer to be encountered nowadays. Since St Ignatius acknowledged the necessity for them to have a fixed revenue it is not a departure from his spirit to require students to pay a fee whereas formerly teaching was given gratis.

The author of this paper can still remember the time when Jesuits, in certain provinces, would accept no stipend for Masses. They would gladly celebrate for those who requested them without asking for, or even accepting the stipend laid down in the diocesan scale. For many years, in these same provinces, stipends were accepted for a restricted number of Masses, and these stipends were given in their totality to the Japanese mission, especially for the benefit of the University of Tokio. Nowadays still the principle is upheld in many provinces whose priests have at their disposal several Masses each month which they can allot, without stipend, to private intentions.

The Society still lays great store on the gratuitousness of its ministry. Its priests accept the offering which is made to them and which should, partially, cover their travelling expenses ; they demand nothing as a return for the spiritual labour involved.

Perhaps more frequently than in St Ignatius's day the

solemnly Professed live in the colleges, particularly in the houses of higher studies. The Rector and professors of a university have to be chosen from among those who have themselves done higher or university studies. But this is explicitly provided for in the Constitutions.

The problem raised by the adaptation of the means of existence and of continuing the apostolate in social conditions that are entirely different and at the same time of keeping intact the spirit of the holy Founder is one that constantly preoccupies those whose duty it is to continue his work.

Chapter VI

THE ECONOMIC ORGANISATION OF CONVENTS

By Andre Duval, O.P.

For a proper treatment of the history of religious poverty following the vicissitudes of economic organisation in monasteries of women, it would have been necessary to enumerate and draw upon a considerable body of evidence. As I have only been able to assemble, somewhat hastily, a few documents referring exclusively to France, and previous to 1789, I shall confine myself here to an indication of the main outlines of the subject in order to encourage research and reflexion rather than offer established conclusions or still less a complete synthesis.[1]

The Monastery at Arles

Without further introduction we can take as our starting point the monastery founded at Arles at the beginning of the sixth century by St Caesarius for his sister Caesaria. If this monastery does not represent the first realisation of the religious life for women in France it is none the less the first whose organisation is known in sufficient detail for it to be regarded as the prototype of cloistered communities of women.[2]

This organisation—which even then turned to account the experience of Eastern monachism (Caesaria obtained her monastic formation at Marseilles in the monastery of women founded by Cassian) and that of the African nuns (on a certain number of points there is an obvious dependence on

[1] Before publishing this report I should have liked to complete the references and give more precision on a few points. I have not found the time to do so and have confined myself to certain modifications of wording.

[2] The documents have been published by Dom G. Morin, *S. Caesarii opera*, t. II, Maredsous, 1942, or *S. Caesarii . . . Regula sanctarum virginum aliaque opuscula ad sanctimoniales directa . . .* (Florilegium patristicum, XXV). Bonn, 1933. The best study is by Dom C. Lambot in *Dictionnaire de Droit canonique*, III, 264-274. Cf. also, by the same, *Le prototype des monastères cloîtrès de femmes. L'abbaye Saint-Jean d'Arles (VIe siecle)* in the *Revue liturgique et monastique*, XXIII, 1938, 169-174.

St Augustine's *Letter* 211)—offered, from the material aspect, the following features :

In the first place it had landed property and revenues.

Since St Caesarius possessed nothing himself he drew upon the property of the Church of Arles to provide his nuns with a site, build a monastery for them and endow them with estates and property on the revenues of which they would be enabled to live.[1]

These possessions increased gradually because the nuns, when they came to make the definitive disposal of their personal property, did so in favour of the monastery itself. Although this form of gift was by no means of obligation the rule made provision for such an act of generosity, without however laying it down (Cf. *Rule*, n. 21.)

On this basis poverty was practised according to the ideal of the Acts of the Apostles[2] by renunciation of all *personal* property (*Rule*, nos. 5, 6), and by an integral common life, as it was laid down by St Augustine in his *Letter* 211 (nos. 20, 21, 29 ; Cf. 17, 9). The manner of common life was to be characterised by a certain sobriety in dress and furniture (nos. 44, 45).[3]

From this point of view work was not merely an occupation—outside prayer-time to avoid useless gossip (cf. n. 19)—but the service of the community. The housework was to be done by the sisters for they were not allowed to employ secular servants, and this applied even to the abbess (n. 6). All the sisters were to take their turn as cook. The community was also to be self-sufficient in respect of the making and upkeep of their clothes.

---

[1] Fearing that his successors might withdraw these gifts, and being perhaps somewhat scrupulous about them, he applied to Pope Hormisdas for a confirmation of the gift. (Cf. the letter *Exulto* by Pope Hormisdas, *Floril. Patr.* 25, and *Dict. de Droit Canonique III*, 266.) Some twenty years later the rule drawn up by Bishop Aurelianus for another monastery of nuns at Arles, the monastery of St Mary—this rule followed closely that of St Caesarius— laid down that the abbess should not alienate any part of this common property of the foundation. *Sanctae abbatissae non liceat aliquid de facultatibus monasterii donare ac vendere* . . . *P.L.* 68, 402-3.

[2] In the same century, in a letter by St Radegundis, foundress and abbess of a monastery at Poitiers, we can read : *Formam apostolicam observantes, tam ego quam sorores de substantia terrena quam possidere videbamus factis cartis tradedimus, metu Ananiae et Saffirae in monasterio positae nihil proprium reservantes* . . . Quoted, after St Gregory of Tours, by E. Lesne, *Histoire de la propriété ecclésiastique en France*, I, Paris-Lille, 1910, p. 106, note 1.

[3] To avoid all temptation to superfluity or ostentation the nuns were to refrain from making valuable stuffs or ornaments (nos. 45, 60).

Woolwork was the 'daily burden' that the sisters were to accept 'with humility' and carry out 'with all their skill', so that it should be unnecessary to buy clothes outside the monastery (n. 28). Thus work was considered as a sign of voluntary poverty. On the other hand there was no question of making it a source of income for the monastery : all material activity, for the benefit of those outside the monastery was forbidden (nos. 46, 51).[1]

There remain two other elements to be noticed as features of the organisation of this community. Because it was enclosed and the proprietor of land, it required the help of men to supervise its interests and possessions. This role belonged to the *provisores* (nos. 36, 39). On the other hand, the nuns were not so far to cut themselves off from the world as to forget its misfortunes. Almsgiving was to play a part in their economic life ; it was merely laid down that it was to be carried out according to the will of the abbess, and not as a regular thing lest disturbance be caused at the monastery door (n. 42).

Thus the rule of St Caesarius depicts an ideal organisation of completely common life. It is the ideal of poverty *secundum formam apostolicam*, to use the expression of St Radegundis. On the other hand we know that the economic basis of this common life is founded on property and revenues held in common and by an initial endowment.

We must now see how the different elements of this organisation were to develop in the course of centuries. The problem to be examined is this : to what degree did the vicissitudes of the second element (i.e., property held in common) endanger the first, 'apostolic' poverty ? After an outline of the history of religious life among women, viewed especially from the point of view of ownership we shall dwell more particularly on certain institutional effects of this economic evolution.

I. Ownership and Poverty

From the outset material security was assured ; this feature of the foundation at Arles was to remain a constant factor in

---

[1] There is to be noticed, also, among the effective activities of the monastery the artistic copying of the scriptures and service books. Cf. *Vita* of St Caesarius, I, c. 5, n. 44.

the history of religious life among women whereas among men it did not do so, though both forms were closely interdependent. The few remarkable exceptions that will be noted merely confirm this general rule.

Initial Developments of Monastic Ownership

Although a certain number of monasteries of men, in France particularly under the influence of St Columbanus, founded at first in uncultivated or unhealthy situations, were by their own labour themselves the authors of their wealth, in the case of a monastery of women, established always in or near a town or even next to a monastery of men,[1] foundation signified, always and solely, endowment. To found a house of nuns meant giving it land, a house and revenues. It was the work of bishops, kings and queens and even of private individuals who were rich. From the seventh century onwards it became so frequent an occurrence that the compilations of formularies for drawing up various legal deeds always contained models for the use of any who desired to build a monastery and endow it sumptuously.[2]

Without dwelling on it at length it may be pointed out in passing that from the seventh century onwards the religious psychology of the 'founder'—and, subsequently, of the 'benefactor'—is well worth studying for its own sake ; it forms, indeed, in some measure an essential chapter in the history of religious life[3] which, in effect, is closely bound up with the life

---

[1] Cf. Lesne, *op. cit.* 84-5, 88 ; Dom Schmitz, in *Dict. d'Hist. et Geog. eccl.*, VII, 1217.

[2] Cf. Lesne, *op. cit.*, 119, note 1.

[3] For example, Marc Bloch shrewdly pointed out that despite the considerable, charitable, cultural or economic functions of the monasteries in feudal times these, to their contemporaries, were merely accessory features. It was only in their 'spiritual' aspect that religious organisations appeared to them as indispensable. The idea of an earthly world completely pervaded by the supernatural was allied, here, with an obsession with the next world. The good estate of the king and the kingdom at the present time, the salvation of royal ancestors and of the king himself in eternity : such was the twofold advantage that Louis VI asserted that he anticipated from the foundation of St Victor in Paris, a community of canons regular. 'We believe,' said Otto I, 'that the increasing prosperity of divine worship is closely connected with the safety of our kingdom'. Marc Bloch, *La Société féodale. La formation des liens de dépendance*, Paris, 1939, p. 139. (The nuns' rule of 816 reminds them what these goods on which they live stand for : *Res ecclesiae oblationes sunt fidelium, pretium peccatorum, patrimonium pauperum.* Mansi, XIV, 276.)

of Christian people, not only because it is from them that its recruits are taken, but because it implies for its continuance, for its development, for the avoidance of spiritual decadence, a certain understanding, and a certain standard also, a kind of spiritual complicity on the part of the elite and indeed of the masses. In any case, at the material level, it implies a determination and an enduring diligence on their part to support it.

At all events the generosity of founders and benefactors did not cease. The property of nuns thus comes to appear as part of that immense accumulation of ecclesiastical property (episcopal and parish churches, abbeys, each with its manifold dependencies, rights and privileges) which, from the seventh century to 1789, occupied so large a place on the economic map of France. In feudal times monastic life was one of the essential elements of the economic structure of the country ; centuries were to pass before it became something entirely on its fringe.

The very considerable materials for this history of ecclesiastical property in the Middle Ages have been collected by Mgr Lesne.[1] Dom J. Leclercq, using these documents to advantage[2] has brought out clearly the paradoxical nature of this monastic economy, dominated by the primacy of contemplative leisure, a drain on the activity of an entire people in order to enable a few to live a more godly life and very many to profit by the methodical organisation of almsgiving and hospitality since the monastery was the economic and spiritual centre of the different 'social services'.

Like the monasteries of men, the nunneries could be quite modest houses, containing about twenty religious. They could also be the centre of an immense enterprise. To quote but one example, the monastery of N. D. de Soissons, in the middle of the ninth century (858) owned estates which could supply it annually with 3000 hogsheads of corn, 350 of vegetables, 3000 *pensiones* (annual tax) of cheese, 2600 hogsheads of wine and ten of honey (intended to be mixed with drinks), 200 barrels of

[1] E. Lesne, *Histoire de la propriété ecclésiastique en France*. Paris-Lille, 1910-43, 6 vol.

[2] Dom J. Leclercq, *La Vie economique des monastères au Moyen age*, in *Inspirations religieuses et structures temporelles*. Economie et humanisme. Les Editions ouvrières, 1948, pp. 211-59.

salt and 100 of tallow for lighting purposes.[1] It should be added
that this provision was intended for a household of upwards
of 400 persons, that is 216 nuns, 130 men servants and 70
women servants.[2] The importance of an abbey is not to be
measured necessarily by the size of its estates in its immediate
neighbourhood but also by its possessions situated sometimes
at a considerable distance in districts where complementary
products could be grown (wine growing regions, for example)
or at key positions for transport, etc. The Abbaye de la Trinité,
founded at Caen in 1066 by Queen Matilda, wife of William
the Conqueror, drew as much revenue from England as from
the continent.

The extent of its territorial possessions made a medieval
abbess a 'powerful lady', simultaneously both vassal and
suzerain. As such she had her court of justice and enjoyed
numerous 'seignorial privileges'.[3]

Secularisation, the peril of wealth

The goods of this world are an attraction for the world.
Property intended to support the development of the religious
life, a richly endowed monastery, remains property none the
less, and as such inspires covetousness. As an integral part of
an economico-social system it runs the risk of being considered
from this point of view only and consequently alienated from
its proper purpose. In consequence the history of ecclesiastical
property, and particularly monastic property, is one of the
successive partial or complete spoliations to which it has been
subjected from Charles Martel down to the decrees of 1789-90.[4]

But a far more serious danger to religious life has been the
insidious attraction of this wealth and these revenues and their
diversion in practice to ends other than the service of God or
the poor. Charlemagne and his successors initiated the system

[1] Cf. Lesne, op. cit. VI, 208.

[2] Ibid. 206. At the death of St Radegundis (587) the monastery of Ste
Croix at Poitiers comprised 200 nuns. Cf., with other figures, Lesne, op. cit.
I, 105.

[3] Schmitz, Dict. Hist. Geo. eccl., VII, 1218.

[4] Mgr Lesne has devoted the whole of the first fasc. of the 2nd vol. of his
History to the 'stages of secularisation of Church property from the eighth to
the tenth century'.

by bequeathing abbeys to their sisters, wives or daughters.[1] The intention of these princes was not so much a concern to facilitate their relatives' pursuit of Christian perfection as an endeavour to ensure that they enjoyed the most certain means of an easy, comfortable, not to say sumptuous, existence.

The same state of mind prevailed in those families where the daughters, at an early age, were sent to the convent. In this way they were 'settled' advantageously.

The wealth of the monastery attracted subjects, therefore, of a kind which threatened to transform it into a centre of worldliness rather than of conversion. If it is inaccurate to look upon the *canonicae* or canonesses, whose existence is attested in the middle of the eighth century, as merely *monachae* or nuns who had finally completely abandoned the vow of poverty,[2] nevertheless this gradual decline did happen in some cases, and there is a certain significance in its recurrence, several times in the course of centuries, and from within the organisation.

The Perils of Poverty

If wealth endangers the spirit of poverty, actual poverty can also be disastrous to religious life in a system wherein everything depends on the certainty of material security. Wealth has its risks, it can be lost or squandered. And in fact many monasteries have experienced a form of poverty to which they were psychologically ill-adapted.

There were several causes for this economic decline. The first was perhaps the very success of the religious life leading, as a consequence, to numerous foundations which in the end were mutually harmful. In a certain number of cases the initial endowment was found in practice to be insufficient. Now monastic property of itself entailed certain expenses : the upkeep of buildings, the support of a large community, the provision of hospitality and charity, secular or ecclesiastical taxes, etc., all of which required of the abbesses or prioresses administrative abilities which were sometimes lacking, while exterior events—war, fire, famine—could completely jeopardise a position which was already of some difficulty. When actual

[1] Cf. Lesne, *op. cit.*, II, fasc. 2, pp. 168-71.
[2] Cf. *Dict. Hist. Geo. eccl.*, VII, 1207. Lesne, *op. cit.* VI, 23.

poverty affected a community in which the spirit of poverty had grown cold the door was opened to 'private life'. We shall see examples of this.[1]

Obviously it is on the subject of poverty that the various movements of reform, which are a constantly recurring refrain in the history of religious life, have first in practice to exert their influence. Did these reforms go so far as to call in question the whole principle of monastic property ?

The renewal of the 'Vita Apostolica'

After the reforms of the ninth century, which for the most part were imposed from above, and consisted principally in legislative reorganisation and unification,[2] the first movement of any importance for our purpose is that which in the eleventh and twelfth centuries was inspired by a re-discovery of the primitive monastic ideal, considered especially under the two-fold aspect of flight from the world and poverty. 'Relinquishing prebends and honours, clerics retired into solitude and there led a life of penance, on the pattern of the fathers of the desert, and following their example by the work of their hands obtained the frugal fare with which their austerity was content. The rest of the time they spent in contemplation. These hermits, living singly or in groups, exerted great influence on the Christians of every rank who came to visit them. Without desiring it in this way they gained adherents, disciples who would share their manner of life and genuine communities, made up of very different elements, were formed around them : clerics or monks, seeking a more perfect life, layfolk, both men and women, attracted by the example of evangelical detachment.'[3] It was a movement of this kind that led to the foundation near

[1] Only twenty-five years after St Caesarius, his successor Aurelianus, drawing up a rule for a new monastery which he had founded, also at Arles, calls on the abbess with a solemnity that is quite astonishing to allot to each of the sisters what is necessary for her clothing and food, lest they be exposed to murmuring and want. (P.L. 68, 404.) The Council of 816 in its turn insisted that the abbess should be no acceptor of persons (ch. XII of the Rule, cf. Mansi, XIV, 269). It is enough, moreover, for an abbess or prioress to make for herself a kind of life apart, to abstain from taking her meals in the refectory, for the example to be quickly followed.

[2] That, precisely, was the purpose of the regula sancti monialium enacted in 816 by the council of Aix-la-Chapelle. Mansi XIV, 265 sqq.

[3] C. Dereine in Revue d'histoire ecclésiastique, XLI, 1946, p. 403.

Laon of the monastery of Prémontré which was soon at the head of one of the most powerful federations of canons regular. Women came to be in association with these incipient communities and placed themselves effectively—in a spirit of evangelical renunciation—at their service. But directly these small accessory feminine communities had taken firm root they developed in accordance with the economic laws of every monastery of women on a basis of endowments of property and revenues.

The eremitical movement, whose influence is to be noticed in the origin of several foundations of canons regular, was equally active at the same period among the monks. It stands out clearly, for example, in the foundation and initial development of the Cistercian Order. The twenty-one monks who in 1098 left the abbey of Molesmes for the 'desert called Cîteaux'[1] intended especially to break with the current monastic economic organisation. 'As neither in the Rule nor the life of St Benedict did they read that this Master had possessed churches, altars, offerings, burial rights, tithes, ovens, mills, villages, serfs . . . all these things they gave up.'[2] Cîteaux was to effect its economic organisation on the basis of direct working of their estates either by the labour of the monks themselves or of laymen in religious association with the monasteries—they were to become the *conversi*—to the exclusion of any organisation on the lines of the Cluniac *familia*. But whatever changes subsequently took place in the Cistercian ideal of the religious life for men[3] it cannot be said that it led to any modification in the economic system of women's houses. The first Cistercian nuns modelled themselves on the rules of Cîteaux in all that concerned their regular observance and liturgical life because they were under the jurisdiction of that Order. But that had little effect on their material organisation. Whereas once more the monks were to create, at least in part, their own wealth by the work of their hands, the reclamation and cultivation of their estates, the construction by their own labour of their abbeys after years spent in rough and ready accommodation,

[1] 'Ad heremum que cistercium dicebatur,' *Exordium parvum*. J. Turk, *Cistercii statuta antiquissima*, Rome, 1949, p. 32.

[2] *Ibid.*, p. 33. Cf. Canivez, in *Dict. de Droit can.*, III, 749.

[3] In fact deviations from the principles laid down in the *Exordium parvum* occurred fairly rapidly. Cf. Canivez, *op. cit.*, 758.

the nuns' monastery was begun on the basis of an endowment in lands which could be let out at rent immediately and in buildings whose construction was sufficiently advanced for the enclosure to be strictly observed.

Thus in the thirteenth century, Benedictine, Norbertine, Cistercian, and shortly afterwards Dominican nuns, differed among themselves only in habit, liturgy and the details of their constitutions. If a monastery left the jurisdiction of one Order for that of another the changes that this step implied were quickly arranged because the economic system and the organisation in regard to poverty were not affected. With whatever male religious family the nuns were associated they remained exposed to the inherent dangers of the property system which in prosperity as in hardship, led to secularisation (many nuns lived for years in, or more accurately off, the monastery without making profession)[1] or at least private life. The register in which the archbishop of Rouen noted down his observations during the visitations that he carried out in his diocese and province in the middle of the thirteenth century is full of significant details. In one monastery each nun has her own poultry yard. The archbishop's intervention was necessary to ensure that the eggs should be served to all in the refectory, no matter to which nun the hens which laid these eggs belonged in fact.[2] It was not a very serious matter perhaps, less so, certainly than the custom observed at Lisieux on the same occasion of dividing up the community property into individual allowances out of which each nun was obliged to provide for her own maintenance.[3]

[1] In 1249 in the monastery at Villarceaux out of 23 'nuns' four only were professed. The others only lived there because it provided board and lodging. Twelve of them were accused of incontinence—three had already given birth to children—not to mention other accusations : blows, drunkenness, etc. Cf. Th. Bonnin, *Journal des visites pastorales d'Eudes Rigaud.* Rouen, 1852, p. 43. When two years later the archbishop visited the monastery again, one of the 'nuns' had just left and got married, 'nubsit in saeculo' (*Ibid.*, p. 117), a proof that she had not made profession. In the same year (1251), visiting the monastery of Saint Amand, where 43 nuns lived, Eudes Rigaud prescribed that after a year spent in the monastery, they had to make profession. There would be many other examples.

[2] The monastery of Gournay. Bonnin, *op. cit.*, p. 550.

[3] Cf. *Ibid.*, 62, 199. In 1250, at Sainte Marguerite de Gouffern, actual poverty led to private life in the matter of clothing : *Non vestiuntur de communi, propter paupertatem. Ibid.*, 83.

Mendicant poverty

The re-discovery of the Gospel ideal of poverty which was already a powerful leaven among the clerics, monks and laity during the twelfth century—sometimes with unfortunate results, witness for example the case of the Vaudois—reached its complete development in the thirteenth century in the person of St Francis and in the economic organisation of the mendicant Orders founded on the renunciation of landed property and revenues and on work and mendicancy. This is no place to examine the evolution of St. Dominic's thought concerning the law of poverty in the Order of Friars Preachers. As regards the nuns, both in the foundation of Prouille in 1207 and in the reform of the nuns in Rome, who were re-grouped at St Sixtus in 1219, he never considered any other economic organisation than that founded on landed property and various revenues. St Dominic thought along the same lines as the rest of the world of his day, a time when the general Chapters of Cîteaux waxed indignant because the improvidence of abbesses or visitors had compelled the nuns to resort to begging.[1]

It needed a St Francis and a St Clare to imagine that women too might claim to live wholly in accordance with the Gospel, as unconcernedly as the lilies of the field or the birds of the air. No longer was it a matter of possessing nothing personally in order to live in common—*vivere sine proprio, vivere in communi de communi*—but of possessing nothing at all, of living from day to day with no other security for the morrow than the help of divine Providence.

The history of the '*Privilegium paupertatis*' is in any case especially significant not merely on account of St Clare's supernatural daring but also because it demonstrates the strength of the traditional notion of religious poverty for women. That a pontifical 'privilege' should be required for the nuns to have the right to interpret the Gospel literally was something quite out of the ordinary, especially at a time when

---

[1] General Chapter of 1276. Visitors of nuns are to find out *si habeant unde possint vivere regulariter absque rubore mendicandi*. Cf. Canivez, *Statuta ordinis Cisterciensis*, III, 1551. In the fifteenth century it was regretted that nuns should be obliged to obtain food and clothing *ad modum mendicantium . . . in dedecus et opprobrium et contra formam et statuta ordinis nostri, hinc inde sibi quaerendo et mendicando. Ibid.* V, 170.

pontifical 'privileges' were usually granted in order to guarantee to religious corporations their possessions and charters. 'Privilege of poverty' : P. Sabatier emphasized the juridical implications of this association of words and, arising from it, its deep spiritual significance.[1] Having obtained it from Pope Innocent III, Clare was obliged to wrest it again from his successors, Gregory IX and Innocent IV who, although they gave way to Clare as to a spoilt child whose whims and fancies must be indulged, and authorized her to live at Assisi without any certain resources, took care themselves to endow the other monasteries of Poor Ladies.

The legislative documents bear witness to this victory and this defeat. The 'Rule of St Clare', drawn up in 1252, approved in 1253—the original text was only discovered again in 1893, wrapped up in the saint's habit—is a repetition in its entire severity of the ideal of poverty of St Francis.[2] But the second Rule of the Poor Clares of Innocent IV (1247),[3] and subsequently that of the 'Sorores minores inclusae' of St Isabelle (1263)[4] re-introduced the right for the community to have *possessiones et reditus*. In 1410 the Constitutions of St Colette once more forbade all possessions.[5] But this was to be interpreted in the light of the practical relaxations introduced by the popes into the literal observance of the very Rule of the Friars Minor, beginning with Nicholas III's intervention in 1277.

St Clare is the exception that proves the rule : nuns must not live on alms or on the work of their hands, but on their possessions and investments.

The crisis of the XIV-XVth centuries

Already in the thirteenth century actual poverty, when minds were no longer in a state to face it, was the cause of a certain number of abuses which may be conveniently classified together

---

[1] P. Sabatier, *Le privilège de la Très Haute pauvreté accordé à sainte Claire par Innocent III. Son authenticité. Son histoire de 1215 à 1253*. Paris, 1924.

[2] Ch. vi. Cf. *Seraphicae legislationis textus originales*. Quaracchi, 1897, pp. 62-3.

[3] Cf. C. Eubel, *Bullarii franciscani epitome*. Quaracchi, 1908, p. 246 a.

[4] *Ibid*, 275b.

[5] Cf. *Seraphicae legislationis textus originales*, 144-5.

as 'private life'; in the following centuries, when everywhere the economic system underwent severe trials, religious poverty experienced heavy blows. The crisis which arose in the first years of the fourteenth century grew suddenly more acute on account of the great famine of 1315-7. Soon the Black Death (1347-50) added to the disaster. In France there must be added the effects of the Hundred Years War.

Fr Denifle has collected the considerable body of evidence relating to the material ruin that these events caused to ecclesiastical property.[1] Many monasteries disappeared. Those which survived did so by adapting themselves to the hardness of the times. This adaptation meant, in practice, adopting 'private life' as an institution. What in the preceding centuries was considered as an abuse, and therefore blameworthy, remained indeed contrary to the Rule or Constitutions but was regularly authorised by dispensations granted in individual cases.

In many monasteries at the beginning of the year each nun received her allowance in money (*peculium*) out of which she had to provide her clothing. Many managed to increase the allowance by presents from friends and parents and sometimes by their own work. Out of this small capital nuns were able to furnish their cells and provide for their upkeep, sometimes even to have built a complete apartment or lodge—occasionally with a private garden—within the enclosure. Naturally on certain days meals would be eaten in them, rather than in the community refectory, in company with a few friends, and at the same time advantage would be taken of the permission, generously granted by superiors, to have one or several secular servants. Facts of this sort are numerous. Consultation of the Acts of the Cistercian General Chapters or of the Registers of the Dominican Masters General reveals abundant examples of such permissions. Private property unabashed was thus established within the cloister, property that a nun could bequeath to her friends or her niece, and at the same time requests poured in to the superiors to obtain the allotment of a private apartment that was vacant or likely to be so shortly. What therefore

---

[1] H. Denifle, *La desolation des églises, monastères et hôpitaux pendant la guerre de cent ans.* Paris, 1897-9, 3 vols.

remained of common life ? The position may be summed up as follows : decreasingly we have to deal with poor nuns living in a more or less rich community and increasingly with wealthy nuns (or at least in comfortable circumstances) forming a poor community.

The Teresan ideal of Poverty

Nothing shows better perhaps the objective difficulty of the problem—a religious life founded on a well-secured income as opposed to the hazards of daily alms or work—than St Teresa's hesitancy, in the middle of the sixteenth century when she was on the point of founding St Joseph's at Avila. She herself explains it at length in chapter 25 of her *Life*. Her own experience and personal reflexion, the influence of St Peter of Alcantara, a Franciscan, all combined to make her decide clearly in favour of the life of *pobreza*. At the same time she considered it necessary to found *con renta* in places of meagre resources, as for example at Malagon. This means that while she had complete trust in Providence she did not lose sight of the fact that it acts generally through intermediaries and that in consequence for a proper practice of evangelical poverty in the traditional setting of enclosed religious life an environment is required that is capable—materially and spiritually—of supporting it by alms. The wonderful history of the Teresan foundations shows clearly that, whatever the basis of the economic life of the monastery, the practice of poverty is primarily a question of the spirit in which it is undertaken.

Reform and foundations in France

While St Teresa was instilling new life into the worn out organism of monasticism, in France its decline could only continue with increasing impetus by reason of the destruction, despoiling and violence of the wars of religion, together with the royal seizure and control of those monasteries with the best endowments. In fact the Concordat of 1517 in practice conferred on the king the general allocation of ecclesiastical benefices. The consequences of this procedure were particularly serious for religious life among men. Many abbeys were thenceforward ruled by commendatory abbots, laymen whose sole concern was to spend a few days yearly in their monastery in order to lay hold of the major portion of its income and entertain their friends lavishly, leaving the monks to fend for themselves as best they could. In the women's monasteries the system of superiors *in commendam* did not function. The abbesses or prioresses appointed by the King were always, as a rule at least, real religious in the canonical sense of the term, women, that is, who had made their profession according to the rule of their community. Yet cases are on record of excellent Christian families which did not hesitate to commit forgery so that a daughter, lacking the requisite age for valid profession, should conveniently have a few years added to her age in order to be professed and receive from Rome effective jurisdiction over an abbey, the government of which had been obtained for her by the diplomatic intrigue of her father. That was the case with Jacqueline Arnauld at Port Royal. What becomes of religious poverty when an abbey like Maubuisson is bestowed by Henri IV on one such as Angèlique d'Estrées, who in moral laxity could give lessons to her sister, the King's mistress ?

Down to the end of the *ancien régime* many abbeys and priories, retaining despite plunder and severe difficulties considerable wealth in landed property, remained exposed, in regard to the practice of religious poverty, to threats from within and without. From within : the royal priory of the Dominican nuns of Montfleury, near Grenoble, was gradually secularised. The habit of these nuns, as it is shown by Helyot in his history of the religious orders, with a scapular reduced to a smart little apron, is clear enough evidence of the evolution that had taken place. Mme de Tencin, who was educated there, had no need to resort to complicated subterfuge to consider herself freed from the vows that she had taken. In this same eighteenth century the Dominican nuns of Prouille were obliged to show considerable determination to withstand the cunning designs of the archbishop of Toulouse—Lomenie de Brienne—the prime-mover in the notorious commission of Regulars and of the states of Languedoc. Since the financial state of the monastery was in fact excellent these gentlemen desired to transform it into a secular chapter for the benefit of the noble families of the district. Their daughters would thus receive, gratuitously to all intents and purposes, out of the revenues of the monastery, an excellent education without being obliged to forgo, by reason of vows of religion, any suitable match should such be offered to them.

In fact from the seventeenth century onwards the royal priories and the great, richly endowed abbeys no longer occupied the chief place in the geography of women's monasteries in France. Numerous foundations arose in which the economic system obviously reflected the generally prevailing conditions. Yet the basis remained always the principle of initial security. In the absence of landed property bringing in a certain income, an effort was made to counter-balance this lack by foundation endowments, dowries, accepting paying guests, a certain amount of work. These various factors will be considered later on. In any case in the eighteenth century there were many houses wherein the spirit of poverty could flourish freely and amply in actual poverty. The growing incomprehension of religious life among the ruling classes used the pretext of the precariousness of material circumstances in religious houses to obtain their suppression by royal authority. Soon the French revolution, after suppressing all religious houses, caused such a transformation in the economic life of the country, that the religious foundations and restorations of the nineteenth century were placed in an entirely new position. On the other hand it may be thought, possibly, that the economic evolution of the last thirty years represents a still more fundamental break with the past, calling for an entire reconsideration of the material organisation of religious life for the purpose of an authentic realisation of the apostolic and evangelical ideal of poverty.

II. SOME INSTITUTIONAL CONSEQUENCES OF THE SYSTEM

For ten centuries after the time of St Caesarius religious life for women was organised, through property, on the basis of a complete material security ensured by human means. This human security may have been somewhat imperilled at certain moments, but in most people's minds, with however certain important exceptions, it never ceased to be the ideal state for the religious life. That life sometimes suffered in consequence, as we have already seen, but in any case its very structure and customs were affected by this security. At all events it will be useful at this point to show the relationship between the system of religious property and certain institutional elements, particularly as it concerns the composition of the communities and the form taken by their activities.

Aristocratic recruitment of religious life

St Augustine (*Letter* 211) and after him the Rule of St Caesarius take for granted that the monastery draws its subjects from different classes, of unequal standing both financially and by their kind of life. In fact historians of monasticism observe that monasteries, founded by royal or at least noble families, rapidly tended to find their subjects solely among the daughters of the nobility for whom these foundations provided a fitting and assured position worthy of their rank. This state of affairs may be observed in Italy and England as well as in France ;[1] it soon became widespread. Every monastery came to take its subjects from a particular social class. As the new classes went up in the social and cultural scale it appears that certain monasteries remained closed to them. This is quite clear in France in the eighteenth century for example, in regard to the Dominican nuns. While the old foundations like Prouille, Montargis, Montfleury, Les Emmurées in Rouen, Poissy, remained houses of noble-women, the new foundations drew their subjects from the upper and middle classes. The tone of the Master General's correspondence is notably different according as he is writing to the Royal Prioress of Poissy, who is addressed as 'Madame', or the prioress of Dijon who is called 'My daughter'. Not only is the tone different but also the requirements in the matter of regular observance.

A girl's opinion was no more asked about entering religion than it was about the choice of a husband. In either way her future was assured materially, and she had but to adapt herself

---

[1] Cf. Schmitz, *Dict. d'Hist. et de Geog. eccl.*, VII, 1219. For England cf. *Ibid.* 1209, for the seventh century ; for the tenth and eleventh centuries cf. D. Knowles, *The Monastic Order in England*, Cambridge, 1949, p. 137 ; for the twelfth and thirteenth centuries, cf. E. Power, *Medieval English Nunneries*, Cambridge, 1922.

to the situation. Whether vocation or love subsequently super-
vened was an entirely different question. In this way the early
age of entry to the monasteries is accounted for. Many postulants
were not more than six or seven. [1]

Limitation of numbers

If to enter religion means taking one's place at a table which
is already laid the number of guests cannot be unlimited !
Certain abbeys, no doubt, experienced such prosperity that
they could provide for the upkeep of a considerable number of
nuns who, economically, were unproductive. But the very first
difficulties encountered in the material order must have sufficed
to direct attention to the disadvantages of excessive recruitment.
In 816 the rule for nuns put forward by the Council of Aix-la-
Chapelle urges a watch to be kept not only on the quality of the
postulants but also on their number in relation to the revenues
of the monastery. [2]

When exactly did ecclesiastical authority intervene to fix the
maximum number in each case ? At all events the practice was
common in the thirteenth century when the Cistercian General
Chapters are to be found requiring abbesses not to exceed the
numerum statutum, [3] Eudes Rigaud insisting on it in his visitations [4] and Humbert de Romanis introducing the principle into
Constitutions of the Dominican nuns where the exact determination of this number for each monastery was reserved to the
Master General or the Prior Provincial. [5] This obligation of
limiting recruitment was bound up with the economic

---

[1] *Nulla notabiliter juvenis recipiatur in sororem* say the Constitutions of the
Dominican nuns promulgated by Humbert de Romanis in 1259. Cf. *Analecta
sacri ord. praed.*, III, 1897, 342. A few years beforehand the constitutions of
the Dominican nuns of Montargis were explicit on this point : *Nulla in sororem
infra septem annos, nulla ad professionem infra duodecim annos recipiatur.* Cf.
Archivum fratrum praedicatorum, XVII, 1947, 73.

[2] Ch. VIII : *Studendum summopere abbatissis est ut tot talesque in monasteriis
sanctimoniales, quae et morum probitate commendentur, et ecclesiasticis possint
rationabiliter substantari stipendiis* . . . Mansi, XIV, 268.

[3] Chapters of 1219, no. 12 (Canivez, *Statuta ord. cist.*, I 505) ; of 1225,
no. 7 (*Ibid.* II, 36) ; of 1242, no. 15 (*Ibid.* II, 248) ; of 1243, no. 7 (*Ibid.* II,
260) ; 1298, no. 2 (*Ibid.* III, 293).

[4] Cf. Bonnin, *op. cit.*, pp. 43, 94, 197, 207, etc.

[5] Ch. XIV, Cf. *Analecta sacri ord. praed.*, III, 1897, 342.

organisation of the monasteries and persisted for the same length of time. But the frequency with which superiors—whatever the Order concerned—recall this obligation[1] is an obvious sign that it was easily disregarded. There were many reasons for this, of course, and among them, possibly, economic reasons.

The Dowry

If the rule of limited recruitment was broken with impunity it was done so because in certain cases admissions in excess of the prescribed number provided the monastery, at least temporarily, with an increase of income.

The religious state was a coveted position ; there was therefore a demand for it. 'Our superiors no longer allow us to receive all and sundry for the time being,' the abbess would answer, 'since our revenues are only just sufficient for our present numbers. But if you agree to pay for your maintenance, or rather to pay for the maintenance of your daughter, until there is a free place, we are willing to accept her.'

That bordered on simony, it will be urged ; certainly it was for this reason that in the twelfth century English Provincial Councils protested against such a practice[2]. Eudes Rigaud calls it that in so many words : *recipiant moniales per simoniam*, he wrote in 1251 of a monastery near Gournay[3]. Even after she had taken the veil he had a nun sent back to her parents because she had been received under these conditions, and her profession was thus tainted with simony. The question was by no means simple ; it engaged the attention of theologians at that time.

In fact it is in connexion with simony that St Thomas pays particular attention to the matter. The principle is quite definite : money cannot be demanded for entry to religion. But in a community whose revenues enable only a limited number of subjects to be supported, if a candidate in excess of this number comes forward cannot a sum sufficient for her support be accepted ? Is it not licit to receive more easily into a

---

[1] It is mentioned by the Cistercian General Chapters of 1326, no. 6 (Canivez III, 274) ; 1397, no. 49 (*Ibid.*, 695-6) ; 1609, no. 481 (*Ibid.* VII, 278) ; 1618, no. 38 (*Ibid.* VII, 337) ; 1686, no. 17 (*Ibid.* VII, 584).

[2] E. Power, *Medieval English Nunneries*, pp. 17-21.

[3] Bonnin *op. cit.*, p. 115. Cf. pp. 215, 319, 361, 512.

monastery one who has given evidence by her alms of the devotion she bears to the house ? Is it not licit by the same token to give alms to a monastery for the purpose of attracting vocations to it ? What must be prohibited absolutely is any negotiated agreement[1].

Again in the fifteenth century St Colette's constitutions for the Poor Clares were extremely sensitive on this point, though they admitted the possibility of a small offering.[2] But as the course of economic evolution rendered the material situation of monasteries increasingly precarious the practice spread and became general. In this way arose the institution of the dowry for admission to the religious life. The intervention of the Council of Trent[3] was confined to laying down that no donation of this nature should be made before profession, except for the sums required for maintenance during the precise period of the noviciate. It thus provided a safeguard against the complicated disputes that might arise in the case of a novice's dismissal and also against reluctance to dismissing them. But in practice it sanctioned the custom of the dowry.

It remained only for it to be made of obligation. This came about gradually and resulted finally in canon 547, s.1 of the *Codex juris canonici*.[4]

The institution of the dowry within the traditional system of collective property, at first a compensation for certain insufficiencies of landed property, came finally to be substituted for it entirely at a time when the stability of money and securities made these small capital endowments a guarantee of security in the future. That no longer holds good.

We come thus to a complete reversal of the situation. In the first centuries of religious life women entered to take advantage

[1] II-II, 100, a. 3, 4m. It will be urged perhaps that girls without means are thus excluded from the religious life. This was denied by Cajetan on the grounds that, in any case, they were excluded in the first place by the required limitation of numbers.

It would not be unreasonable to use the term 'black market' of some admissions to religious life.

[2] Ch. I, nos. 6 and 7. *Seraphicae legislationis textus originales*, p. 109.

[3] Sess. XXV, ch. XVI. *Concilium tridentinum*, ix, 1083, l. 24.

[4] See the pontifical interventions of 1577, 1594, 1683, 1759, 1766, 1834, and 1902 which are referred to in the annotated edition of the Codex. A thesis on the history of the religious dowry is in course of preparation under the direction of Fr. Creusen.

of the wealth of a monastery. At the other end of the evolutionary process it is the monastery itself which looks to its subjects for the means of livelihood.

The disadvantage of the old system was that it opened the cloister to women without a vocation, who were more concerned for their board and lodging than about serving God. The development of the dowry system led to the disadvantage of sometimes closing the cloister to vocations without means. Predominant under both systems was the same idea of realising material security from the outset.

Necessity for a staff of servants

In the next place, in order to obtain full benefit from the material advantages thus provided by the religious life a certain amount of work was required. Who was to undertake it ? The Rule of St Caesarius ordained that the nuns themselves should undertake the house work of their establishment—particularly the cooking—and that they should do without servants. In the event, the immense development of monastic property and the aristocratic condition of the nuns soon brought about the introduction of a domestic staff within the monastery.

The Rule of 816 considers the presence of servants as quite normal : *Quia licitum est Deo dicatis canonice viventibus, vernulas secum famulandi causa in monasteriis habere*[1]. At Notre-Dame de Soissons, by 858, there were seventy servants[2].

The presence of servants was an inevitable result of the system. It tended to imperil the religious spirit to the extent that the moral mediocrity of the servants or their gossiping outside the enclosure lowered the spiritual level of the monastic community. To this point particularly chapter XXI of the Rule of 816—quoted above—draws attention, a warning that was to be frequently repeated in the following centuries.

The Lay Sisters

The need to secure from the domestic servants of the monastery behaviour more in keeping with the religious life and concern to obtain unrestricted authority over them, had

[1] Mansi, XIV, 274.
[2] Cf. Lesne, *op. cit.* VI, 206.

probably something to do with the development of that subsidiary form of the nun's life which is called the state of lay
sister.

The question is a difficult one and, so far as I know, has not
been studied directly. There are some studies about lay brothers.
It might be thought that these would suffice to explain the
analogous origin and development of lay sisters. That is
partially true. But very possibly this institution as it was carried
into effect in women's houses comprised original elements which
it would be interesting to explore. The question remains an
open one.

It does not appear that originally the distinction between nuns
and lay sisters was based on difference of education, or more
accurately on differing aptitudes for taking part, or not, in the
Divine Office. The distinction between educated and
uneducated, *litteratae* and *non litteratae*, was probably to be
found quite early among the nuns, as among the monks, though
it entailed no other consequence than a different method of
taking part in the Office : those who did not know the Psalter
said the Lord's prayer in a low voice during the collective
recitation of the Psalms. In the middle of the thirteenth century,
when for some time past there had been lay sisters in the
monasteries, the distinction between *litteratae* and *illitteratae*
was still to be found among those we call 'choir nuns'. Thus
the Constitutions—of Dominican origin—of the Sisters of
Penance of St Mary Magdalen in Germany (1236) lay down
that after the age of twenty-four it is too late to teach the Psalter
to a sister, but there is no question of giving her an inferior
position in the monastery.

It is possible that the origin of the *conversae* in the twelfth
century should be sought rather in the history of numerous
conversion movements to which the preachers and hermits
gave rise, particularly in the north and in Belgium, and also in
the fact that layfolk, men and women, went to work, in a
religious capacity, on behalf of these newly-formed communities.

In the same way that the Cistercian lay brothers assumed the
functions previously exercised by the serfs and secular servants
in the many dependencies of the great abbeys, so also women—
bound by vows—undertook the *outside duties* of the monastery ;

their collaboration was the more necessary since the nuns were obliged to observe the enclosure.

Eudes Rigaud's visitation register of the middle of the thirteenth century mentions here and there *sorores* or *sorores conversae* or *sorores laicae* side by side with *moniales* in the monasteries or priories. Some of these entries show that eventually these sisters took charge in the granges in the same way as the lay brothers[1].

The Rule of St Clare (1253) provides for 'extern serving sisters', *sorores servientes extra monasterium*[2].

It is significant that this personal Rule of St Clare which on the question of property makes a clear departure from universal practice, is also probably the only one at this period not to provide for *sorores servientes* within the monastery.

The Constitutions of the Dominican nuns (1259) are as explicit as possible on this point : they authorise nuns to receive lay sisters within the enclosure according to the need for their *services*.[3]

Of course if their service was the primary reason for their existence there could be no question of receiving them in extreme youth like the nuns. They are to be chosen *maturas* and *laboriosas* from among strong and hard-working girls.[4]

We may observe how St Isabelle in 1263 drew up the Rule of the *Sorores minores inclusae* on the basis of previous rules. She restored the legitimacy of property and revenues, that is she adopted the usual practice of religious houses, and provided also for *sorores servientes* within the monastery and decided that they should wear a distinctive habit. The rule of 1247 confined

---

[1] *Visitavimus apud Bondevillam. Ibi sunt xxx moniales, v sorores et due recepte ; item, tres fratres, tres clerici . . . Quadam soror moratur sola in grangia quadam, et quidam frater similiter ibi moratur solus ; iniunximus, propter suspectionem, quod revocaretur illa soror ad domum vel daretur ei socia . . .* Bonnin, *op. cit.* p. 217.

[2] Cf. *Seraphicae legislationis textus originales*, pp. 54, 69.

[3] *Licebit quoque aliquas recipere intus in sorores conversas, ubi hoc expediens videbitur, in numero moderato : prout earum officiis et adjutoriis aliis alie sorores indigebunt. Analecta sacri Ord. praed.* III, 1897, 342.

[4] *Possunt . . . recipere quasdam conversas, maturas, honestas, laboriosas, quarum indigent intus vel foris . . .* Ordinations made by a Prior provincial in Germany in the second half of the thirteenth century. Cf. E. Ritzinger and H. C. Scheeben, *Beiträge zur Geschichte der Teutonia in der zweiten Hälfte des 13 Jahrhunderts*, in *Archiv. der deutschen Dominikaner*, III, 1941, 33.

itself to laying down the colour and shape of the cloak with which the extern sisters were to cover their religious habit when they went abroad in the town.[1] Henceforward, in St Isabelle's community, the *sorores servientes* within the enclosure were to wear a woollen girdle and a white veil, like the novices, instead of the cord and black veil which was reserved to the professed.[2]

With the Dominican nuns, although differences in the habit are not mentioned in the Constitutions—any more than they are for lay brothers in the primitive Constitutions of the Order—they must have quickly come into existence. In any case, following word for word the legislation concerning the brethren on this point, the Dominican nuns effected an amalgamation between *conversae* and *illitteratae* in all that concerned the Office.[3] Later on, permissions to pass from the position of *conversa* to that of *clerica* were given on condition that the sister so favoured should learn to read.[4]

The reactions aroused by permissions of this kind are moreover, significant of the class spirit which for long past had been the effective cause of this distinction between two categories of nuns.[5] Towards the end of the sixteenth century the Chapter General of Citeaux required a certain community of nuns, who were so far relaxed as to have each her own private servant, to be content with making use of the services of lay sisters or servants in common.[6] Were not their functions the same? In 1664, to avoid looking like lay sisters seemed good and sufficient reason for the Dominican nuns of Arras to refuse a reform in the style of their head-dress.[7] In this same year of

---

[1] Cf. Eubel, *Bullarii franciscani epitome*, 243a.

[2] *Ibid.*, 270b.

[3] Cf. *Analecta sacri ord. praed.*, III, 1897.
The rule of St Colette even provides that the *illitteratae* should say the Office peculiar to them in a special place, *in aliquo loco propter hoc eisdem assignato. Seraphicae legislationis textus originales*, 119.

[4] A Dominican example, in 1480 : *Bullarium sacr. Ord. Praed.*, III, 590. A Cistercian example, 1425 : Canivez, *Statuta ord. Cisterc.*, iv, 298.

[5] Against changes of this kind the nuns of a monastery in Florence in 1505 obtained a Bull forbidding them to receive amongst them—for they were *ex nobiliori loco*—lay sisters *ex humilioribus locis inibi ad earum servitium recepte.— Bullarium Ord. Praed.* iv, 231.

[6] *Illud satis esse debet si in commune conversarum suarem aut saecularium ancillarum ministerio utantur* (1584). Canivez, *Statuta*, vii, 172.

[7] Cf. *Annee Dominicaine*, 1875, p. 324-5.

1664 when the archbishop of Paris was at his wit's end to overcome the resistance of the nuns of Port Royal at one moment the idea was entertained of reducing them all to the status of lay sisters. 'That state is extremely humiliating, since, in fact, such persons were formerly considered as servants and not as nuns, and a monastery in this state is practically ruined.'[1]

A staff of men

A monastery of women needs at least one priest to provide for divine worship and the administration of the sacraments. But from the beginning, also, the economic organisation of these foundations required masculine assistance for the administration of the temporalities. The *provisores* mentioned in the Rule of St Caesarius were to experience an increase in numbers and a variation in functions, from temporal administration properly so-called to carrying out all sorts of material work, following the development of monastic possessions. Thus from the seventh century onwards, in Spain, in France, then in England and in Germany 'double monasteries' are to be found. In the twelfth century the same phenomenon recurred in a more developed form.[2] The most famous examples are, in England, the Gilbertines whose canons' and lay brothers' only function was to provide religious and temporal ministry for the nuns, and in France the Order of Fontevrault. Several Cistercian or Premonstratensian houses were of this type. In any case, without going so far as to have a male counterpart, every convent of women in the Middle Ages included an annexe with a small masculine community comprising chaplains, confessors, lay brothers, whether these were provided by the Order which exercised jurisdiction over the convent (Cistercians, Premonstratensians, Dominicans or Franciscans) or whether the nuns themselves recruited them and they made religious profession directly into the hands of the abbess or prioress.[3]

[1] M. de Sainte-Marthe. Quoted by L. Cognet, *Claude Lancelot solitaire de Port-Royal*. Paris, 1950, p. 155.

[2] Cf. *Dict. hist. et geo. eccl.*, VII, 1210. U. Berliere, *Les monasteres doubles au XIIe et XIIIe siecles*, Brussels, 1923. St. Hilpisch, *Die Doppelkloster: Entstehung und Organisation*. Munster, 1928.

[3] Cf. R. Creytens, *Les convers des moniales dominicaines au Moyen Age*. *Archivum fratrum praedicatorum*, XIX, 1949, 5-48.

If, one after the other, Cistercians, Premonstratensians, Dominicans, Franciscans, at first made no difficulty about accepting the *cura monialium*, but very soon did all in their power to give it up, it was precisely because this *cura monialium* implied also temporal administration and for this reason involved heavy responsibilities and a great wastage of man power.

Work

If the requirements for the administration of a fairly large estate soon obliged the monastery to have joined to it a staff of men, and if, on the other hand the aristocratic nature of its recruitment quickly caused the housework to be entrusted to servants, and then to lay sisters, what, it may be asked, was the nuns' own function in relation to the economic life of the monastery ?

The history of work in monasteries of women is a subject well worth lengthy treatment. But, so far as I can judge, nothing of any importance has been done on this subject.[1] There is a greater abundance of documentary evidence about it than might be at first supposed. It would be sufficient to scrutinise and classify the documents, providing time enough were available. Unfortunately I can only furnish here a few summary indications taken almost entirely from Rules and Constitutions and that is a source notoriously inadequate to provide a knowledge of the concrete routine of daily life.

According to the Rule of St Caesarius work is primarily an occupation, idleness being one of the principal enemies of fervour and religious regularity. In this same spirit the Rule of Aix-la-Chapelle (816) requires the nuns, outside the time for psalmody and spiritual reading, to be occupied in manual labour.[2] The Constitutions of St Sixtus, as they are known, which represent an early stage of the legislation for Dominican nuns, joins to this consideration that of the necessity of work

---

[1] See, for what concerns the old monastic Rules : E. Delaruelle, *Le travail dans les règles monastiques occidentales du quatrième au neuvième siècle*, in *Journal de psychologie*, XLI, 1948, 51-64.

[2] Ch. X . . . *In monasteriis quoque positae non otio torpeant . . . ; sed aut psalmorum modulationibus, aut manuum operationibus insistant, aut certe divinis lectionibus aurem accommodent* . . . Mansi, XIV, 269. The same ideas, expressed in the same way, are to be found in ch. XIV, id. 271.

pure and simple, in every state of humanity.[1] Humbert de Romanis, energetic compiler as he was, did not repeat that last idea. The various versions of the Rule of the Poor Clares evince still greater reserve in mentioning the religious value of work.

Here, moreover, it is the economic rather than the religious value which interests us. In the first place, what was the nature of the work ? What could it be other than what was then, in addition to housework and the care of poultry, the only women's work, whether they lived in a convent or in the world ? A woman's work was to spin wool and to make clothes with the material that she had made herself, or else to execute work of a more delicate nature such as embroidery or lace making, etc.

In many aristocratic monasteries in medieval England such fine 'lady's work' seems to have been the nuns' sole occupation, even to the extent that they were obliged to buy their clothes outside the house.[2] There were probably similar cases elsewhere. Nevertheless it is also probable that many monasteries followed on this point the prescriptions of St Caesarius which required the nuns to provide their clothes by their own work. The Rule of 816 considers this practice quite normal.[3] More sumptuous work, in so far as it was required for vestments and the decoration of the church also became an integral element of the monastic economy—not without a certain danger to those who devoted themselves to it, as the prohibitions of St Caesarius, and centuries later, of St Colette, reveal.[4]

---

[1] Ch. XX . . . *quia ociositas inimica est anima necnon mater et nutrix est vitiorum, nulla in claustra maneat ociosa ; sed semper, si poterit, aliquid operis faciat, quia non de facili a temptacione capitur qui exercio bono vacat.* 2. *A Domino enim dictum est homini, quod in sudore vultus sui vesci debeat pane suo ; et Apostolus dicit : qui operari noluerit, non manducet ; et propheta : labores manuum tuarum manducabis, beatus es et bene tibi erit.* 3. *Ideo exceptis illis horis quibus oracioni, lectioni vel provisioni divini officii seu cantus aut erudicioni litterarum debent intendere, operibus manuum omnes attente insistant, prout visum fuerit priorisse.* Cf. A. Simon, *L'Ordre des Penitentes de Sainte Marie-Madeleine en Allemagne au XIIIe siecle.* Fribourg. 1918, p. 152.

[2] Cf. E. Power, *Medieval English Nunneries*, p. 255.

[3] See ch. XIII which deals with the way that abbesses should provide equitably for the various material needs of the nuns : *Dent etiam eis annis singulis lanam et linum, e quibus sibi conficiant necessaria indumenta, exceptis infirmis et debilibus, quae propter corporis incommoditatem, haec sibi conficere nequeunt . . .* Mansi, XIV, 270.

[4] Ch. XII *Seraphicae legislationis textus originales*, p. 153.

Did nuns go a stage farther and increase the resources of the monastery by selling stuffs and clothes that they had made ? In this case the legislative documents, even where they emphasize the fact that work is not a mere pastime, and that the sisters must aim at a certain output,[1] prove insufficient for our purpose. St Colette, at least, explicitly alludes to work as one of the sources of the economic life of the monastery when she foresees that it may have to be continued beyond the time limit prescribed.[2] But the Poor Clares of St Colette well knew what it meant to be poor at a time when the material distress of certain monasteries was to be seen in the fact that the nuns in them were reduced to begging . . . and to working ![3]

It should not be forgotten that very frequently the monasteries were cultural centres. It could hardly be expected that manual labour should have been the only occupation in them. The place given to study—which legislators, like Humbert de Romanis in the case of the Dominican nuns, do not appear to have looked on with a very favourable eye—cannot be counted, for obvious reasons, among the economically productive

---

[1] So far as Dominican nuns are concerned the ordinations of a French prior provincial in the thirteenth century prescribe that each sister should attain a certain output, and that she must be obliged to attain it under pain of correction and penances, such as being deprived of wine and of going to the parlour. *Ne vero opus commune negligatur, singule lanam sibi ad operandum commissam, tempore determinato fideliter filatam restituant nisi infirmitate impediantur. Quod nisi fecerint intra tres dies sequente se expediant. Alioquin ex tunc sedeant in terra nec bibant vinum nec vadant ad fenestram donec opus suum fecerint.—Archivium Frat, Praedicatorum,* xxi, 1951, 224. Thus the nuns worked at a common task and not merely each one on her own account. But there is no evidence to show that what this work yielded was intended for outside the monastery.

[2] Ch. XII *De occupationibus sororum* . . . 4. *Et quia in praedicta clausula formae vitae* (i.e., the Rule of St Clare) *continetur* : post horam Tertiae, *nos tamen considerantes strictam paupertatem dictarum Sororum, et necessitates et indigentias quae possent habere, concedimus quod si aliquod negotium ante horam praedictam in conventu eveniat quod sit necessarium vel conveniens ad perficiendum, quod Abbatissa vel eius vicaria possit praecipere cui voluerit quod illud faciat, vel perficiat si opus jam sit inceptum.—Seraphicae legislationis textus originales,* p. 153.

[3] Thus in 1425 in an Augustinian monastery, near Soissons : *non sunt nisi quinque vel sex pauperes muliercule religiose, quae inibi vivere non possunt, sed quasi mendicando et laborando in magna paupertate ibidem habitant* . . . Cf. Denifle, *La desolation des Eglises,* I, p. 23.

activities of the monastery.[1] But one form of manual labour, arising from this culture and in close connexion with it, was the copying of books. In the Middle Ages this was a technical and extremely important form of work ; by modern standards the proper comparison would be not with duplicating but with printing. The Dominican nuns in Germany in the thirteenth century devoted themselves to works of this kind primarily to furnish their own library and provide a sufficiency of choir books for their own use, but also to sell them. A friar of the Order, well versed in this sort of business was to fix the sale price.[2]

Although wealthy monasteries like Prouille in France had no need to supplement their income in this way, it is by no means impossible, on the other hand, that this kind of work effectively contributed to balancing the budget of the monasteries of Dominican nuns in Germany where, because they were numerous, it is probable that they were not so richly endowed.

Subsequently during the Middle Ages it is likely that work held a place also in the various monasteries of the Third Order regular, Dominican,[3] or more particularly Franciscan—the numerous Black Sisters or Grey Sisters of the north of France for example. It is by no means certain that the movement for the restoration of the contemplative life to be witnessed in France in the sixteenth century gave to work the place that it occupied in the Middle Ages. The practice was maintained probably, in certain monasteries, as at St Praxedes at Avignon,

---

[1] Since the special Constitutions of the Dominican nuns were drawn up by changing to the feminine gender the Constitutions of the Friars it is not surprising to find in them at first some mention of study in connexion with work. But it is curious that the Constitutions given to the nuns of Montargis, in about 1250, by Humbert of Romanis, then the French Provincial, are less explicit on this subject than the Constitutions of the Penitents of St Mary Magdalen (1236). The Constitutions issued by Humbert in 1259 for all the nuns of the Order no longer mention any other save manual work.

[2] Ordination by a German Provincial Prior : *Scriptrices sedeant cum aliis laborantibus in communi domo, sed hac non scribant aliis, donec conventus habeat libros necessarios. Scribentibus vero aliis taxetur pretium per librarium fratrem . . . et in utilitatem conventus vertatur acquisitio . . .* Cf. *Archiv der Deutschen Dominikaner*, III, 1941, 37.

[3] One small example in passing : in 1455 a community of Tertiaries in Florence petitioned to be excused from paying certain dues on the grounds that they possessed very little revenue and that the sisters lived *ex sudore manuum suarum. Bullarium Ord. Praed.* III, 339.

the originator of so many Dominican foundations, of being
self-sufficient in the matter of the provision and upkeep of
clothes,[1] but the over-loaded timetables with, in addition to the
Office, the periods of mental prayer, particular examens,
spiritual reading, preparations of mental prayer etc., left but
little opportunity for any sustained work. In addition there
were constantly occurring feast days of all kinds which reduced
the already short time which remained. There was certainly no
question of maintaining a given output. Thus superiors and
officials, bursars particularly, were obliged to be dispensed
from choir or other community exercised in order to find the
minimum time necessary for those immediate duties which the
smooth running of the material side of the house demanded.

Under the pressure of actual poverty an effort was made in
the eighteenth century to turn the activities of some sisters
towards more lucrative channels. Thus the sale of 'gimblettes',
probably a kind of fancy pastry, of which the recipe has been
lost, was a factor of importance in the budget of the Dominican
nuns of the Cross at this same period.

It is obvious that the modern economic transformation,
favouring industrial expansion at the expense of craft work, and
on the other hand the numerous possibilities open to the work of
women, have modified considerably the various factors of the
problem of work in the religious life. It is something of a
paradox that cloistered monastic life in particular could easily
hold its own at the current level of women's work, and in
consequence had nothing to fear from competition so long as it
enjoyed an economic status which allowed it almost to live
without working, but that when cloistered life is in an inferior
state in comparison with current conditions of women's work
such work, becomes for it, a very necessity of life.

The Boarders

Although this is only a secondary aspect of the matter, it

[1] Cf. the answers given by the nuns at the canonical visitation of 1628, in
Rousset, *Le Monastere de Sainte Praxede*, Lyon, 1876, p. 49.

If the Annee Dominicaine, I, Amiens, 1678, p. 143, informs us that the
Dominican nuns of Aumale at the beginning of their reform (in the early
seventeenth century) had 'no other revenue than what they earned by the
work of their hands' it is, os to say, the sign of a heroic age now departed.

will not be unprofitable to point out, in the last place, the connexion between economic life and historically one of the most important functions of the religious life among women. I refer to the education of girls. This form of activity is obviously anterior to the appearance of 'teaching' congregations and goes back several centuries. No place was made for this educational activity in the monastery at Arles, according to St Caesarius's plan. But when in 816 the Council of Aix-la-Chapelle legislated for nuns in general, chapter XXII of its Rule, lavish with its advice on the manner of educating children and girls living in the monastery, obviously considers it quite normal. Did these children and girls pay for their board? The contrary was probably the case. Since the monasteries were the domain of the nobility these children too, sent there by the nuns' own families, were very likely living on the revenues of the convent. It might happen that in straitened times their presence was a heavy burden. It was for this reason, no doubt, as well as for the improvement of religious observance that Eudes Rigaud during his visitations enjoined in some places that girls should no longer be kept in the convent if in fact they were not destined for the religious life.[1] As, progressively, the nuns themselves no longer came to the monastery to take advantage of endowments made before their day but were obliged to contribute at first with an offering, and then by the dowry system, to the material security of their community, the monasteries continued to admit girls to be educated no longer gratuitously, however, but in order to derive a profit. Thus the Dominican nuns of Montargis were authorised in 1527 to receive girls *pro institutione bonorum morum et aliorum officiorum muliebrium . . . ad occurendum egestati monasterii.*[2] The practice became so common that the general Chapters legislated on the dress, behaviour, hairdress and jewels of the boarders.[3] In many foundations started

---

[1] E.g. at Preaux in 1249; cf. Bonnin, *op. cit.*, p. 60; at Bondeville in 1255, *Ibid.*, p. 217; at Evreux in 1258, *Ibid.* p. 305. In 1252, Eudes Rigaud observed that the nuns of Buyval were even educating ten young boys in their house, *Ibid.*, p. 146.

[2] Unpublished registers of the Masters General. In 1577 the Dominican nuns of Beaumont-les-Valenciennes likewise received licence to accept *nobiles et honestas puellas ad pensionem.*

[3] General chapters of 1644, 1650, 1656.

in the seventeenth century exclusively for teaching, like Mother Alix le Clerc's, the boarding department was instituted especially to provide the necessary resources for the maintenance of the nuns who devoted themselves primarily to education of the poorer classes, gratuitously of course.

In the seventeenth century the system of receiving boarders corresponded indeed so well with the economic conditions of the times that it was extended far beyond children and girls. How many convents have also their lady boarders whose oddities and whims must be borne—for, after all, one must live !

Conclusion

The observations gathered together here are far too fleeting, and too isolated from the economic and general history of the condition of women, for any historical conclusion to be drawn from them. It was a question, merely, of drawing attention to certain related facts.

So many allusions to failures of all kinds should not leave a painful impression of the value of religious institutions. Quite the contrary. In this way we are reminded that institutions are at the service of an interior spiritual attitude which they support but do not bring into being. In so far as the religious state is a life based on the practice of the evangelical counsels it should be continually inspired by whatever is most personal, spontaneous and free in each on of us—*Si vis*—'If you wish . . .' Thus the poverty offered by the Lord is primarily in the heart. If it is not to be found there first of all, the institution will be powerless for in this case actual poverty, no less than riches, can be dangerous. If therefore it is expedient to bring our religious institutions into harmony with the new economic conditions of modern life the primary problem still remains a spiritual one. *Vigilate* !

CHAPTER I

THE THEOLOGY OF RELIGIOUS POVERTY

By M. MICHEL LABOURDETTE, O.P.

The idea of poverty has this paradoxical quality : it arouses
in the mind the simultaneous notion of a distressing human
experience, one of the misfortunes of our present life, and of a
lofty spiritual reality which, perceived by those of a certain
nobility of character, is right in the forefront of Christian
teaching. A paper which observed the proper proportions of
the subject and appeared unaccompanied by others, would
begin by an analysis of the Gospel teaching and Christian
spiritual tradition. For the purposes of the limited study for
which I have been asked I shall follow a more systematic, more
concise plan, with careful emphasis on essential principles.

Poverty is the opposite of wealth, of possession, and can only
be defined in that connexion. In the first part I shall give a
short analysis of this idea of possession to show where the deep
instinct of appropriation is rooted in us, and I shall study what
should be the moral and Christian attitude towards material
possessions and what the idea of poverty means for the virtuous
life. In the second part I shall begin with a reminder of the
evangelical idea of poverty and I shall then study religious
poverty in itself.

Possession and the virtuous life

Possession of something other than self is a necessity for
every creature. God alone possesses everything in himself, *is*
of himself all good and all perfection. The creature, limited to
being this or that, must seek outside himself that which is his

completion ; essentially he lacks a perfection which he can only receive. He is obliged to complete and perfect his being by the possession of something additional to himself, essentially by the possession of that good which is his end : God himself, the greatest riches of all.

Man, because he is intelligent and free, because he is a person, is master of his acts and of his destiny ; he possesses himself with a certain mastery and this mastery he extends to the various things which satisfy his needs and which he requires for his full development. An animal takes its food where it finds it, possesses neither field nor flock and cannot be *master*. With man possession is as it were an extension of his person. And because man's wealth is primarily spiritual what he most truly possesses, after his own human faculties, is that on which they subsist, the qualities which enrich him, which will be his final end, that is, God, in the most personal and most profound of his activities, the beatific vision.

But man possesses a body and he must sustain the life of this body ; he does not live alone. His usual state is that of marriage, by which he brings children into existence whose responsibility is on his shoulders until they become men in their turn. That requires a fairly wide use of a certain number of material possessions. Now it is the nature of material things that they cannot be possessed completely and without division. If several persons make use of the same consumer goods, even if they are possessed in common, each in the last resort will possess only part of them. We may all of us know the same truth with equal fullness, and also love virtue fully and practise it individually : the progress made by the individual in no wise detracts from that of another. But in the material sphere possession by one is a necessary limitation on that of another.

The need for possession gives rise to an instinct of appropriation, of setting aside for actual or future use, for the needs of those in one's charge ; and in the corporal order this appropriation becomes abstraction or withdrawal from others. In this connexion arises the idea of material wealth. Whoever possesses much is rich. It is not in my province to set out the general theory of property and its social distribution ; it will be sufficient to emphasize this natural character of ownership and the tendency to a certain wealth at least in so far as it represents ordinary sufficiency.

For the individual person wealth represents simultaneously *treasure*, something actually possessed which augments his power, and *security* a reason for confidence in the future and provision against emergencies. These two aspects are correlative ; the distinction between them is of considerable importance in the accurate definition of the correlative idea of poverty, both in its actual reality and in the spiritual development that it may assume. For us, whose knowledge surpasses things sensible, possession and poverty extend far beyond material goods to goods which, of their nature, can be possessed without division, but which we consider somewhat in the same way as material goods and readily assume in their regard a similar affective attitude, a proprietary attitude.

Such an extension of the idea of possession and poverty is of capital importance in determination of the spiritual attitude ; for the purpose of our analysis of first principles we can confine ourselves to material possessions. They loom so large in human life that an important problem is thereby raised in morality and the virtuous life ; its solution is not without effect even on the idea of religious poverty which, though it surpasses, should not be in opposition to, the natural law ; the religious state does not dispense from ordinary honesty : *haec oportebat facere et illa non omittere*.

What, then, is the virtuous attitude, in the Christian and human sense, in relation to all those things which form the object of possession and the instinct of appropriation ?

In the first place there are a number of virtues which I shall not mention specially ; they are here taken for granted. I refer to the different forms of justice. The primary duty of the individual is to respect the legitimate possession of others. Obviously, too, there are many problems in connexion with the distribution of wealth ; they are no part of our subject. What we wish to discover is the virtuous attitude to be personally adopted in relation to our own goods, to what we possess as our own.

Certain attitudes are manifestly vicious ; the best known of them is *avarice*. It is exceedingly common, and frequently concealed ; it can be defined as the immoderate love of material wealth. And since the ordinary measure of this wealth, its symbol and universal means of exchange is money, avarice must be considered particularly in relation to money. In contradistinction to consumer goods, money, which is in some sort an artificial and conventional form of wealth, possesses a distinctive characteristic whereby it lends itself admirably to the growth of avarice. Money can be the object of unlimited desire. The desire for material wealth is limited by its very finality ; beyond a certain limit it cannot be used and becomes indeed useless and unused. But directly it is no longer considered from the point of view of its proper use but as a potential means of exchange, regarded, that is, in terms of money which is the universal means of this exchange, there exists no natural barrier to the desire to accumulate it. Everything that is acquired means an increase of power and security. It is for that reason that money is the foremost object of avarice. But it is not the only one ; avarice can extend to every kind of possession. St Thomas defines it therefore as *immoderatus appetitus habendi*, the immoderate desire for possession, the inordinate desire for possession whatever the object.

The contrary to avarice, and another obviously vicious attitude, is *prodigality*. The word seems to bear in general and at first sight merely a rather weak meaning and suggests improvidence and carelessness about material possessions. But includes much more than that. It is simultaneously a certain forgetfulness of the human condition and glorification of self, a desire for power : the ability to spend unstintingly. It is the supreme manifestation of the 'pride of life'.

Inversely, there is a virtue which is too little known ; its precise function is to perfect man's habitual attitude in regard to money and material possessions ; it is called *liberality*. It is often defined rather by the effect that it produces—giving— for he who possesses it gives easily. But in it there is something far more profound, the interior attitude, the spirit that it fosters. It is in some sort an assertion of man's spiritual dignity and nobility. The domination of material things, the ability to use them without being enslaved by them is to show oneself greater than they. Inherent in avarice is something petty and degrading ; liberality on the other hand cultivates and establishes this spiritual greatness and detachment in virtue. He who is liberal is not a slave to his wealth as an end in itself imbued with the sole overriding desire to protect and increase it ; he is the master of his wealth and makes use of it in accordance with the necessities of an upright human life. There is a close relationship between liberality and that form of strength which is called magnanimity, greatness of soul ; both are an affirmation of nobility and grandeur.

Liberality, then, has to deal with the effective condition of life in which the individual may find himself in relation to material possessions, a state of plenty or of want, riches or poverty. Poverty is not a virtue like, for example, chastity or obedience ; essentially it is a certain state of life. There are numerous degrees of poverty, taken in this entirely objective sense, from somewhat embarrassed circumstances to downright want and destitution. But, contrary to wealth, poverty is always characterized by a certain limitation of actual resources and a certain insecurity in regard to the future. When a poor man is able to hope, to face life with confidence, he relies, obviously, on other reasons than the power of money or his reserves of wealth. The same virtue, which humanises the use of wealth when it is possessed, raises to the moral order that state of life represented by material poverty. Liberality prevents its being an obstacle to spiritual life because it implies affective detachment. Of course, I confine myself here to the enunciation of principles, since this paper is concerned entirely with religious poverty. It is obvious that there is much to be said, especially nowadays, solely from the viewpoint of human moral life : it is easy enough to preach detachment to those who have nothing when the preacher himself enjoys at least relative security ; moral teaching should always be adapted to, and make allowances for, a whole host of considerations.

II. Religious Poverty

One of the most striking aspects of the Gospel teaching is the place given to the 'poor man', the mystical importance attributed to poverty. There is no need to set out the quotations themselves in detail ; you are familiar with them all and other papers have reminded you of them. But we may summarize their teaching.

For our purpose the teaching of the Gospel provides the answers to two sorts of questions :

In the first place the poor man's confidence, his security as he confronts life, is not derived from the power of money or any other wealth held in reserve ; it is based on Providence, abandonment to Providence, confidence in the Father.

Secondly the real object of possession for the fulfilment of man, his glorification, is quite other than material wealth. It is not limited or created, but it is God himself. The poor in spirit are blessed, not because they possess nothing, but because they possess only the kingdom of heaven into which they enter with all the poor in the vast community of charity.

Round these two leading notions it would be easy to muster the texts which set before us either Christ's example or his teaching. The Son of God became poor not only by becoming man but by choosing a poor state of life among men, entirely free from the trammels of wealth and whatever humanly speaking conduces to power. He had nowhere to lay his head. His preaching owed nothing to what we call 'propaganda' ; he spoke to all with the greatest simplicity, but more especially to the poor, for they are the freest of all, the only ones who are free. That is the great wonder of messianic times : the poor have the Gospel preached to them. He accepted the service of the holy women and probably also their pecuniary assistance ; but no rich man, no one 'in authority' was summoned to be an apostle. And when the rich young man came forward our Lord did not tell him to offer his goods to the community but to distribute them to the poor, to leave all to follow him and with him to enter the society of the really poor.

His teaching is a reflexion of this example. The first beatitude is that referring to the poor. There was to be no overweening care for the morrow : the heavenly Father provides everything. 'Lay not up to yourselves treasures on earth where the rust and moth consume, and where thieves break through and steal. But lay up to yourselves treasures in heaven . . .' Such earthly things are not true riches, true security is not to be found in them. In this preaching which is addressed to all, he calls on certain persons among them : 'If thou wilt be perfect, go, sell what thou hast, and give to the poor, and thou shalt have treasure in heaven : and come follow me.' I do not consider that the Gospel contains an economic theory of poverty and wealth, but it certainly offers a mystical theory of detachment, mystical because it relies solely on spiritual premises ; complete, blind abandonment to the Province of the Father.

Thus was outlined the great Christian ideal of poverty, the actual model which henceforward was to prove an everlasting attraction for souls. Imitation of Christ is the fundamental rule of all Christian virtues for none of them appears as an abstract ideal, and to Christ himself as the exemplar all must be referred. That is to put it very imperfectly and to give the impression almost of an imitation solely 'from outside' ; though this is true it represents only a relatively superficial and observable element of Christian life. There is something far different from the mere attempt at resemblance ; there is the whole power of grace, of that grace which forms in us an outpouring of, a sharing in, that of Christ : 'we have all received of his fullness'. The fundamental rule of this grace is to cause us to re-live the mysteries of Christ, to clothe us with his affections and virtues, to enable us to reach the fullness of the age of Christ. In Christian grace there is thus that 'predilection for the Cross' so admirably described by Chardon, there is a bias towards abasement and humility : *exinanivit semetipsum* ; also, without question, there is interior predisposition to actual and spiritual poverty, to total renunciation of all that is not God. Poverty embraced effectively as a state of life can never, of necessity, be the way for all ; but for all, poverty of spirit is essential as an indispensable condition of Christian perfection. Since Christ's coming this call to poverty has always been heard in the Church, indeed it has also been experienced and felt by Christian souls ; and it is this call which religious life, among others, desires to answer.

In religious life the individual creates for himself by vow, a strict, a 'sacred' obligation to practise the evangelical counsel of poverty. No need here to linger over the religious life itself and its various forms. Each type has its own form of poverty ; and as there can be no vow unless its matter is determined this form must be precise. But no form of religious life is conscious of being more effectively bound and disposed to poverty than the apostolic life, and this by reason of the very work from which it takes its name. Such a life is not necessarily religious, and it is significant that even outside the religious life it appears to be so bound to poverty that the apostolate itself is dependent thereon. Christ's preaching and that of his apostles were not to be a form of 'propaganda' effected by wealthy means—*infirma mundi elegit*. When the special requirements of the apostolate are joined to and strengthen what is already the purpose of every form of religious life, there is evolved the Christian mystique of poverty, of that poverty which likens us to Christ in his life and his works.

To return to the structure of religious life itself it can be said that vowed poverty always comprises two elements :

(1) The effective renunciation of material possessions, the removal of all 'abundance' ; thereby poverty ensures freedom of soul in relation to money and all material wealth and should be a lofty exercise in the virtue of liberality.

(2) Dependence on superiors in the use of necessities ; in this way the vow remains a state of bondage, restraint for man's natural instincts ; it is a safeguard against the attitude of prodigality as an expression of the pride of life, of the will for power.

Thus in the religious state liberality, the common virtue from which no Christian is dispensed, has two appreciable conditions joined to it :

(1) The gift is made once and for all : *reliquimus omnia* ; whatever its materiality its importance is due entirely to the total nature of the gift. Many, of course, gain more than they have renounced, but they gain it in the form of 'ours' not of 'mine'. Hence the second condition :

(2) The use of all things falls henceforward under the authority set over the common life. To liberality is added obedience, so making of religious poverty an important means of asceticism.

The vow of poverty forms the rule of a precise mode of behaviour, exteriorly verifiable. The vow is broken *only* if, in connexion with a material object, there is an act of possession without the reasonable permission, at least presumed or tacit, of legitimate authority. To keep the vow thus carefully is good, but it is only a minimum. Religious life is so organised that it does not usually demand the greatest sacrifices. By carrying out only the bare minimum one does not derive from the vow of poverty, and from the evangelical counsel of which the vow is the institutional form, all that it is intended to offer as a means of spiritual perfection. We must go farther than that ; here there is tremendous scope for the spiritual development of poverty.

Even in exterior poverty it is possible to go far beyond the minimum. But this, very necessary as it is, is of its nature a very personal matter and one not without its dangers.

Particularly in the early years of religious life there can be a certain enthusiasm, a tendency to enter on a state of life that in practice cannot be sustained or at least cannot be sustained without impairing an efficiency that is of greater importance. Poverty can be external merely, and there is also an aesthetic notion of poverty ; the danger of aestheticism in this connexion is that it, too, possesses its *mystique*. Poverty is never an absolute, it remains always a means in the service of charity.

There is also the danger of reducing poverty from the lofty religious ideal to considerations of economy ; economy is, of course, very necessary, but it is only a material factor and it is by no means rare to see it become a cloak for absolute avarice, just as under the pretext of collective honour a terrible collective or caste pride may sometimes be observed. A man may lose all notion of the virtue in an unenlightened casuistry wherein, practically speaking, the advantage of the spiritual freedom to which poverty tends, entirely disappears and at the very least the way lies open to scrupulosity.

But principally there must breathe through the material practice of poverty a spirit capable of indefinite progress. In the same way that avarice, as a psychological and moral attitude, can extend beyond mere material possessions, so also poverty, as a spiritual and moral attitude ought to extend to everything that can be a particular object of possession. It is an absolute rule of spiritual greatness and Christian perfection that *nothing* should be possessed with attachment (in the spiritual and ascetic meaning of the word), nothing save God. God is both our treasure and our security. Whatever is not God must be possessed as if it were not possessed, used as if it were not used. Failing that, however great the material external detachment, one remains or becomes an increasingly rich, proprietary, attached soul, a covetous soul. A distinction may be made between a laden soul and a rich soul. A soul laden with gifts (natural and supernatural) can be 'poor' or 'rich' (in the ascetic sense) according as it is attached either to God alone (and it has poverty of spirit) or to these gifts (and it is spiritually covetous.)

Now it is easier for a rich man (in that sense) to enter into the Kingdom of Heaven, into the vast kingdom of spiritual freedom, of union with God, than for a camel to go through the eye of a needle. The poverty I am speaking of is not a lack, a want, it is detachment. It is possible to have very little and be avaricious, to possess much and be poor in spirit. The miser is held in thrall by his treasure, the poor man is free for the only possession that he holds to is God who cannot be taken away from him.

It is outside my present scope to mention the stages of progress in this interior detachment, at each of which a more progressively, more perfect interior poverty is achieved. Spiritual writers have spoken of it at length, St John of the Cross especially. I wish merely to show how this interior perfection, the soul of religious poverty, comes within the theological order. Its principal motive which increasingly becomes its substance (under charity and with it) is theological hope. 'Go, sell what thou hast'; that is poverty; 'thou shalt have treasure in heaven'; that is hope.

Hope is that supernatural movement which causes us to tend to the possession of God in heaven : there is our only 'treasure', by placing our reliance on his Almighty help ; there is our 'security'. Both object and motive are divine. Hope effects in the sphere of the theological life what liberality and magnanimity are in the moral order. It is a virtue of Christian nobility and therefore of liberty in relation to all that is less than God for, as St Thomas tells us, 'no less must be expected of God than himself'. At the same time that hope fixes the soul on God, it detaches it profoundly from creatures. It strengthens the Christian nobility of the generous, magnanimous soul, and in addition demands and confirms that interior renunciation which is the fruit of reverent fear of God, humility, the complex whole of a profoundly religious attitude essential to true poverty of spirit. And thus, because it empties us of attachment to every treasure and every other security than God theological hope is the very substance of the most profound spirit of poverty. It allows entry into the blessedness of the poor.

Because he who is poor has not stooped to the measure of some possession he has grown in stature, has increased to the fullness of God, of the divine Will; in God he possesses all things in a far truer way. St John of the Cross could sing: 'Mine are the heavens and mine is the earth'. The Gospel had said it already: 'Theirs is the Kingdom'. The soul is thus truly free for the exercise of perfect charity.

CHAPTER II

RELIGIOUS POVERTY IN CANON LAW

By A. DELCHARD, S.J.

From the earliest period of the eremitical life down to our own days practice of the evangelical virtue of poverty has been inspired by the desire to keep the word and follow the example of our Lord. The saints, urged on and upheld by an increasingly pure and burning love, needed neither rules nor vows to live a real poverty leading to renunciation in its most heroic form. But the great majority of those who, as religious, desire to tend to the perfection of charity, are obliged to have recourse to human means—to a rule to form their understanding and to direct their efforts to an authentic, unobtrusive practice of poverty; to a vow to effect the offering of private possessions for the benefit of the poor of Christ and accomplish the actual renunciation; to uphold a will which continually seeks to take back what one day it gave up; to consecrate to God himself in the most filial confidence this renunciation of self and all possessions.

Human means no doubt they are, none the less they are requisites of social life, of life in the great community of the Church, of life in those communities formed by the religious Orders. The spirit of poverty comes, and indeed must come first, but in conjunction with individual and social requirements it must be incorporated in an institutional framework. Hence, again, the need for a formula for action, for an individual and social rule of life, for an engagement subjecting man freely, but completely, to this rule. Moreover what has been evolved by a long religious tradition dating back some sixteen centuries, and imposed by it on monks and friars, on all religious of both sexes, is to be accepted only with humility. The Church, the mistress of truth and life, has adopted rules formulated in various ways; and by elucidating their inner meaning it shows us in outline, but quite clearly, the portrait of the religious living in voluntary poverty. In spite of its legal nature the formula elaborated by Canon Law remains flexible and open to adaptations in the future as it was in the past. I shall endeavour to bring out this point especially.

Canon Law now in force considers the question of poverty from two principal viewpoints : individual poverty and collective poverty. Collective poverty or the degree of poverty of the corporate body may vary in austerity. A religious institute may possess in common both real and personal property, stable sources of income, and in this way provide for the maintenance of its members and the prosecution of its work. On the other hand it may renounce, wholly or in part, this possession of property, especially in so far as the needs of common life and action are assured by means of a regular income. This poverty, whether mendicant or non-mendicant, governed by the very purpose of the Order, leads to a meagre and more or less restricted use of property and governs various rules concerning the manner of obtaining resources.

The Code, except for reference to a very special case in Canon 582, leaves the responsibility of determining the form of collective poverty to the Constitutions of the various religious Orders. But it lays down certain general rules concerning the mode of acquisition and the administration of common property. It contemplates as sources of income dowries, the profits from work or a trade so far as it is allowed, the proceeds from alms and begging. It envisages various provisions in connexion with the administration of religious property. Although these rules are concerned principally with the prudent preservation of property they are not without their effect on the practice of poverty. Those dealing with ordinary or extraordinary administration, with the rendering and checking of accounts, remind superiors of their position as merely agents of the Church's and Christ's property, of their duty to maintain to the best of their ability what is necessary for the support of those in their charge and the works committed to their care. Poverty is not crippling destitution and such a condition must not be allowed to arise through faulty or speculative administration. A sense of responsibility is called for even in the financial field. Lastly the Code re-asserts categorically one of the ends of the possession of this material wealth. Religious property is intended for the use of religious but likewise, so far as possible, it is placed in their hands to be administered according to the moral law and enable them to practise the most elementary form of charity both by apostolic work and almsgiving. I merely mention this aspect ; my purpose is to consider only the question of personal poverty.

Although an explicit vow of poverty does not make its appearance in the formula of religious profession before the end of the twelfth century, rules concerning poverty were laid down from the earliest period of the cenobitic life. It has already been pointed out in a preceding chapter how in the third century ascetic practice gave rise to entirely new ways of life. The hermit, so far as possible, divested himself of his property. The monk, while giving equal weight to effective detachment, entered a community ; it was by this means that he was enabled to possess nothing of his own and yet to make use of the material possessions necessary for life in accordance with a degree of austerity of varying severity. Pachomian or Basilian monks in the east, Benedictine monks more particularly in the west, made no vow of poverty ; but at least by the very fact of entering the monastery and taking the habit they undertook to live the common life in a state of constant dependence. St Benedict requires profession but without an explicit vow of poverty ; it is through his fidelity to this public profession that the monk is enabled to carry out the obligation of monastic observance. This obligation, ratified by the vow of *conversatio morum* requires him to submit himself to the regular and common discipline of poverty. Consequently at the outset he was called on to give up his personal possessions, to renounce them even to the extent of having nothing of his own, to undertake life in common, to work in close dependence on the abbot and to accept all these things before God and under the sanction of a profession by which his whole life was committed : so many elements which enabled the monk to live according to the evangelical spirit of poverty. The Rule repeats to him the spirit and offers him the discipline of a life of poverty.

In the twelfth and thirteenth centuries occurred a further phase of evolution. A movement called forth by spiritual needs, encouraged by social conditions and economic factors, tended to give increased importance to poverty in religious life. The mendicants appeared with their system of stricter collective poverty. Owing to the work of canonists and theologians and, in no small degree, to the unifying and centralising activity of the Roman Pontiffs, a common doctrine and relatively universal legislation were evolved and began to compel recognition. The traditional conception remained, but a new emphasis was given to it with the appearance of the three vows of poverty, chastity, and obedience in religious profession. The first instance that the sources allow to be quoted with certainty is furnished by the formula of the Canons of St Genevieve of Paris in 1148. The Trinitarians and Friars Minor were to adopt it later. The value of this vow was asserted and defended by theologians, and its applications determined by the canonists and when necessary by legislative authority.

The vow of poverty made to God forms an essential part of a whole. It is always taken in connexion with religious profession. After much hesitation and considerable discussion this vow, owing to the profession which it entailed, was officially and juridically recognized by Boniface VIII as a solemn vow which, according to the law prevailing at that time, amounted to saying that it was the only public vow and the only vow of religion. At the same time its effects became the object of an increasingly coherent body of well-defined and obligatory rules, the result of doctrinal elaboration, legislative action or the gradual growth of custom. The object of the vow was formed by material possessions and rights which we should nowadays hold as capable of estimation in terms of money. When taken by the monk or friar it implied a previous renunciation of personal property. Practice of the vow, based on the principle that a regular could possess nothing as his own, required that all use should be dependent. Whatever was obtained by a religious through his work, by gift or legacy was acquired by the community. Furthermore the regular was juridically incapable of acquiring any property for himself, of enjoying the usufruct or of making independent use of it. It was an explicit interpretation of the fact that the professed religious could possess nothing as his own ; he was absolutely incapable of doing so, even to the extent that every act contrary to his vow was not only illicit but invalid. Such consequences of the vow, binding in conscience, did not arise from the nature of the vow as such. In reality there was a duality in the rules concerning poverty which still subsists in our present law : there are those rules which belong to and are required by every vow (dependence in use, for example) and there are those which are disciplinary consequences of the vow, in agreement with its very nature, but which were only formulated gradually by the leading Rules, and sanctioned at a particular moment and by this very fact imposed by the authority of the Church (incapacity to possess of the solemnly professed religious, for example).

Thus the system of poverty in solemn profession was elaborated. Yet all was not yet settled regarding systems and degrees of poverty. Economic and social, even political, conditions—the spiritual and practical needs of the apostolate in fact required adaptations—gave rise to other forms of the application of the vow of poverty, led to the adoption of other rules governing the effective practice of the vow. The established position was maintained but Canon Law gradually came to sanction a new form. The influence exerted in the sixteenth century and subsequently by the legislation peculiar to the Jesuits, particularly in the creation of a type of religious in simple vows, has been pointed out in this connexion. The Jesuit scholastic, after his noviciate, takes only simple vows. The Council of Trent, in 1593, approved this right of the Society, and Gregory XIII, in 1583 and 1584, laid down that its scholastics are true religious. It was a revolutionary conception, particularly as regards poverty. The religious in this case could be called on to give up his property but ordinarily he retained the ownership of his personal possessions and the capacity to acquire property either by gift or succession. As for the effects of the vow they tended to be reduced to the essential—a state of dependence for the licit use of material property. Any act contrary to the vow is not invalid but merely illicit. The solemn vow is no longer the only religious vow, the simple vow also is a public one. And although this privileged juridical position was, until 1900, reserved to the Jesuits nevertheless it exerted in fact a considerable and decisive influence.

Under the pressure of the immense needs of the Church which required active works of charity and apostolic work in the educational and missionary fields, the seventeenth and eighteenth centuries witnessed the growth and development of several foundations : societies of men and women organised in a common life without vows of religion ; Institutes of men and women adopting the rule of simple profession either as a means of preparation for the regular life properly so-called or merely as a means to ensure, in practice, a religious life. Rome tolerated or approved certain congregations but with reservations.

The system of poverty under simple vows was perfected during the nineteenth century by the combined efforts of the Roman Congregations, the canonists and the founders of Institutes. In the first place we should notice the introduction into the application of the rules governing poverty under solemn vows of various exceptions derived from those of poverty under simple vows. For reasons connected with the political situation and the civil law the Sacred Penitentiary, on 2 December, 1854, clarified a juridical position which until then had remained somewhat vague ; it dealt with the case of enclosed nuns under simple vows, but it was only the Apostolic Constitution *Sponsa Christi* (21 November, 1950), which called for the gradual suppression of this anomalous situation. In 1820, too, a general dispensation was granted by Rome to the regulars of Belgium and Holland. Although they were religious in solemn vows, and consequently in a state of dependence on their superiors, they could retain, not only in regard to the civil law, but also in conscience, the ownership of their inheritance. These are just so many examples showing how clear a distinction should be made between what is implied by the very nature of the vow and what is a consequence of its degree and the discipline pertaining to it. A still more important modification of the law concerning regulars was introduced in 1857. In order to ensure greater freedom to subjects and their Order, since solemn profession involved almost total stability and a radical condition of poverty directly the noviciate was over, Pius IX decided that in all Orders of men the novices should make profession of simple vows, which on their part were to be perpetual, and could not be admitted subsequently to solemn profession until at least three years had passed. In virtue of this simple vow of poverty the professed religious did not give up his property but retained the ownership of it and also the capacity to acquire. He lost the independent use of all possessions and was required to surrender the administration, use and usufruct of his inheritance. It was the genuine system of poverty under simple vows. It is also to be noticed that those professed in this way were not then regarded as true religious. In 1902 this legislation applying to regulars was imposed on nuns.

A further and far more important innovation in the law began to develop at the end of the nineteenth century. Numerous Congregations of men and women had come into existence and expanded rapidly. All had adopted the system of poverty under simple vows. Indeed no more Orders under solemn vows were founded. But the discipline laid down by the Constitutions of these numerous societies varied greatly. It was necessary to prune and select, standardize and construct anew, in accordance with certain leading principles which actual experience could show to be of value. Constitutions were submitted for approbation at Rome and it was then that 'annotations' were made by the Consultors. Certain corrections were required, certain points were clarified, others were tolerated. These 'annotations' gradually came to form a standard collection ; in this way there appeared *schemata* and in about 1859 a model formula, known as Bizarri's, gained recognition over all others. It lays down the ordinary discipline of simple poverty according to the mind of the S. Congregation of Bishops and Regulars. On 8 December, 1900, Leo XIII officially sanctioned Congregations with simple vows. Their members without being regulars were none the less religious, and their profession, although simple, was recognised as a real religious and public profession. On 28 June, 1901, the S. Congregation of Bishops and Regulars laid down certain complementary *Normae* which enabled the Constitution to be applied, and in a second part provided more or less completely formulated model Constitutions. The question of poverty is treated in chapter X. Many points are taken from Bizarri's formula, but there are relatively numerous corrections and additions. This was no definitive legal solution and the preliminary work for and even the final text of the Code showed evidence of fresh modifications. Notice the impression of prudence and wisdom produced by this slow work of development.

Nothing is finally laid down before it has been put to the proof by experience. Moreover, this second system of poverty did not bring the legislative evolution to a conclusion, as is amply demonstrated by the Code's official recognition of Societies of common life without public vows in which the system of poverty is necessarily special to each society ; and also in the sanction given to secular Institutes by the Apostolic Constitution *Provida Mater* of 1947, where in the system of poverty provides for practice of the evangelical counsel which is no less effective, despite reduction of the consequences of the vow to essentials and reference of the disciplinary details of the vow to the rules in force in each Institute.

Personal religious poverty according to legislation now in force implies the taking of a vow and submission to discipline laid down by law. The public vow of poverty is either solemn in religious Orders or simple in Congregations. In the Societies of common life and in the Secular Institutes there is a private vow or a promise of poverty, ratified or not by oath. The taking of this vow and its practice are subject to certain provisions and decisions which, in other words, fix the rights and obligations of the religious to a discipline, the rules of which vary according to the degree of commitment. These rules are defined by the common law and by the Constitutions of the various Institutes in the case of a public vow. The life of poverty in accordance with this commitment, with all its obligations binding in conscience, is put forward by the Rules and Constitutions of the various Institutes. General rules are clearly intimated by a body of doctrinal tradition, and this is the moral aspect formally implied and sanctioned by the Code, from its own point of view of the external forum, in canon 579.

We need not dwell on the particular nature of the vow of poverty, whether public or private. It should be noticed, however, that even in secular institutes a formal promise must be made. It is a question of giving authentic form to a state of life which, although not the religious state, is none the less a juridical state of perfection. How, then, are the two principal degrees of poverty defined by law ?

In the Orders, both of men and women, the members, after a period in simple temporary vows, take the solemn vow of poverty. Save for certain privileged exceptional cases, the normal juridical principles, while stated more precisely as regards secondary points by the Constitutions proper to these Orders, are defined by the Code. The traditional rules are there to be found. Whoever takes this solemn vow loses for ever, by the very fact and in virtue of these provisions of the law, all right of ownership, direct or prescriptive, all right of possession and every other right over temporal goods which are capable of estimation in terms of money, and which he might have had before profession. In addition he loses the capacity for acquiring further goods or possessions as his personal property. He can have neither use nor usufruct of these goods independently of the will of his superiors (Canons 581-2). As he no longer possesses anything and is radically incapable of possessing anything at all, the professed religious who, without the permission of the superior competent in the matter, acts, in fact and intention, as would an independent owner, performs an act which of its very nature is not only illicit but invalid. The actual consequences of this invalidity will depend on the legal possibility, or otherwise, of annulment of the act contrary to the vow (Canon 579).

Such a state of dispossession clearly presupposes a previous act of renunciation. That is why, during the sixty days which precede solemn profession (and not before, under pain of invalidity) the religious must renounce all the property that he possesses. Should he omit to do so he will none the less be deprived of everything, and all his possessions will be acquired by his Order. By this act of renunciation, on the other hand, the religious can dispose freely of what he possesses, a freedom which he should exercise—when all debts of justice have first been paid—in accordance with what the spirit of poverty and charity shows him to be his duty. When the renunciation has been finally completed by valid profession it cannot be modified without an indult of the Holy See. It comprises, obviously, all goods in actual possession. Property which may come to the subject in the future by means of gifts and bequests will subsequently be acquired by the Order. Does the same rule apply regarding a future inheritance? Or in other words, can the religious, by this act made at the time of profession, renounce and dispose of an inheritance ? The Code lays down nothing save the principle of acquisition by the Order. The Constitutions of the Order may indicate the course to be followed. But, in the absence of special rules of this kind, several solutions are offered, though all authors admit the right of disposing of an inheritance in which the religious will certainly have an interest by reason of a share in the estate legitimately reserved for him. This renunciation is certainly valid in Canon Law and in conscience ; but the Code requires that after profession the religious should as soon as possible do what is necessary for his act to be effective in civil law (C.581 § 2).

The renunciation disposes of the whole question of property possessed up to the time of profession, and the principle of incapacity subsequently regulates the relationship of the professed religious to future property. There is no question of declaring him absolutely incapable of performing any act in civil law, even for the benefit of his Order ; he is not dead civilly. Canon Law renders him incapable both of acquiring property that he would be able to possess as his own or dispose of for his own advantage and, likewise, of administering his property in his own name. Henceforward, even when he desires formally to acquire property for his Order, to act for a third party or for his community, he can do nothing validly without the legitimate permission of his proper superior. He is completely dependent.

This rule of incapacity implies, conversely, the right for the Order to acquire all property which may fall to the professed religious whether by gift or legacy or as a result of his work (C.582). The only questions which arise here are those concerning the extent of the Order's own capacity to acquire in the case of an inheritance.

In Congregations, both of men and women, only a simple vow of poverty is taken. Unless the Institute enjoys a special privilege, defined by its own laws, this vow implies no juridical incapacity and prescribes no surrender of property. The professed member retains the ownership of his personal property and the capacity to acquire further property (C.580, § 1). He loses the right of using it and of disposing of material goods that are capable of being estimated in terms of money. He can perform licitly no act of administration even over his personal possessions, let alone over the possessions of a third party or of his community, without his superior's permission.

In order to place the religious in such a position that he can effectively practise his vow, Canon Law requires certain acts on his part. The full significance of these acts goes beyond the minimal requirements of the vow, but none the less their performance is prescribed in conscience by the law.

Under pain of nullity, the novice during his noviciate may not surrender his property, whatever the legal form taken by this act performed gratis and *inter vivos*. The reason for such a prohibition is simple enough : since the noviciate is a period of probation, the most complete freedom should be enjoyed by the novice and the religious Institute ; the effect of an act of so definite a nature would only be to impair this freedom. Towards the end of the noviciate, if the novice possesses personal property, the law requires him to take steps to organise his life under the rule of poverty. The effective functioning of the vow must be ensured and provision made for the safeguarding of his personal estate. The permanence of his engagement under the vow is indeed only relative, so that it should embrace renunciation of what is fundamental in ordinary ownership—the use and enjoyment in full independence, and, for this purpose, the active administration of property—and at the same time not only the maintenance of the radical right of ownership but also the possibility of recovering complete exercise of this right. Provision must also be made against all the vexatious measures of the civil law concerning the Congregations. That is why Canon 569 § 1 requires the novice to effect, for the duration of his vows, an assignment of his actual property to whomsoever he may wish; he may not retain it himself. Secondly, he must execute a deed arranging for the disposal of use and usufruct of this same property in favour of a third party, or in his own favour provided that his state of dependence is assured by means of the necessary permissions. Yet although the common law of the Church leaves full liberty of action on this point, the Constitutions may contain special rules restricting the disposal of usufruct. The rules of common life, too, will play their part in fixing the implications of the relatively personal use of possessions. If these deeds have not been executed because, for example, there was no personal property, the professed religious, although bound by his simple vows, will have to take steps to do so (C. 569 § 2). The same procedure must be adopted if further property comes into his possession.

The law also requires another instrument the importance of which is not always realised: in Congregations the novice, before his first profession, must with complete freedom make a will disposing of his present and future possessions (C. 569 § 3). A will forms one of the ways by which in law the right of ownership is most firmly vindicated, since the testator, from beyond the grave, which deprives him of everything, maintains his right to dispose of what he possesses and enforces his own desires. Moreover, experience has shown how some are exercised throughout their religious life by this matter and, on the other hand, how the omission to make a will may leave an estate in an involved condition. The requirements of this canon may thus be understood, but its application raises certain practical and legal difficulties. Is this will required only when it can be validly propounded according to civil law ? Authorities are divided on the point. Is it really of obligation when the novice does not yet possess any personal estate ? *Per se*, yes. As novices are usually inexperienced, how far can superiors intervene in the drawing up of the will, since the freedom of the testator has to be safeguarded ? They can only advise.

All these deeds are executed only in order to be effective during the period of simple profession, but in this sphere they cannot be unalterable. Consequently the law, in Canon 580 § 3, provides for the conditions to be observed in modifying clauses previously settled and, in Canon 583 § 2, it settles the procedure for changing a will.

Two further canons complete the regulation of the simple vow. The professed religious, although he retains the ownership of his possessions, has obviously to give up some part of his rights, but there is a strict limitation on how far he may do so ; he is prohibited from renouncing gratuitously by deed *inter vivos* by a deed of gift, for example, the actual ownership of his possessions (C. 588 § 1)—a further precautionary measure, arising from the nature of simple profession. The professed religious, since he retains the capacity to acquire further possessions, may do so either on his own account or for his Congregation. Canon 580 § 2, therefore, lays down the principle that whatever he acquires by his work, whether manual, intellectual or apostolic, whatever he receives on behalf of his Congregation, is acquired by this Congregation. He has no right to compensation nor grounds for counter-claim. It is inevitable that cases will occur which are difficult of solution, but in those which are doubtful the presumption is to be in favour of the Congregation ; furthermore the Constitutions may define those cases in which the property is to be considered as personal.

This whole structure, which some will consider far too legalistic, is yet based on, and finds its central unity only in, the Church's intense desire to enable whoever adopts a state of perfection to be a living exponent of the evangelical counsel of poverty. She desires to pledge him to a way of personal perfection and to enable him to exert an efficacious apostolate ; she wishes to ensure his fidelity in the constant realisation of his aim. She has no intention of teaching, by means of her laws, what is the spirit of poverty that should be the profound inspiration of the religious, but she desires to furnish him with the means of finding and pursuing his course on the way of perfection. To this end she reminds the religious particularly that the living expression of his voluntary poverty is to be found in his Constitutions, in the moral rules which govern the practice of the pledge he has taken : 'All must order their life according to the particular rules and Constitutions of their Order' (C. 593). In the case of the vow, the religious necessarily gives up at least the free use of all material possessions, and relies on Providence for what he needs to live and act. The fundamental manifestation of the vow is to be found in the dependence, promised to God or before God, on legitimate superiors, who are to be the distributors of whatever is useful or necessary. For this reason the religious cannot freely dispose of property, own, acquire or give it; he can neither borrow nor lend it, nor can he gratify his own desires. Whether effectively deprived of everything or still possessing, none the less, by fidelity to his promise, he is always as one who possesses nothing.

In the case of the public vow, Canon 579 defines the value of acts contrary to this vow with reference to the law. Moral theology, in its own sphere of application and obedient to the requirements of our human state, has been obliged to elaborate the casuistry of the practice in conscience of the vow of poverty. To make the whole of poverty depend on a scrupulous observance of these rules alone would be a mistake, but no less would it be so to condemn this effort at systematisation. Moral theology, in harmony with Canon Law, is obliged thus to define the matter of the vow of poverty, the nature of the permissions required for a licit or valid use of property, the gravity of faults against the vow and the consequences of violations of the moral obligation. It is the province of the spiritual life, instructed by the teaching of the Church, her doctors, her theologians and spiritual writers, grown to its full stature in and through a life of loving imitation of the poverty of our Lord, to place the soul in a state of activity regulated in this way, and to enable it to tend personally and increasingly to the perfection of poverty.

Religious poverty is a form of poverty that is prudent and cautious, and carefully elaborated by Canon Law. Does the present system lessen the effectiveness and growth of the spirit of evangelical poverty in the life of one who enters a state of perfection, and in his influence on others? Canon Law lays down obligations, but it has never diminished the generosity of those who desire to live poor like Christ. Canon Law has never thwarted authentic Christian effort. It may seem to restrain ideal and fine endeavour, but it has to be observed, on the other hand, how constant the Church has been in sanctioning new forms of the life of perfection. New needs will require further adaptation. Throughout this chapter it must have been obvious that nothing is absolutely settled in this sphere of the practical forms of poverty. The essential, that which derives its origin in the life of Christ and the nature of the vow, is bound to endure, will always endure. New forms may possibly be evolved, but there will still remain the constant requirement of obedience to the directions of the Church and docility to the promptings of the Holy Spirit.

Chapter III

THE PSYCHOLOGY OF THE INSTINCT OF POSSESSION

By Abbé M. Oraison and Michel Ledoux

Among the apparent paradoxes to be found in the religious state, the vow of poverty is one of the most striking. For the religious life requires an absolute dispossession, varying in its details according to the different Orders and Congregations, but aiming always at complete renunciation. On the other hand the Church, as the guardian of the natural law, insists on the lawfulness of property, showing thereby that she considers the instinct of possession as one of man's normal powers.

There seems to be some inconsistency here. In this sphere, as in others, the requirement of the Church appears to be directly contrary to the natural structure of human psychology. At first sight it contradicts one of the features of this structure which is intended legitimately to ensure to man his maintenance in existence and the affirmation of personality in its extension over the material objects intended for his use. As Mounier says in his *Traité du caractére*: 'There is a dominion of the ego over space.'

But an attempt at scrutiny of the instinct of possession in its profound reality, and in comparison with the authentic idea of poverty as it is to be found in the teaching of the Church, shows that this apparent antinomy gives place to complete agreement. In the following pages we intend in the first place to attempt a psychological description of the instinct of possession and its normal development. Next, we shall see how the doctrine of Christian poverty, as it is expressed canonically in the vow, far from being a negation of the inmost tendencies of man's being, offers on the contrary a transcendent fulfilment of these instinctive tendencies. Lastly, we shall show how this transition is a matter of some delicacy, since the normal and ideal evolution of instinctive powers may frequently and easily be compromised in varying degrees ; this section offers practical guidance on the psycho-pathological aspects of the problem.

I. THE INSTINCT OF POSSESSION

So far as we know there is no systematic study of the possessive instinct analogous with those dealing with the sexual instinct. Certain partial descriptions have been outlined, in passing, concerning different aspects of the psyche, but no comprehensive description has been attempted. That is our excuse and will account for the rather hypothetical, unsubstantial or schematic nature of what is a personal reflexion on very varied data. Our sources indeed are somewhat heterogeneous. Mounier's *Traité du Caractère* ; *Psychanalyse et conception spiritualiste de l'homme* by J. Nuttin, *L'Ame de l'enfant et la Psychanalyse* by Ch. Baudouin, Ey's *Etudes Psychiatriques, Le Moi et ses mécanismes de défénse* by Anna Freud, *La théorie psychanalitique des néuroses* by Otto Fenichel, form our principal written sources in conjunction with the various clinical observations and deductions that we have been able to carry out.[1]

1. *Phenomenology*

It is easy to discern, within the bounds of ordinary experience, certain principal categories among the more or less conscious reasons that a human being may have for calling into play his instinct for possession. This need scarcely detain us and will be merely a reminder of ideas that are all familiar.

Right at the outset is the desire for self-assertion or power. That is the meaning of Mounier's phrase quoted above. The possessive adjective is an expression of the link between the object possessed and the ego, that is, an extension of the latter over the material object. In this connexion Mounier very properly points out that the sense of possession is far more strongly centred in the taking of possession than in the state of ownership. Psychologically, then, there is a certain relativity

[1] E. Mounier, *Traité du Caractère*, Paris, editions du Seuil. J. Nuttin, *Psychanalyse et conception spiritualiste de l'homme*, Paris, Vrin. Baudouin, *L'âme de l'enfant et la Psychanalyse*, Lausanne, Delachaux et Niestlé. Ey, *Etudes Psychiatriques*, Paris, Desclée de Brouwer. Anna Freud, *Le Moi et ses mécanismes de défénse*, Paris, Presses Universitaires de France. Otto Fenichel, *The Psycho-analytic theory of Neurosis*, New York, W. W. Norton.

in the laws of possession : the further removed the act of taking possession and the effective exercise of ownership, the more the latter is diminished as a psychological reality, and its legitimacy becomes perhaps increasingly less obvious. This incentive may extend not only to material objects, but also to human persons, reduced in consequence to the state of objects.

It can be a simple need to secure one's personality on a firm foundation. It can be the need to rise in the social scale, to stand out amongst others by means of an increase of power. It can also be the need to assert oneself before others by some original characteristic : *my* style.

A second group of reasons is to be found in the fact that possession in general is the direct means of procuring pleasure of whatever nature : the various sensual or aesthetic pleasures, needs for personal satisfaction, even of the highest spiritual order.

A third group is connected with the profound need experienced by man to assure his future so far as he can. Possession means security, safety against reverses, difficulties or struggle.

A fourth group is made up of affective reasons. Some object is prized because 'it belonged to my mother' or 'that was Balzac's penholder'. These affective reasons of a family, personal or symbolic nature frequently give rise to possessive relationships which are more limited but certainly more deep-seated and less easy to eradicate.

In a fifth group can be discerned the necessity of possessing in order to be able to give. This desire for giving may be real generosity and large-heartedness. But it may also be no more than a cunning dissimulation of the most selfish desire for domination. Paternalism is a typical example of this.

This phenomenological description already furnishes interesting and useful indications in the actual practice of living, but it remains inevitably superficial and we can sense that underneath there is a whole array of dynamic forces at work. On the other hand it leaves a certain impression of confusion ; there is difficulty in discerning the principal impulsions which govern the manifestations of the instinct. Lastly, although it is accurate it takes no count of the fact that man does not become theoretically adult at one stroke. The human psyche evolves, there is a complex development of behaviour by the interaction of mind and the manifestations of instinct : man is a dynamism in progress and always incomplete.

We are obliged, then, in an endeavour to understand the more essential and explanatory aspects, to refer to the genetic data of depth psychology.

2. *Genetics*

Here the outlook is entirely different and far more enlightening. To understand it properly it is well to remember that according to this theory, speaking generally, the human psyche is subject to dynamic evolution from earliest infancy. In it may be discerned, following the hypothesis resulting from experience, the *Id*, the primitive instinctual force constituted in connexion with the two instincts of aggression and sexuality ; the Super-ego, a reactive and counter-impulsive structure of the unconscious tending to regulate behaviour following the needs, customs and laws of the social milieu in which the child grows up : it is placed according to the different schools, between the ages of one to five ; the *Ego* develops progressively on a conscious, autonomous and mental level ; it assimilates one after another the data of the Id and the Super-Ego, re-arranges them in their order of value and reciprocal relationship and constitutes the psychological reality of *personality* corresponding with the underlying metaphysical reality of the *person*.

The various schools have emphasised certain complementary aspects or newly evident details. Freud, the originator, based his study particularly on the sexual instinct, in the widest sense of the term, and in the instinct of aggression. Jung detected variation in the notion of the Super-ego, a more complex factor than it at first appeared ; he insisted also on the common instinctual structure, the collective unconscious and the power of symbolisation of unconscious forces. Adler, in reaction against an excessive sexuality, paid particular attention to the instinct of aggression and the power of expansion of the Ego. Certain works at the present day are concerned with these three initial lines of investigation in an endeavour to harmonise their data into a comprehensive synthesis.

But the psychological 'schema' of this evolution, based on the primary data and the unconscious in its broad outlines, remains valid. Man, in the whole complexity of his nature, appears as an aggregation of powers in process of development which must progressively be mastered and governed by the conscious mind ; as J. Nuttin expresses it in a telling phrase : 'human activity is the dynamic expression, on the plane of the psychical standpoint, of what man *is*,' that is, a being who constructs himself but does so only in relation with the world outside himself.

It is possible, consequently, to discern and follow the fundamental guiding line underlying the evolution of the possessive instinct. Of course such a study here can only be schematic ; and it will easily be understood that psychical growth from birth to maturity is at least as complex, progressive and continuous as bodily development, with which, indeed, it bears a close relationship. It will not be possible, therefore, to do more than point out those landmarks which seem the most important, or, in other words, the principal stages. These stages, moreover, will be considered essentially in close connexion with the problem we are dealing with, namely the instinct of possession. It is neither easy nor usual to view the problem from this angle, and once again the reader is requested to bear it in mind and to excuse the inevitably awkward and somewhat theoretical nature of this study.

These principal stages are four in number. The first two enable us to grasp the entirely primitive origin of the two fundamental aspects of the instinct of possession : the integration of the external world with oneself and the primary need of dominance. During the two others, of later development, these two aspects will have more complex affective elements added to them and in consequence a tendency conducive to elaboration. These two last stages are, indeed, essentially conflicts between the Ego in state of formation and the exterior world, from which the personality issues strengthened, balanced and ready for further progress.

The oral stage

It can be said that during the first period of its existence the child is primarily a digestive tube. Its first psychical reactions are governed by this fact. Although in the child's primitive reaction, in its instinctive desire which urges it towards its mother, there is, albeit indistinctly, the whole of embryonic sexuality,[1] from the point of view which concerns us here, it has no other importance than to emphasise how largely this movement can be imbued with affectivity. On the psychical plane the child's activity is an expression of what it is : an organism in full course of formation. Its behaviour is conditioned by the necessity of biological development. It is a question of assimilating food to maintain and ensure growth, and that at an increasing rate. Everything is governed by this necessity, the need to absorb in order to make it its own.

This almost exclusive characteristic is concerned primarily with food. But it also extends progressively to what is not food : in the first place the objects which the child makes his own by putting them in his mouth ; next the persons in his environment : to his mother who is at the same time the source of food, then those near. A distinction develops : 'the ego is pleasing—I put it in my mouth ; the non-ego is unpleasing—I spit it out.' And this distinction is extended to persons, represented symbolically by objects which belong to them or concern them. 'The first positive instinctive attitude in regard to objects that are desired consists in reduction of the distance between self and the object, and finally in its absorption,' writes O. Fenichel. It need hardly be pointed out that this quite primitive mode of possession, which is termed 'primary narcissism' governs a whole phase of future behaviour in connexion with sexual or general libido. It forms even at this stage the integration with self of external realities.

In this connexion the frustration conflict occurs with weaning, which is of considerable psychological importance. The change from one entirely passive method of feeding to another which is less direct and separated to a greater degree from the presence

---

[1] Since, by force of circumstances, there is no vocabulary available to designate distinctly the affective and unconscious reactions of the very young child there is nothing for it but to use the terms of adult and conscious psychology. But it should be always borne in mind that these terms are analogical. Here sexual means a pleasure in connexion with an organ of the body.

of the mother, constitutes a real drama in which for the first time the child experiences with intensity the feeling of insecurity through privation. His reactions to this state may persist for some time unless it is resolved by fresh security of a more personal and autonomous nature.

The anal stage

This stage corresponds with the period of training in cleanliness.

Its primary characteristic is awareness on the part of the child of the control that it can exercise over its sphincters ; he is conscious of *producing*, of making something more or less at will. But at the same time what the child produces and makes, issues from him and is separated from him after forming a part of himself. And this awareness is closely bound up with the reaction of what Freud rightly calls an erogenous zone, i.e. the region of the perineum. During this period the training of the child is carried out by the parents or others in charge of him. The idea of 'dirty', gains in clarity and is associated with that of rejection, removal.

From the point of view of the instinct of possession, this stage is also of prime importance, for in it occurs the origin of the second aspect of this instinct which is the need to impress the personality on the external world. The child's discovery of the pleasure in producing and making something *personally*, from being at first concentrated on his stools will gradually extend to the rest of its world. It will seek to make his own the objects in this new sphere, even going so far as to destroy what withstands him in order to assert his power in spite of everything. Next he will extend his tyranny over those around him, if need be by being dirty to get his way and attract attention. This stage, in the view of most authorities on analysis, is of capital importance ; it is here that the most ambivalent tendencies come into play and may indeed lead to deviations of all sorts. Egocentricity, sadism, masochism, neurotic avarice, may all originate in this stage. Clinical experience shows this clearly ; the child who kneads or moulds his stools, as if to increase his power as 'maker', is by no means rare. And the re-education of neurotic children beginning with this stage is often effected by means of modelling and the gradual substitution of modelling clay, then, at a later stage, of drawing, in place of the primitive material chosen by instinct.

At the same time the child comes to experience a clearer feeling of de-individualisation or depersonalisation. During the period of anal evolution the stools begin to appear to him as something common to everyone and, in consequence, lose their individual character ; they are separated from the Ego and therefore in some sort lost to him. In the final stage, as O. Fenichel remarks, occurs the discovery of money which has the same property of being common to everybody : grown ups own it as a common possession, lacking the character of something special to the individual, and also capable of being lost. Hence arises the dread of dispossession and the despicable nature of stools and money. The latter may easily become a symbolic substitute for the former. 'Psycho-analysts could not fail to perceive the excremental eroticism of the child in the symbolism of money or gold. The child, like King Midas, turns his faecal matter into "gold" and it is recognised that this symbolism, represented in all its crudity in Hieronymus Bosch's *Earthly Paradise*, is one of the collective constants of humanity' (Ey, op. cit.).

But as a counterpart to this dread of dispossession there appears the earliest tendency to gift making. As education in control of the sphincters progresses the child gradually adopts the attitude of offering to his mother, not without a certain pride, what he has been able to produce, and thus, in this way, pays tribute to her. The importance of this aspect in education of the anal period cannot be over-estimated, to the child it forms a staggering discovery to realise that it is in his power to make something on his own account ; and his joy at being able to offer it to her whom he loves best in all the world is certainly one of his earliest joys in giving.

Therapeutic experience adds confirmation to these hypotheses which also, are derived from observation. We need only quote the following example. A four year old child, in excellent health, exhibited persistent constipation ; there was no organic trouble to account for it and no purgative or laxative succeeded in clearing it. Two homely talks during which the story was told of Harpagon, 'the man who kept everything for himself, even the filthiest,' were all that was necessary to put him entirely right again. A rhyme about generosity, an affectionate attitude to calm his dispossession anxiety, an appeal for unselfishness were enough, coming at the right moment, to root out an incipient neurosis.

There is no need to emphasise further the close connexion that all this can have with the instinct of possession and its development.

During the oral period, then, is manifested the earliest tendency of all, that of absorption for pleasure. At first it is purely alimentary, but then becomes symbolical. From this point of view it forms the stage of primary narcissism, followed by that of object narcissism, the objects being considered only from the aspect of the pleasure that they can procure.

During the anal period three fundamental discoveries are made : the child can *produce*, make, impress something with the mark of his personality ; he runs the risk of *losing* something that was inside himself ; he is able to *offer* something which he takes from himself.

The Œdipus period

This is the first affective conflict of importance, no longer merely with the external world distinct from the Ego, but with persons in the child's immediate surroundings. The possessive tendencies, which we have already seen manifested in their primary forms, have now to reach a further stage, effect a further adaptation on penalty of remaining permanently in an infantile condition. The child is thus faced with his first effort to establish his autonomous affective personality.

The Œdipus conflict is formed schematically by the fact that the child, spontaneously drawn towards the parent of opposite sex, begins to see the parent of the same sex as an obstructive rival. He will have to overcome and in some sort exorcise this feeling of frustration or otherwise his budding personality will be compromised. He will achieve this by means of identification with the parent of the same sex. From a purely passive, receptive love he must change to a positive attitude which causes him thereafter to take the rival as a model, thus entering on a decisive phase of his development. The mother ceases to be that confused object which provided nourishment, care and comfort, and becomes something entirely new, much more complex, a being with her own mystery, her personal reactions, which act as a guide in sympathy with which behaviour must be modified.

For a boy, this consists in understanding that if he wishes to keep his mother's affection, on an entirely different level for the previous standard no longer suffices, he must be like his father whose privileged position he discerns. This leads to an imitative love of the father—one of the keenest joys of childish mimicry—in order to share, in some sort, in the mother's love for the father.

For a girl the problem is more complicated. There is an ambivalent attitude towards the mother who, as well as the provider of care and comfort, is also the rival. The girl has therefore to achieve a twofold detachment, if one may so call it, and rid herself of this ambivalence by identification with the mother which, in a certain sense, will enable her also to share in the conjugal love.

The whole, strictly speaking, sexual aspect of this conflict is extremely important. As Hesnard shows in *La Psychologie homosexuelle*, many deviations of this instinct originate at this stage. But of set purpose we shall leave aside this aspect of the question and consider only that of the instinct of possession.

For the girl as for the boy—though with differing modalities—the conflict (for it is one) is the same. There is at first a feeling of affective frustration of very great intensity, as shown by the study of deeply rooted neurosis at this stage.

This frustration causes a feeling of insecurity, of isolation, even of being abandoned. In some sort it is the first experience of the great loneliness of human kind. It is vitally important for the child to get over this stage. For him this amounts to consenting to look on those in his immediate surroundings, no longer as objects existing for his comfort or pleasure, but as persons requiring a positive attitude on his part. His behaviour, still highly egocentric, must be transformed by means of the normal evolution of circumstances and his position, into behaviour which is far more dependent on others and more generous.

In a word the child no longer *possesses* his parents ; he is beginning to *know* them and to *love* them.

Adolescence

If it were required to give the distinctive features of this period in a single term its difficulty might be expressed summarily by saying that it is a development conflict. Two suddenly increased powers are in confrontation, one of which is in opposition to the other in such a way that, in the normal course of evolution, it forces it on to a loftier, a wider plane thus offering the possibility of further autonomy.

The first of these powers is obviously controlled by sexual development. But it is not resolved at the period of sexual awakening after the period of latency under the influence of bodily growth. Sexuality is the controlling factor, but in different degrees it affects the whole organism. All the instinctive impulses have an extreme tendency to 'socialisation', to use the psycho-analytic expression, that is to link up with the social environment. The still extremely egocentric and confined views of childhood begin to disappear. Values of a less material nature are discovered ; more complex needs make their appearance, lacking formulation and upsetting at first, then growing clearer—general ideas, of an absolute nature ; affection, freedom, domination of time. And these new needs assert themselves with a force that is uncontrolled and disordered and ill-adapted to the exterior reality thus prematurely discovered and as yet not studied with patience. The social environment of the child also becomes too small : the family becomes too confining ; customs or habits of 'the set' annoying ; there is a need metaphorically to throw open the windows and let in fresh air. It is the age when the father is boring because he 'rambles on so', or the mother irritating because she treats him 'like a kid'. It is the age when ideas different from, or even entirely opposed to, those of the usual surroundings prove extremely attractive.

When the adolescent is confronted with this powerful force, which, in short, appears very quickly and almost suddenly, a defensive mechanism comes immediately into play ; its role, like that of the Super-ego in childhood is, so to say, two-edged.

It may be an excellent thing if it causes the subject to sift, select, grade the force by which he is urged and which, as a consequence, functions easily in relation with the whole external world. But it can be harmful when with a tyrannical Super-ego wrongly regarded as a moral sense, it leads to atrophy and stifling of vital dynamism, to a further stage of repression. For at this stage a force comes into play which during first infancy is only potential ; this is the mind, the faculty of judgement, liberty. And it is this, on a last analysis, which should regulate the conflict ; it can do so if the defence reaction mentioned above is not excessive in intensity or consequences. Anna Freud in *The Ego and its Defence Mechanisms* makes an interesting study of what she calls the extreme asceticism of adolescence evincing a certain anxiety confronted with the growth of instinct. That is a profound law of life ; everything occurs as if the Ego confusedly and spontaneously experienced the impression that if it gave way to invasion by this overpowering growth, it ran the risk of being engulfed by it. It is in a position to defend itself but not yet with the necessary balance and composure ; its re-actions are exaggerated. There is a certain inclination to a real 'angelism' alternating with periods of profound agitation and uncontrollable desires. And if the conflict takes place mainly on the sexual level it concerns none the less the whole psychical make-up.

Gradually balance is achieved. Instinctual impulse is established in some sort of order and becomes systematised. The fear reflex grows less keen and the control functions with greater flexibility and precision. Compromises are made, for nothing is perfect and the ideal adult age of before the Fall is never more to be attained in life as it is at present. In any case, even though incompletely, the Ego is no longer centred upon itself ; it is no longer fundamentally predatory but tends to a spontaneous generosity, which the subject may either allow to atrophy into moderate egoism, or to increase from one day to another by knowledge and love, an outlook on the wonder of the world and the mystery of the human person.

In short, this conflict of adolescence is as capitally important as the preceding stages. Generosity, the need to develop, albeit often excessive and ill-adapted, an inflexible reaction suggesting the egocentric, which re-awakens more or less durably previous modes of behaviour, is an expression of a longing for childhood confronted with the difficulties of life—these manifestations when all goes well leads the Ego, enlightened by the reason, to a courageous acceptation of that autonomy which can only function in a state of authentic self-oblation that is respectful of reality as it is. It is signalised by that sexual maturity, so rarely completely achieved, by which the subject is placed in a state of waiting or seeking for reciprocal self-oblation and union.

General conspectus of the evolution of instinct

1. Dr. Nodet at the *Semaine des Intellectuals Catholiques* in 1950 brought out very clearly that in the view of depth psychology an instinct has not reached its stage of adult formulation until it is properly 'socialised'.

From another point of view, Nuttin gives expression to the same idea by relating it to the fundamentally vital necessity of the dynamism of the Ego. This dynamism is shown, briefly, in three ways which are stability, defence and demonstration ; these are the three *essential* needs. In the course of development, the Ego passes through stages in which the needs change and are subject to an ascending scale of elaboration. (It is hardly necessary to point out that the word *need* as here used is as far removed as possible from the psychological meaning of *desire* ; it is used in the sense in which it is said that a plant *needs* to grow.)

From the primitive elementary needs of the child, the Ego passes progressively, and from its very force of expansion, to needs that intellectually are more clearly formulated and less egocentric. 'Objects on which inclinations or well-defined needs are resolved,' writes Nuttin, 'together with certain forms of conduct which, in the case of those needs, represent a method of relief, regularly lose their active potentiality owing to the fact that at a later stage of personal development new forms of need take shape or, all things considered, certain modes of conduct are experienced as less satisfactory'.[1]

The need for possession (oral assimilation) or for assertion of

[1] *Op. Cit.*, p. 257.

power over matter (anal production) are primitively the most elementary needs. The whole psychical evolution of the instincts is governed by the higher and progressively manifested need of *union*.

2. The evolution of oblativity develops from one stage to another. At the oral stage it is non-existent and the individual is completely narcissistic. At the anal stage interest begins to awaken concerning something which is other than self or which is not destined to become so by assimilation ; and the first phase of oblativity begins to take form. The Œdipus period is still confined to the parental circle, but it is characterised by the transition from 'relationship with another in so far as he is of use to me' to 'relationship with another in so far as he has a life of his own'. At adolescence this phenomenon of development is extended to the external world in general.

3. Every time, at each stage, the instinctive 'drive' which enables the gap to be bridged is integration and transcendence of the obstacle. Indeed, surpassing of the childish feeling of insecurity is an essential condition of autonomy and encourages the first, and always alarming, steps towards freedom.

Notes

A. In actual practice this evolution, whose meaning is revealed to us by the study of depth psychology, is never brought ideally and entirely to fulfilment. It is long, frail and complex. And in the present state of the world (for its dynamism, as we know, is profoundly compromised by the mystery of the Fall) in very varying degrees there remain in every human being unresolved *sequelae* of childish or adolescent behaviour.

B. Man, having arrived somehow or other at the adult stage of this evolution, finds himself confronted from force of circumstances with a further obstacle which, on this occasion and so far as his own natural resources are concerned, is insuperable. By no possible means can he discover in himself and at his own level the entire and definitive realisation of his deepest inclinations. To overcome this fresh obstacle he is obliged, by means of a further integration, a further development, to reach a transcendent level. This the crisis of religious distress and of Faith.

II. The Vow of Poverty

'We make the reality of the world for ourselves by our attachment. It is the reality of the Ego transferred into things. This is in no wise external reality for that is only discernible through complete detachment.' 'Attachment is nothing else than an inadequate sense of reality' (Simone Weil). These few lines seem to us to tackle the problem of poverty at its very centre.

At first sight it might be thought, as was pointed out at the beginning of this chapter, that there is some conflict between the normal instinct of possession, which expresses the proper projection of a personality over the external world, and the requirement of poverty, which is the renunciation of all personal ownership.

But study of the evolution of the instinct has already provided some clue to the solution by showing us that it consists fundamentally in transition from a primary closely possessive stage to a further and very different stage with far greater participation in life. The apparent antimony is the result perhaps of a negative conception of poverty. At this point we should like to emphasise briefly certain metaphysical principles which enable poverty to be envisaged from its positive aspect. This will allow us to see to what extent the religious vow of poverty enters into the general scheme of normal psychology, albeit as an exception and at a level, and in a sense, which is transcendent.

The relationship of a living person with things and with other persons can be of two kinds. We shall call the first a 'relationship of having', it is that of possession, in accordance with which the thing or person is known, experienced, attained in so far as it 'is of use to me' or 'gives me pleasure'. The second is the 'relationship of being' in accordance with which the thing is known, experienced, attained in its very being and in the mystery of its individuality.

At first sight the 'relationship of having' appears to be an enrichment and, in fact, is so from one point of view; by possession I ensure the maintenance, protection and extension of my being; I mark with my personality the things which belong to me and in this way foster its assertion.

But possession, by the same token, is a dreadful limitation. By possession I enrich my being, but I enclose myself within the confines of my Ego which, all said and done, is but a fragmentary particle of the universe. In that way I prevent myself from reaching another in his 'being in itself'. I know him, reach him, experience him only in his 'being for me' which is but a very secondary and accidental aspect of himself and his existence.

He whose only knowledge of an ancient oak tree is confined to the quantity of fire wood that he can obtain from it, will know and experience but a ridiculous limitation of that oak in comparison with the wonder of an artist, who enters into communion with the beauty of the tree and its position, simply because that tree is beautiful and stands well in the ground.

The mother who knows her child only for the joy which he gives her, the pride she has in him, the hopes she founds on him following her own preferences, refuses in some sort to know him as he is, in his grandeur of a man in process of growth and in his freedom. Moreover, in this case, limitation to relationship of possession radically deforms the whole education and induces in the child abnormal psychological reactions of varying gravity.

Prostitution furnishes a still more striking example. The man who makes use of a prostitute, achieves the contradiction of entering into contact with a human person and of reducing her at the same time to the temporary possession of a mere instrument of his carnal pleasure. This sacrilegious caricature of love in its own sphere is one of the most lamentable outrages due to human incoherency.

'Intellectual goods' and even 'spiritual goods' are capable of being limited by the 'relationship of possession'. A general idea ceases to be one directly I consider it strictly as *mine*. On a final analysis God himself, the very fullness of Being, can be reduced for me, if it may be so expressed, to the paltry and ridiculously contradictory dimensions of the instrument of *my* personal perfection, *my* increase in holiness.

These few examples are enough to show that if possession is in a certain sense an enrichment of the Ego, it is at the same time, and more particularly, a limitation within the narrow bounds of this Ego. It confines me in the circle of myself and on the very level at which my possession is located. 'Where your treasure is there will your heart be also.' Consequently it is a definitive personal limitation of myself. I am the master, of course, of what I possess ; but more particularly, subtly and without my knowing it, I am its slave.

To dispossession, poverty, belongs, therefore, a positive reality in so far as it breaks the fetters of that relationship with another as possessor. To be really poor means nothing else than ceasing to limit the world to the measure of my needs in order to be open to the plenitude of being. That is the fundamental meaning of the frequently quoted saying of Christ's 'he that shall lose his life *for my sake*, shall find it' (Matt. 16, 25). He who thus requires complete renunciation, even of oneself, to follow him is God, the absolute Being, in the person of the Word.

Thus poverty comprises detachment and renunciation. But that is only the reverse side of the reality ; it does not constitute specifically and essentially the attitude of poverty. Thus someone who wishes to go up to the first floor of a house must, of course, leave the ground floor ; but that is not the real nature of his action ; we do not say that he has left the ground floor, but that he has gone up to the first floor.

The very soul of poverty is charity. There is no poverty which is not genuine love of another ; for it is meaningless save to the extent by which it frees me from the narrowness of my 'relationship of possession' wherein I confine another, and enables me to have access to an infinitely more profound relationship, essentially richer, by which I reach another *as another*, as a being, a self, an independent existence.

The life of St Francis of Assisi provides a striking illustration of all these reflexions. Completely detached from all possessions, he at once discovered in his contact with nature that genuine sovereignty of love and union, which has nothing in common with the destructive caricature of tyrannical possession, but which certainly bears a far greater resemblance to what the sovereign Royalty of almighty creative Love must be. In this way that other saying of Christ's, in answer to Peter's anxiety, is brought out in its full meaning : 'And everyone that hath left house, or brethren, or sisters, or father or mother, or wife, or children, or lands for my name's sake shall receive an hundred-fold, and shall *possess* life everlasting' (Matt. 19, 29).

We are now in a position to give a definition of the canonical vow of poverty. 'It is the decision taken by a subject to place himself voluntarily in the actual conditions of, and to identify himself with, a social organisation which, freeing him to the greatest possible extent from the requirements of ownership entailed by ordinary life, enables him more easily to concentrate his quest on that plenary relationship with Being as the object of existence.'

In view of what we have learnt of the psychological evolution of instinct, far from being a contradiction of nature, this vow, from the point of view of faith, is its fulfilment to the very highest degree. Every man, of necessity, must undergo such a reversal of outlook by this total liberation at the moment of his death. Some prepare for it systematically, with a deliberate act of their will while they are still alive. Such a course is in conformity with nature.

The normal psychological behaviour of one who has taken a vow of poverty will be characterised in the first place by an attitude of respect, of 'consideration' towards the beings, even material ones, and the everyday objects for his personal use. He has acquired the automatic response of seeing spontaneously in these beings primarily their own entity, their beauty, their significance ; this he does profoundly before considering their relationship with himself.

Normal poverty is characterised, in like manner, by increasing ease, freedom of spirit, a certain independence in respect to all being which is exterior to oneself. The subject seeking to know it for itself, is no longer a slave to its utility in his regard.

But the fact must not be lost sight of that this poverty, which is true metaphysically, and normal psychologically, is never merely a tendency to be cultivated in all tranquillity. It is a liberation which the whole of life is insufficient to bring to fulfilment. Even within the setting of the canonical vow it would seem necessary respectfully to make allowances for the position and strength of each subject. The desire to *impose* poverty as an external behaviour when the psychological stages have not been passed through, incurs the risk of checking psycho-spiritual evolution, thus producing a regressive attitude or one of traditional conformism which bears a strange resemblance to that of the Pharisees.

III. Psycho-pathological Aspects

We shall offer here merely certain rapid and very general observations for guidance of a practical nature. Two principal classes will be considered : the obstacles to poverty and false forms of poverty.

1. *Neurotic obstacles to poverty*

It is a question here of regressions or more or less serious checks to psychical evolution at one or other of its stages. The subject under consideration still retains in his most spontaneous behaviour, traces of his attitude at the time of these previous stages.

Certain excessive forms of greed may belong to regression to the oral stage. The most typical form of this is that morbid fear of insecurity for the future which forces the subject to hoard. It can be connected with the unresolved insecurity of weaning. In its extreme form it may cause the behaviour of those of whom it is jokingly said that they have taken a vow of poverty in order to be certain to want for nothing. More frequent and less serious pathologically are those cases which may be observed of transitory regression to the oral stage, either direct, as in the morbid hunger occurring during the noviciate—we have ourselves had such cases under observation—or indirect, as with the subject who endlessly collects used wrapping paper and bits of string, sometimes the most extraordinary odds and ends on the irrefutable plea that they 'may come in useful later on'.

To the anal stage belong the various forms of morbid greed distinguished fundamentally by an irrational and disproportionate dispossession anxiety. In accordance with psychological evolution, as we have studied it, it can be said that we are here concerned with a literal case of 'psychological constipation'. To the anal stage belongs, also, the need for domination, the tendency to impress everything with one's personality which makes certain monastic petty tyrants really impossible to live with, the more so because the restricted environment serves only to aggravate this attitude.

The *sequelae* of an unresolved Œdipus conflict will take on a less primary and more formulated expression. They will be tinged with a more symbolised form of affectivity. Thus a subject's choice will be fixed on some object (or some person) symbolising in their case the mother that they have been unable to make up their minds to leave, or on a symbol, extremely tortuous on occasion, of unconscious opposition to the father with whom they have not succeeded in identifying themselves. In the same way, the Œdipus frustration, if it has been inadequately resolved, may leave an excessive need for compensatory affectivity, a sentimental and childish desire for affection, a tendency to be coaxed and waited on which is manifested sometimes in a remotely symbolic form, even in liturgical or para-liturgical life, for example. At the end of the scale, it is by no means rare to observe a subject who, entirely unconsciously, adopts the convent as a substitute for that warm maternal atmosphere for which an unsurmounted state of childhood still hankers.

The conflicts of adolescence obviously react on ground already well prepared. But in behaviour at a later period specific traces of this period may remain. Stiffening of the Ego in the face of the rising tide of instinct, and in conjunction with an inflexible Super-ego, needs only to be slightly neurotic for the impulse of generosity to be extinguished at source. There are almost hopeless cases of selfishness, of greed arising from disappointment, which remain prominent in certain circumstances although the generosity of a religious vocation is undeniable. It may be manifested, for example, by the disappointed fine idealism of an adolescent obstructed by his super-ego or ridiculed by incomprehending associates, or by an adolescent with his 'wings clipped'.

Though we have no intention of offering a complete list we mention here some other causes which may be observed. Childish jealousy of a younger brother or sister. (The Cain complex, to use the correct and generally understood term, may leave future behaviour with a reflex tendency 'to take one's revenge', to indicate one's superiority, to possess more in order the better to assert one's personality.)

With some cases of affective deficiency there can be observed a sort of generalised infantilism which may be combined with satisfactory intellectual capacity ; they remain in possession— symbolically—of the toys of their childhood.

Lastly there may be also observed—and it is by no means rare—the symbolic transference of a repressed sexual libido. Properly speaking it is a case of fetishism but in twofold symbolisation : the object itself is only very indirectly a fetish ; its affective action is no longer directly sexual, but is formulated either indistinctly or in connection with the spiritual life or, more accurately, with its manifestations in the senses.

2. *False poverties*

Certain neurotic attitudes resemble poverty and may lead subjects, who seem at first sight fairly well balanced, to seek the canonical obligation of the vow. Generally, in fact, these attitudes have only the negative aspect in common with poverty which, as we have seen, is only the reverse of this virtue.

To give some examples we mention in the first place the reaction, the opposite of those quoted above, to the feeling of frustration. Instead of seeking instinctively, by behaviour which is secretly childish, to cope with this feeling and the fear of insecurity, the Ego gives way and loses its defensive vigour. The feeling of unworthiness, disinterest in self, are psychological realities that may be observed not only in melancholia and Hebephrenia.

The morbid feeling of guilt, of which Hesnard has made a remarkable study,[1] is different but not entirely dissimilar. It may cause a reflex tendency to self-punishment, either by self-detraction or by seeking to realise an ideal of excessive renunciation which will, perhaps, arrest this guilt anxiety. This is what is known, in Jungian terms, as super-compensation. It occurs in connexion with some sacrifice which well intentioned directors may mistakenly approve, even with a certain admiration, without paying sufficient attention to the somewhat

[1] Hesnard, *L'Univers morbide de la faute*.

excessive, and especially the negative, character of this attitude. This kind of behaviour is closely connected with an insufficiently developed instinct of aggression which, as we have seen, originates principally at the anal stage. From this point of view Leon Bloy's novel, *La Femme Pauvre*, manifests a partially neurotic conception of poverty : it contains a curious mixture of anti-social reaction, almost paranoidal protestation and persecution, and a pre-occupation with filth, together with the identification of 'dirty' with money which would tend to induce the belief that material goods are bad of their very nature. Such a conception of poverty, despite appearances, seems to us as unchristian and unevangelical as is possible.

The excessive asceticism of some at the crisis of adolescence, as described by Anna Freud, may also remain unresolved. Deriving from it, there may be a certain fear in the face of life, a certain need for purity bordering on angelism, a need for irrational renunciation and mortification which act as a perversion of any genuine religious outlook. On the intellectual plane, such an attitude sometimes gives rise to fear of original or personal ideas, the need for very narrow limits within which safety is felt, an aggressive distrust of anyone who claims to reconsider these limits ; in short what can be called the ' integralist ' mentality.[1]

III. Ambivalent behaviour

In everyday psychological experience there is always a certain amount of ambivalence even in the most balanced subjects. But quite frequently behaviour may be observed which is deeply rooted in a pathologically determined ambivalence of tendencies. This is the case of those subjects who are covetous or miserly and foolishly extravagant at the same time ; people who save up bits of string and waste money on fads.

A boy of eighteen, an only son, with the Œdipus complex at its height, regularly fails at his work and examinations in which he takes no interest. He shows supreme detachment from the goods of this world and comfort, but commits himself to

[1] The vow, in the case of a normally developed psyche, can be a psychological arm of the greatest value. But in impaired psychical conditions it may form an ideal refuge for neurosis. (Cf, in *Supplément de la Vie Spirituelle*, August 1950, articles by Drs Nodet and Zilboorg.)

enormous expense for his hobby which is the construction of wireless transmitters. In spite of his obvious good will he is impervious to reason. One day he buys a costly lighter as a present for his mother, his father, a non-smoker, not having thought of doing so. But a few days afterwards, without seeming to, and almost unknowingly, he has regained possession of the lighter and it remains habitually in his own pocket.

This rapid review of the psycho-pathological aspects of poverty can conclude with this clinical example. There can be no question in so short a space of making a profound study of all these aspects. But they are useful to illustrate more clearly, by means of serious or mild irregularities, the normal psychological foundations of a genuine poverty.

Conclusions

At the conclusion of these reflexions the vow of poverty is seen as it should be, that is as the positive and confident step by an adequately balanced psyche. Moreover that is the condition for it to be pervious to the reality of an objective faith. Like every step of this order, which is a profound commitment of the whole complex development of an existence, the vow of poverty should only be the final stage of a harmonious psychological and spiritual evolution. That is not necessarily a question of age ; a subject, aged fifty, may well be retarded in the reflex attitudes of his former Œdipus complex, whereas another of twenty or twenty-two may have come to maturity of instinct very satisfactorily.

In any case it is well to remember always that the vow of poverty should be nothing else than a 'step forward'. It means passing from the false wealth of possession to the true wealth of fellowship. 'Mind the things that are above, not the things that are upon the earth,' says St Paul to the Colossians (3, 2). Poverty consists indeed, psychologically speaking, in being freed from those early chains which have become real fetters. But the human psyche is so made that the Ego in its frailty can succumb even to the practices and customs involved in leading a life of poverty in a religious community. The phenomenon is more frequent than might be supposed and there can be a veritably passionate attachment to certain details of costume or certain directions of the customary. The danger is the more subtle for being hidden behind 'respect for traditions' which at first sight are very venerable, but it exists unquestionably and frequently, particularly at periods when intercourse with the external world is reduced to a minimum. A subject may easily get to the stage of *possessing* his poverty, his 'style' of poverty, in the same way that he may grow proud of his humility.

The real positive attitude of renunciation is from the psychological point of view, an evolution and a personal evolution. Community practices and customs can only be aids to this stage of apprenticeship, provided they are applied with the necessary flexibility. There must be a willingness to accept, in subjects excellent in other respects, conduct that shows partially possessive tendencies which are to be resolved and overcome gradually. In this sphere, as in others, *absolute* success does not exist.

A final problem arises. Is it possible that a vow of positive poverty and its effective exercise may be grafted on to a neurotic start, on to one of those false poverties whose existence we have pointed out ? It would seem to be the case, if the by no means negligible example of the saints counts for anything, that a clearly questionable beginning of the evolutionary process can furnish progressively a complete rectification of the situation and lead to a remarkable balance. It depends on the general quality of the psyche. It is also a question of grace : the personal mystery of God, without performing a miracle properly speaking, can exert more often than is thought—it is a matter of experience—an action that is literally psycho-therapeutic. In other words, each case is *sui generis* ; and if attention is to be so enlightened that a neurotic desire for renunciation is not taken for balanced virtue, that is not to say, by any means, that tactful direction and a profound spiritual life are incapable of arranging matters.

In any case, here as elsewhere, the crucial point of all conduct is certainly to have the greatest possible lucidity about oneself. It is necessary to be able to accept oneself as one is, complex, changeful, divided. It is necessary to be able to accept seeing in ourselves 'ill-digested' instinctive motivations from our past childhood sometimes underlying the most highly spiritual of our conscious acts. That in no wise diminishes their intrinsic

worth, nor does it deprive us of our freedom though it may, on
occasion, modify our ideas concerning the way in which we
practise them. Poverty consists in giving the whole of oneself
to God with the expectation of transcendent socialisation, since
God allows us to and gives us gratuitously the power of doing so.
But, in a certain sense, we cannot give what we do not possess,
that is, what is not at our disposal. If we give the whole of
ourselves, in the obscurity of faith, without having calculated to
our utmost our strength and our weakness, we run the risk of
seeing whole facets of our personality so far unknown to us lag
behind and begin to weigh heavy indeed. It is at this point that
we meet once more the profound unity of the Gospel spirituality
which is wholly governed by humility of heart and by love.

Chapter I

MISERY AND POVERTY TODAY

By Simone Thenier

My contribution is merely the testimony of a working mother.

To most people the 'poor' signifies those who are apparently without means, who lack necessities—a beggar, an old man rotting in a slum, a man, a woman, children in rags, who sleep under the arches or who may be encountered in certain streets, main roads or districts of a town.

This idea is wrong for these human beings, who make up what is called nowadays the sub-proletariat, live in *destitution*, obvious destitution and not poverty.

To others 'the poor' means the working class. And understood in the sense of material possessions, or rather the absence of material possessions, that is an accurate definition.

But in my opinion working-class poverty, as it may be seen in present day circumstances, is not true poverty. For, in reality, doesn't the poor mean those who practise poverty ? And what is poverty ? Isn't it detachment from material possessions, a detachment which, according as it is solely a personal commitment or as others are also engaged, may or may not extend to complete renunciation ?

Poverty understood in this sense can assume various forms. Thus a religious is not poor in the same way as the father of a family who is obliged to maintain a certain standard in order to practise his profession, and through it provide for his family. A nun is not poor in the same way as the mother of a family who must have a dress which though simple, perhaps, is becoming and up to date ; she needs a few finishing touches, make-up, a style of hair-dressing that is fitting and tidy. The mother of a family should be pleasing to look at for her husband, children and household. Her witness as a Christian is thereby enhanced, but her external appearance may give the impression that she is not 'completely detached', that she is not really 'poor', and yet...

She is engrossed in, continually overwhelmed by, a succession of urgent material tasks. She has not time for her own affairs, to think about herself, save in connexion with those in her care to whom she is entirely devoted. She has no time for reading, study or keeping abreast of the latest discoveries. Since the actual time to do so is lacking she realises full well that gradually she will lose the taste and the ability for such things. She realises it and accepts it for the sake of her family. She has not time for regular frequent church going, for long vocal prayers. Can she even find a minute or two of privacy for reading and meditation?

As she stirs the gravy she may snatch a moment to read a passage from the Gospel; changing a baby's napkin, doing her shopping, keeping an eye on the children she will manage to meditate on what she has read, thus incorporating it into her life and into all the humdrum activities of her day.

And the form of poverty experienced by this mother of a family in its very renunciation is akin to the poverty of a nun.

That is what poverty means.

It might be added that Christian poverty is a free act which derives from the depths of man's being so that he may go to God.

Now the unskilled workers, the poor of our times, are experiencing a material, intellectual and moral destitution which is imposed on them from outside by the very fact of actual economic conditions.

This state is *imposed on them* : it is not desired, wished for or loved. It is imposed on them, but in their hearts they do not accept it, nor in their minds do they understand it.

The poor of these days do not desire poverty on this level of destitution. They do not understand its meaning. It is rejected by them more especially because it affects every phase of their lives.

At the present time the unskilled worker can satisfy neither his own essential needs nor those of his family : everything is an insoluble problem for him.

Housing

A family consisting of father, mother, four children living in one room 12ft. by 20ft. How are they to breathe, eat and sleep normally under these conditions ? How can the children be brought up properly ?

Another family of father, mother and seven children living in two rooms. The father finds it impossible to stay in on account of the continual racket and goes off to the 'local'. The elder children cannot do their homework and fight with the smaller ones who tease them : the mother is worn out with work and grows irritable ; the washing, airing, darning of clothes for nine people is unending.

One or other of the children is always ill, thus adding a further complication to life.

Where, how and at what rent can a larger flat be found in which family life can develop under normal circumstances ?

Food

One case from among many :

A household with three children of thirteen, twelve and nine. The youngest is frequently ill. Earnings and family allowances amount to 36,500 francs. After deduction of insurance, rent, heating and lighting about 30,000 francs remain, that is 6,000 francs a month per head for food, clothing, doctor and medicine.

The mother has to work wonders to provide nourishing food, especially for the children, and make ends meet. Half her nights are spent in mending and cutting down clothes so that the family, in spite of everything, shall be decently clad, and all the time she is obsessed by the worry of what they would all do if her husband fell ill.

Then there is the sort of case of fairly frequent occurrence (with slight variations of circumstances) :

The father has been ill for three years. Five children. Monthly income : Insurance and family allowances bring in approximately 41,000 francs for seven persons, that is 5,900 francs a month per head.

The children are well turned out but the diet suffers. At the end of the month the family, despite a diet which is below standard, is reduced to bread soaked in coffee. The mother, who is feeding the youngest child, is extremely thin. Two children already have been in a sanatorium. On such a diet they cannot hope to escape illness.

The working class family is so engrossed in finding a solution to problems of living that they are obsessed by it, heart and soul. The individual's entire vital energy is turned to obtaining for his family and himself what is essential, the necessities, the normal things of human life.

Intellectual interests are choked and in their place remains the one constant worry : how to manage until the end of the month. The money question assumes tremendous proportions in our working-class lives. In many cases it could be called 'the food complex'. And this, for the greater majority of working people, prevents their taking any interest in others. In some families the husband does extra work at the end of his day. The wife goes out as a charwoman. They have no free time at all. It is not gain that attracts them but they are impelled by a concern to meet the legitimate and urgent needs of their family.

In the jungle conditions of modern economic society it is every man for himself. A heart of steel is required to assume responsibility for others. It is only an elite, of whom there are few indeed, who will campaign in the working class political parties.

The great majority of workers experience an overriding urgent need for escape, to forget for an hour or two their crowded uncomfortable quarters and unsurmountable difficulties they are constantly faced with. They hurry off to the cafés where in winter it is warm, and cool in summer, where there are no children shouting and they can talk to their friends.

In other cases the whole family goes to the cinema. There with the actors on the screen, they move in easy circumstances, they experience a change of scene, they take part in a wonderful adventure. Their poverty and cares are far away. They will pick them up again as they leave the cinema but after this short breathing space their troubles will seem lighter, and they will face them once more with increased courage.

Poverty cannot be discussed unless man's essential needs—sunlight, space, food and clothing—are first satisfied.

The distressed condition of the poor to-day is the origin of serious moral difficulties. It causes or gives rise to all sorts of anomalies, and may even smother the deepest natural instincts.

Thus it is that the coming of children is prevented and that abortion has become normal in working-class circles.

This distress which causes sin is the direct consequence of the lack of the spirit of poverty among those who have the control of money in their hands. These people are the financiers. They seek money at any price. They desire to monopolise money, to make it increase for the luxury that it allows and the power that it confers. This pursuit of money for the selfish satisfaction that it bestows on the few is the cause of the distress among the immense majority. In such cases money is not sought in order to satisfy essential needs (shelter, food, and clothing) but to provide the most unbridled and frequently the most flaunted forms of luxury.

This money which is heaped up by men confers on them power enabling them to have at their disposal the work, independence and freedom of others. They silence in their souls the spirit of justice, for if they did not they would be obliged to change something in their life and attitude to others. From pure selfishness they are committed heart and soul to the pitiless struggle which leads to the conquest of money. And to achieve their end by their example, they create the same desire for possession and power in other human beings, in a large number of the sons of God who on that account run the risk of never knowing the Father.

What should be our reaction to this state of affairs ?

In the first place the spirit of poverty should be required of all those who control the means of making money.

Those who, by reason of their material circumstances, are called the poor, should be placed in other conditions of life to be enabled to practise poverty. They should be able to free themselves from the obsession of having to obtain the bare necessities so that they can free their hearts in regard to material matters. Man, set in this human jungle, should not feel himself an orphan.

He must have within himself the certain knowledge that he is not alone in thinking of these problems, that a Father is watching over him so that all his efforts may bear the mark of filial trust and not be merely desperate expedients.

A little girl is preparing for her first communion. She asks 'Shall we have enough money to buy me a white dress and give a proper dinner and invite our friends for my communion?' Her mother replies : 'What are you bothering your head about ? Prepare yourself as well as you can to receive Jesus ; all the rest is my business not yours. I'll look after that, don't worry about it.' And the child, trusting her mother, leaving the burden of material cares to her, is able to concentrate on essentials. We must have this childlike attitude in our relations with God.

God knows better than we do what is strictly necessary for us. We ought to trust him and not allow ourselves to be crushed under burdens too heavy for us to bear.

We must convince ourselves that without any doubt material conditions should not take the first place in our lives. We are not on earth to pile up money, to work ourselves into a good position, but to find God and live in him.

But it must be remembered that the more man's basic needs are assured, and the more he is released from material circumstances, so much the greater is his freedom to think of essentials. A normal person gives no thought to eating once he has made a good meal. He is freed from his hunger and can turn his attention to something else.

The abolition of extreme poverty will not lead automatically to man's growth in divine life and his being actuated by the spirit of poverty. But an improvement in the standard of life is an essential condition to enable the modern poor to live as sons of God. For though it is still possible to be ill while one has enough to eat, it is impossible to be well while one is deprived of food.

The seed that is sown on good ground is most likely to germinate ; grace has the greatest chance of working on a human ground that is healthy and well-balanced.

It is our task, therefore, to make this ground ready, to create these favourable circumstances. We must work for the establishment of social justice if we desire the spirit of poverty to flourish in each one of us.

POVERTY OF THE LITTLE SISTERS OF JESUS

By Pere Voillaume

I. Principles of Poverty in the Fraternities

A certain form of the life of poverty is essential to the Fraternities of Little Brothers or Little Sisters of Father Charles de Foucauld. It is governed by two fundamental considerations.

1. The desire, originating in love of Christ, to imitate the poverty of the Workman of Nazareth, living from day to day by the work of his hands.

This motive for poverty is manifest in Charles de Foucauld's vocation.

Poverty, the renunciation of material possessions which hold captive the freedom of soul, remains the fundamental requirement of blessedness, but the principal motive which causes us to practise it, endows it with its chief characteristic and transforms it into a life ; it is the *desire to be like the Beloved*.

The Prioress of the Little Sisters of Jesus writes as follows :

'Our Lord's summons is addressed to all, and every religious must necessarily suffer in order to go to God. But the summons varies according to each one's mission.

'Some are called to follow Jesus more closely in poverty and renunciation of life.

'How quickly will he be poor who, loving with his whole heart, cannot endure to be richer than his Beloved.

" I know not whether it is possible for certain souls to esteem you if you are poor . . . for my part I cannot imagine love without the overriding necessity of conformity . . . " (C. de Foucauld)

'Imitation for love's sake—poverty. Jesus was born in a manger, was a carpenter at Nazareth, chose his disciples from among the poor, died on the Cross.'

2. *Love of the poor, the destitute, those whose poverty condemns them to arduous work in order to live, love of those who are too easily despised, the abandoned, those whose sufferings are forgotten.*

This love leads the Fraternities to adopt, so far as possible, the living conditions of the poor, to be present among them, to break down the barriers of contempt or indifference which surround them. By sharing their poverty, their work, their way of life, and thereby accepting a share of the contempt or indifference which they suffer, the Brothers and Sisters desire simply to live on a brotherly, friendly footing which will make them the social equals of the poor.

Each will tend always to live in such a way as to be indeed a brother, a friend, and equal of the poor.

This point is capital for an understanding of the importance in the Fraternities of certain practical applications of poverty which could not be justified by poverty seen merely as a means to achieve spiritual freedom or the imitation of Jesus. In this way the need to make oneself 'one of them', the limitation of standards of living to a certain level when on the mission, even if health should suffer thereby, will be understood as a real form of love of the poor ; that indeed is for us a form of mission, of bearing witness and of love.

As a consequence, in the Fraternities poverty is not to be considered merely from the point of view of the spiritual well-being of the religious, and it is this which endows their vocation with its own particular emphasis.

The Prioress of the Little Sisters of Jesus writes as follows on this subject :

'We have to imitate Jesus in his life—an imitation for love's sake—and like him to go after the sheep who are the most lost, the most abandoned ; like him we must make ourselves poor among the poor so as to bring within their reach the message of love that Jesus desired to reveal to us through the poverty of his life. Hence manual labour—like Jesus at Nazareth—work in order to live, in order to be poor like the poor. Hence, also, adaptation—adaptation which is only authentic if our poverty is truly spiritual, making us give up our own outlook, manner of life, our customs, so as to make us one of those whom we are seeking. For the same reason we observe poverty in what we eat, what we earn, our lodging ; nothing must make us richer than those among whom we live.

'Poverty will set a limit to the possibility of material help because we shall be able to give only as the poor themselves give and in proportion to the wages we earn. But poverty will make unlimited charity possible, charity that extends to the very gift of ourselves ; our own nothingness is necessary for us to be at the disposition of our Lord and of our brothers.'

These two principles of the poor life of the Fraternities required clear definition before mentioning actual achievements.

II. POVERTY THROUGH WORK AND MISSIONARY SPIRIT

(Cf. art. 11 of the Constitutions, in the appendix to this chapter.)

(a) Work in order to live is consequently not only a material necessity for the Fraternities but also a means of effecting friendship with the poor. That is why each Fraternity, made up of a small number of brothers and sisters, is obliged to live by its own work.

The Congregation can accept neither dowries nor investments. In this connexion the following extracts from two petitions addressed by Sister Madeleine de Jesus to the Holy Father, in 1944 and in 1948 are relevant.

1. 'Every religious family has a mission to fulfil which has been bequeathed to it by its Founder ; in the continuation of its Founder's work it must be extremely careful not to betray his thought. The Little Sisters of Fr de Foucauld can possess neither dowries nor investments without seriously departing from his spirit ; how should we have the right to bear his name and be called his daughters if this poverty is refused to us ?

2. 'Every religious family has its particular and characteristic works for the sake of which it must adapt itself, not by a purely formal adaptation, but by one which is *effective and profound*. How can we understand the nomads, how can we love them if in some degree we do not share their sufferings and their poverty ? How can we want for nothing among these people who stand in need of everything without their destitution becoming a living reproach to our well-being and comfort ?

3. 'All of us, without exception, would prefer to give up our *official* religious life rather than lose the right to follow the form of real poverty, for it is that which drew us to Christ ; all of us desire to follow this rule of Fr de Foucauld's.

' The Sisters will have ever before them their unique Model, the Carpenter, Mary's Son, bearing always in mind that whatever more they possess than he did will show how different they are from him. All of us adopt as our own this remark of Fr de Foucauld's : "To live comfortably at ease when Jesus was poor, living laboriously by hard work, that I cannot do, I cannot love in that way".'

(Petition to the Holy Father, Christmas, 1944.)

'The Little Sisters are unable to resign themselves to the possession of dowries and investments and capital deposited in the bank, as they have inherited both the name and the ideas of Fr de Foucauld.

'To enable them to live, they have their working fraternities and the labour of their two hands like the poor and the labourer who cannot take advantage of, or be guided by, the rules of prudence and yet, to a far greater extent than we as religious, need security for the morrow for their often large families.

'I beseech you, most Holy Father, to allow us who have not, like others, to maintain charitable works, to occupy our place in the Church in the face of the Communist onslaught, in the mission fields as well as in Europe, as little Sisters of the working class, that class which can never take thought for the morrow and lives from hand to mouth by their arduous labour, with no other honour than that of following faithfully in the footsteps of Jesus.

'Furthermore, in the present economic crisis what is the significance of dowries and investments which are at the mercy of the smallest financial fluctuation. And if in reality they have no significance, why, since our Lord has caused us to come into being at this critical period, should we be obliged to provide for them in our Constitutions ?'

(Petition to the Holy Father, July, 1948)

(b) Since one aspect of the poverty of the Fraternities consists in their sharing the lot of the most outcast, the Brothers and Sisters of Fr de Foucauld are called on to implant themselves in missionary territories where it is difficult or almost impossible for them to live by their own work, for example in Africa among the primitive negro tribes (Fraternity at Mora in the North Cameroons) and the Eskimo fraternity in course of foundation. These fraternities, called missionary Fraternities, are frequently unable to live by their own work on account of the destitution of the country, but their *poverty* and *shared life* serve to emphasize the witness to fraternal charity which consequently takes the first place. These fraternities are helped by others. This was the wish of Fr de Foucauld whose desire it was that poverty should never dim the missionary flame. He envisaged Fraternities in Christian countries which were to 'obtain resources for missionary Fraternities'.

'Solicitude for strict material poverty must never deflect us from our primary aim which is to imitate Jesus and bring the love of God within men's reach. Poverty must yield pride of place to fulfilment of our Lord's command to go out into the world and preach the goodness of the Kingdom.'

Therefore the Fraternities can receive and solicit alms for their distant foundations and for the formation of the sisters (theological or linguistic studies).

The following extracts are from a letter of Fr Voillaume, Prior of the Little Brothers, written to his subjects on this difficult matter.

'It is of the utmost importance to understand that the redemptive love of Christ is, of its very nature, impatient to be spread among men by means of his Church, that this love is preeminently the reason for the existence of poverty which, although only a means of expression, none the less leaves intact the ever-recurring problem of fidelity to our special vocation of poverty.

'I am increasingly convinced that our poverty should be that of the poor working man, of the humble craftsman or the small peasant earning his bread by his work, and that our Fraternities ought to live in this way. I think I can say that we have been entirely faithful to this aspect of our vocation : Berre, Lyon Concarneau, Les Houches, Algiers, Marrakech, Beyrouth have indeed lived in poverty, uncertainty, without help from outside and by means of labour that has often proved arduous. Several have experienced hardship for varying periods and all have honourably shared the lot of their fellow workers. But I am increasingly convinced, also, of the need to safeguard the formation of the novices, the careful study of theology and of language, and the ability to answer unhesitatingly the summons of a distant people, even if it is costly to travel there. Safeguard of these important points requires financial means that cannot for the time being be supplied by the work of the brethren alone. Yet these needs both for the training of religious and for foundations in distant countries are directly required by our missionary vocation in the Church.

'I realise the objections and the problems raised by the obligation of obtaining funds by other means than work. A strict separation between the established Fraternities on the one hand, and the fund intended to meet the expenses of studies or foundations on the other, does not obviate all the difficulties.

'Nevertheless some such choice must be made : a refusal of all resources save those obtained from work would lead to the immediate closing of the distant foundations, the impossibility of providing for the theological and linguistic education of the brethren and holding back of a large number of vocations. The apostolic fervour of brother Charles of Jesus would have broken its bounds had it been enclosed within such narrow limits. Such an attitude would amount to imprisoning love within the confines of a material poverty based uniformly on the resources obtained from work whereas truth demands that the poverty of the disciple of Jesus should, on the contrary, be subordinated to the requirements of love and zeal. "For the spread of the Gospel I am ready to go to the ends of the world."

'Following Brother Charles, we have chosen to imitate "the poverty of the Workman of Nazareth" and out of love to embrace the lot of the poor. That is why, Little Brothers, in each Fraternity we must be faithful and not deviate from a mode of life which enables us to follow in all gladness the counsel of Christ in the surrender of self, and to become the brother and friend of the poor. That is our vocation : to share their lot out of love for them and, in order to bring them Christ, to bring him to them in his Church. No one can take this mission from us and we have *no right to give up* what enables us to carry it out. "To be a worker like the rest" cannot be an end in itself ; the only reason for such an existence is to be impelled to it by the desire of giving Christ. That is why you cannot agree to be in everything *a worker like the rest*. You *cannot agree* to be housed so poorly that you cannot have a humble oratory where you can go to pray to God. You have no right to undertake work of such a nature that you can no longer effectively fulfil your vocation to a christian life and prayer. You have no right to forgo conditions which enable you to strengthen and deepen your faith ; you should be confirmed in truth not only for your own sakes but in order to become the "light" of the world. I can see no justification for a state of poverty which takes as its sole standard "to be in everything in absolute conformity with the life of poor working people". In all that is not fundamentally incompatible with the realisation of your mission as christians, missionaries, and contemplatives, yes. Because in your environment people acquiesce in conditions of life that are incompatible with a minimum of spiritual, or indeed completely human life, should you accept them in the name of the sole principle that our vocation consists in allowing ourselves nothing that an ordinary poor worker would not allow himself ? Yes, but once again to the extent that the love of Christ allows and requires us to do so. Observe brother Charles of Jesus, be poor as he desired with the zeal of love ; I would prefer to hear you say that your poverty is an imitation of that of Jesus of Nazareth, rather than an imitation of the manner of life of the workers surrounding you. You must understand this only as the desire to see you constantly subordinating poverty to charity and to mission in the Church.

'You will tell me, perhaps, that *our mission in the Church* is precisely to *disappear among the poor* and to give up all methods of the apostolate that are incompatible with this state of poverty, that in order to safeguard this vocation brother Charles of Jesus renounced for his own part, and formally forbade his brothers to undertake, any charitable work or ministry. That indeed is true, still there are two things which brother Charles never gave up and to which he made the poverty of his brothers subordinate : he never gave up those conditions of life which are indispensable to the growth of a life of prayer and union with Christ, nor what was necessary for him to be able to go and live among men and to understand them in order to take to them the witness of the Gospel. Nor can we give up these things, but must do everything to reconcile these requirements with those of our poverty.

'Fr de Foucauld envisaged Fraternities in Christian countries in order "to obtain the means for missionary Fraternities". He realised full well that it would cost money to answer the appeal of some distant and abandoned tribe. Would you have us close our ears and our hearts to the silent appeals which come to us from suffering humanity or from those who live without the light of the Gospel? Must we answer in the negative because such a foundation would require a journey incompatible with the means of a simple worker? The Carthusians can refuse to make a foundation in a country where they would be unable to observe their rule, because their vocation is independent of locality. We cannot do so because *presence*, our *insertion* among men is an essential element of our vocation. In each case, nevertheless, the indispensable conditions for the establishment of a poor fraternity must be safeguarded, just as care must be taken not to make our conception of the poverty which God requires of us so inflexible that it is reduced to the sole point of " work in order to live ". I have already spoken of this. In such a notion we may discover, perhaps, not merely a certain pride of the man who desires to be self-sufficient but to some extent a refusal to be uncertain of the morrow or to accept the humiliation of receiving from others.

'I know that the expression of evangelical poverty must be adapted to the mentality of each period and that is why a religious poverty of the wage earner or the manual labourer is especially opportune in our times. Read again what I told you in my letter from Mar Elias; not one line of it do I take back. We must bring back the Church and religious life to the proletarian masses whose lot we desire to share. But should such adaptation extend to the sacrifice of fundamentals? Time and again I have heard this or that method condemned out of hand on the sole ground of its not *being understood*, that it would upset, cause scandal or opposition.

'We are treading here on dangerous ground, for it goes far beyond a discussion on material poverty . . . We are fully aware that although whatever is accidental may be modified for the purpose of adaptation, and that every effort should be made for our actions to be "understood", yet where a fundamental Christian or Gospel truth is at stake there can be no question of suppression or attenuation without repudiating our mission as witnesses to the Gospel. Christ did not act in such a way that he was understood by all, although in the presentation of his teaching and in his actions he behaved always with a continual concern not to give unnecessary offence : but on the essential truths of his message he never compromised. He had no fear of giving offence and did not shrink in the face of incomprehension ; it brought him to his death.

'It is a temptation, and too easy a solution, to wish to say or do only *what will be understood*. This is a frequent temptation in our days ; it is, so to say, the counterpart of an authentic effort at religious rejuvenation and realism, and is all the more subtle because we have a natural repugnance to being misunderstood—there lies human respect, the fear of being laughed at, of seeing men shrug their shoulders at our actions, of being held up to ridicule. In a materialist milieu wherein the sole outlook is one leading to an increasingly rational organisation of society, how can you expect the Christian message permeated with mystery and with the very transcendence of God to be understood in its entirety ? How can the Church, which in its visible organisation partakes of this mysterious and paradoxical character, fail to be misunderstood ?

'Our mission is bound up with the Church. Are we to repudiate it because it is not understood by our Marxist workmates or by certain Christians, well endowed with the goods of this world, who have lost all idea of the Church ? . . .

'Little Brothers, I think I have made myself sufficiently clear and I am sure that you have understood me . .

'To spread the charity of Christ abroad in the world and to share the poverty of the Workman of Nazareth form the core of our vocation. It is in order to prepare yourselves the better to fulfil the primary aspect of your vocation that you are obliged to live for some years as students. That it costs you something to be unable to work with the poor, that it causes you suffering, these are good things so long as you understand that your ideal is in no wise diminished thereby. Live your life as a student to

the best of your ability. Do not imagine some compromise or
other with life as a worker which would prevent your deriving
full benefit from your studies. To be a student is a form of
poverty : students are maintained by grants from the state or
benefactions like those inspired by the campaign in the news-
paper *Figaro*. Your situation is no different. You have to be
supported. Accept this as the condition of your life as a student
just as others accept their grant, without raising useless
questions.

'It is by increasing fidelity to the exacting requirements of
the love of Christ, in self-renunciation, that we shall discover
that poverty according to the Gospel and unstinted missionary
expansion can be completely reconciled. When incompatibility
between the two appears, it is a sign that in our conception of
life there is something which no longer corresponds with the
spirit of Christ.'

III. WORK IN ORDER TO LIVE[1]

The following is the actual position regarding work in the
thirty Fraternities of Little Sisters.

Of the thirty Fraternities :

In France :

Ivry : maintained by work : two (out of three) sisters are
wage earners ; can contribute to another Fraternity. Work in a
rubber factory : at first two sisters worked there ; now one of
them goes out as a charwoman.

Le Sambuc : one agricultural wage earner.

Caravan : one wage earner in a factory ; occasionally another
as a charwoman.

Handicraft Fraternity : Pottery.

Lyons : waitress.

Marseilles : occasional Fraternity : factory work.

Lourdes : some handicraft work.

In France only the Fraternities of Tubet and of the Montée
d'Avignon at Aix (motherhouse and noviciate), St Maximim
and the rue Oudinot in Paris (both study houses) are not maintained by their own work.

[1] Cf. Const. no. II, 30, 172-5.

In Algeria

Algiers : amply maintained by its own work ; one factory worker and two charwomen.

Oran : one factory worker.

In Morocco

Casablanca : Fraternity of *Roches Noires* : according to season one or two factory workers.

Azrou : one wage earner, a nurse, dressmaking.

In the Sahara

Under Canvas : partially maintained by its flock of sheep.

Beni-Abbes : one waitress, one shorthand typist.

In North Africa

Only the Fraternity at *El Abiodh* is not maintained by its own work (Study house and noviciate).

In the Near East

Beyrouth : is maintained with some difficulty by giving private lessons.

Damascus : two wage earners (waitresses).

Bethlehem : two wage earners (waitresses).

Jerusalem : craft work ; cigarette boxes and dressmaking.

Jerusalem (Israel) : one waitress, dressmaking.

Nazareth : dressmaking.

In the Near East six Fraternities out of eight are maintained by their own work.

In the Cameroons

Bassa : one wage earner, a nurse.

Mora : one wage earner, a nurse ; and work as lorry driver for the Brothers.

Summary : twenty-one Fraternities out of thirty are entirely maintained by their own work, two others are partially maintained.

At the beginning of this paper we pointed out how poverty was a means for the Fraternities to put themselves on an equal footing with the poor out of friendship for them. Work can be understood in the same sense. The following quotation is given as an example of this : it is from the pen of a Little Sister working as an agricultural labourer :

'There are still a great many in our days whose lives are lived in close contact with the land. They enjoy a very great advantage for they are in direct contact with God's nature. It is quite certain that everywhere and always such a contact plays its part, though with very different results according to each individual's position, function, character and education.

'This is the positive, though hidden, side of life in the fields ; yet it should help us to understand and bear the rest. Everyone is poor and powerless in the face of drought, hail, frost etc.

'Little Sisters, then, can share the uncertainty of the life of a smallholder or agricultural labourer ; they will be sure to find in such a life, not only imitation of Jesus at Nazareth, but also an experience of the life of the poor in present day society.

'At the outset it must be borne in mind that in a village, people live very close to each other, as a family. Everything that is said or done is known or seen. The Little Sisters are not excepted from this rule. By reason of this familiarity there is little or no risk of the affectation of an exterior but unauthentic poverty ; it would be very quickly found out.

'The Little Sisters' house is as like the others as possible, especially in its furniture. They eat, receive visitors in the kitchen. All their activities take place there. Because of the chapel they had to accept a house somewhat larger than the others, but that is no real drawback. Since it is for our Lord he will not separate the Little Sisters from their fellows.

'Periods of work and unemployment follow each other irregularly following the seasons and the yield of the harvests. The sisters are not bound solely to one employer by mutual agreement ; they are therefore obliged to be taken on several times a year. The Little Sister's position is quite plain to all because she enjoys no particular favour on the part of employers and shares the common lot, but especially because she puts her trust in the Lord, just as he asked. Some jobs are well paid ; these are the activities that must be undertaken in anticipation of the winter. For in winter there is little work for women and the Little Sisters have no other means than women's wages. Consequently there are periods when the work is extremely heavy, during which the office has to be given up but mental prayer and adoration are carefully adhered to before work and in the evening on returning from it. The slack periods, on the other hand, are the times when they can pray together. Without worrying about this irregularity a certain balance is achieved, especially by practising the presence of God during work.

'Keeping a garden is also a mark of the poor; the sisters cannot forgo it, even though it means additional work.

'They also receive visitors, more particularly from their close friends. With others, chance encounters or advice to be given, or especially to be accepted, play their part. Receiving advice indeed is an expression of their poverty, for since they lack the experience of those who have always lived in the district they have everything to learn. The service that they are most frequently called on to render is to give an injection. Giving help to a mother, welcoming to their table on a feast day two lonely old people, are acts of friendship within the limits imposed by their poverty.

'Monotony and oblivion obviously await them when some years have passed. When their illusions and day-dreams are shattered there remains what alone is true and enduring, our Lord, if they have been able to keep him living in their hearts.'

And this is what another Little Sister writes of her experience of work in a factory :

'In the face of all the suffering caused by too hard a life, materially speaking, in any sphere it will be felt sometimes that the solution is to share it so as to direct it all to the Father by uniting it with the redemptive suffering of Christ. In that way expression is given to the vigorous modern tendency to bear witness ; it is the leaven in the dough.

'But the primary aspect of our poverty must not be lost sight of—constantly we must be thinking out the whole matter in the sight of God alone, in the light of his love. Indeed, in the long run, by living among those who, generally speaking, suffer under their poverty and yearn and struggle to escape from it, there is a serious risk of becoming hardened and, by fellowship with the poor, of rebelling with them against social or racial injustice thus diminishing in ourselves the love of God. The lot of the poor, the insecurity of the workers, the harsh life of the nomads or of any other people, must be embraced but out of love. As Father Prior has written : "It is not an end in itself to be a worker like other workers, unless we are urged thereto by the desire to give God to them. It must never be forgotten that primarily we must live in Christ and for him alone in a spirit of adoration, love and complete detachment.'"

IV. Living Quarters

With the exception of the two fraternities at Tubet and Montée d'Avignon at Aix—the noviciate and motherhouse—all the other Fraternities are established in small houses that do not belong to us. Most of them are rented, others belong to the diocese.

We prefer to have flats exactly like those of the workers, and to experience, with others, that insecurity of tenure which brings us nearer to the poor.

At *Algiers* we are in two rooms, the sacristan's quarters at St. Paul's church.

At *Oran* we have the ground floor of a small tenement house belonging to the diocese ; two other poor families also live there.

At *Casa*, Roches Noires, a flat in a working class tenement : three rooms, one of which is the oratory and the cooking is done at the end of the passage.

At *Arzou*, a large village in the Berber mountains, we rent three rooms in a native house.

At *Beyrouth* and *Damascus* we rent a flat.

At *Bethlehem*, two rooms and a passage which we use as kitchen and parlour.

In *Jerusalem* (Israel) our entire Fraternity is established in a warehouse (30 feet by 12) and comprises dormitory, chapel and shop in which the sisters ply their trade as dressmakers in full view of the public. The sign-board is in Hebrew.

We have two other nomad Fraternities : one in a caravan among the gypsies in Province and the other in the Sahara housed in a goat-skin tent.

At *Bassa*, in the Cameroons, in a leper village, a hut like those of the lepers, but somewhat larger.

At *Mora*, in the North Cameroons, round native huts with thatched roofs.

The four foundations to be made next year (1953) will also be in small dwellings of the kind mentioned above.

We have only four large houses for the noviciates and mother-houses.

For the course of studies at St Maximim, which lasts from one to three years according to the circumstances of each case, the sisters live, like everyone else, in rented rooms and go only to those lectures given for them at the priory.

Poverty in the Little Sisters' housing often results in extremely rough living conditions ; but these form part of their vocation. When the very close quarters make silence and a minimum of solitude difficult, an effort is made to redress the balance by regularly recurring intervals of spiritual relaxation, an occasional day spent outside the Fraternity, or outside the district when necessary : in the country, at a friend's house or a convent—the sort of thing that is done by the workers in need of relaxation at the end of the week.

V. Reserve Funds and Dowries

No Little Sister possesses a dowry and this point has been inserted in the Constitutions which at the present time have the approval of the Archbishop of Aix who has erected the Congregation into a diocesan Institute. At the present moment Rome is being petitioned to grant permission for an effective renunciation of all property to be made at the time of perpetual profession. A reserve fund is envisaged to ensure that sisters who return to secular life can be given the necessary help.

Most of the Sisters belong to the workers' social security fund (national insurance).

The mother-house or regional centre may possess reserves in money necessary for the maintenance of the novices and students and to provide for the needs of foundations at a distance.

The tendency is gradually to associate a working Fraternity with each missionary Fraternity (Cf. Constitutions nos. 91-3).

VI. Habit

The Little Sisters have a religious habit which they wear even to work. But this habit is so simple with a simple veil tied over the hair, that it can be worn without singularity among working women. Neither the shape nor the material is laid down and in this way it can be adapted to every locality and climate. The badge is always the same : a cross of brown cloth with, at its centre, a heart of red cloth.

Where working women change their clothes and put on overalls, the Little Sisters do the same.

For some field work which is carried out in the water and mud of the Camargue ricefields the Little Sisters have had no hesitation in dressing like the other women, and with the full permission of the local bishop have adopted a form of dress comprising paddling drawers.

Conclusion

I cannot do better, as a summary of the spirit of this chapter, than quote in conclusion the following lines by Sister Magdalen of Jesus :

'It seems to me that the actual poverty of a religious sister should take on a new aspect. It should be much more realistic. Modern people can no longer tolerate a show of poverty which hides inherent wealth, which requires permission to be asked to use a pin in a house where furniture and artistic ornament of the parlours and public rooms relate the community to the most bourgeois of milieus. There is a certain simplicity of poverty demanded nowadays of the religious life. In the eyes of the public nothing excuses an appearance of wealth even in houses frequented by people of distinction. They indeed, sometimes more than others, evince an exacting standard of simplicity.

'It seems to me that poverty everywhere should find increasing expression in terms of work and wages, and no longer depend on unearned income. This work can be manual or intellectual.

'The life at Nazareth and its ideal can be a model to all. There is no reason why one aspect of the life of Christ should not be shown to all as an example in the meaning of simplicity and of earning a living by work.

'The poverty of the Little Sisters is expressed essentially through manual labour, in order to make them as like the poor as possible. The Congregation is essentially a working class

Congregation. To avoid the risk of deviation from this ideal they do not undertake work which would raise them from their lowly condition of working women, save for a small proportion— only one out of ten, for example, is allowed to become a nurse or give lessons. All the others accept the risk of real poverty with its ever present anxiety and the discomfort that is only too often to be found in life as a wage earner. This point has to be strictly observed, and also that concerning the possession of land or houses. Wherever possible the sisters will pay rent, or the property will remain in the actual ownership of the diocese, so that they may experience insecurity and the risk of one day being turned out. Girls to-day will accept no compromise on poverty. The modern Christian conscience is in reaction against the abuses of capitalism in the religious sphere. The temporal power of religious communities shocks a world in which there exists so much real poverty, in which to a greater extent than before the real affliction of the poor is seen in its true light, and the meaning of evangelical poverty is better understood. There seems to be a desire for a more personal love of Christ leading to conformity. In the words of Fr de Foucauld : "In loving, there is a desire to imitate the beloved. To be different from him is intolerable." '

Appendix

Articles from the Constitutions of the Little Sisters of Jesus on the subject of poverty and work

Chapter 2 : *Their Fraternities*

No. 11—Working Fraternities, whether industrial or rural, are established in artisan, factory or agricultural neighbourhoods in order to earn the maintenance of the other Fraternities, and to bear witness, at the same time, to hardworking poverty and brotherly love by means of an authentic religious life lived in close contact with the neighbourhood in which the work is done.

The Little Sisters do no direct, exterior, apostolic work in the milieu save by the influence exerted by their contemplative religious life, humbly and silently among their fellow-workers.

They go to the factory or workshop simply because they are

really poor and they desire to be workers to share the work, the anxieties and the sufferings of their workmates, together with their joy and pride in earning laboriously from day to day—like *Christ the Worker* in his poor workshop at Nazareth—their daily bread.

But they will never forget that they must live in these conditions as religious, as worker Little Sisters, consecrated to God, and that their primary testimony is of their belonging exclusively to Christ Jesus, their only Love, of which the exterior expression is their habit and religious badge.

Chapter 5 : *Their Spirit*

No. 22—Love of poverty and abjection by a desire for complete renunciation in order to become like to Christ and to have, like him, the joy of being given the lowest place and humbled, despised and treated as nothing out of love of him.

Chapter 6 : *Their adaptability to circumstances*

No. 30—In the industrial or rural Fraternities the Little Sisters, making themselves as like as possible to their work mates, becoming really one of them, will identify themselves completely with the milieu in which they work, earning their bread laboriously from day to day in a state of constant uncertainty for the morrow.

In order that their testimony shall be authentic their Fraternity will be maintained exclusively on the earnings of those who go out to work, and all alms given to them, and even, as soon as possible, any profit from work done within the house, shall be sent to the Fraternity for which they have assumed responsibility.

Part II—Chapter I : *Conditions of admission*

No. 38—In order to preserve real poverty, so essential to the spirit of their vocation, and never to possess capital or a fixed income, the Fraternity will accept no dowry from the Little Sisters, but it will ask them—so far as possible—to share the expenses of maintenance until the time of their perpetual profession by paying for their keep and their outfit.

Chapter 6 : *Temporary profession*

No. 61—Until perpetual profession the Little Sisters will retain ownership of their property and the capacity of acquiring other property (Canon 581 § 1). But they must give up its administration and free usage in favour of whom they wish, before the religious profession (Canon 569 § 1) so that henceforward they will be no more concerned with their property than if it did not exist for them (Cf. art. 89). At their perpetual profession they will make a renunciation of all their property in favour of anyone they wish, keeping only the capacity to acquire further property which they will at once renounce in the same way.

Chapter 12 : *The vow and virtue of Poverty*

No. 89—By the vow of poverty the Little Sisters give up the use of all material things, which can be valued in terms of money. They give up also the administration and free use of their personal property.

90—The Little Sisters will not be content with the strict obligation of their vows. They will apply themselves particularly to imitation of the mystery of *the hidden life of Jesus* at Nazareth, desiring to learn from him to endure the want of necessities and to suffer poverty which they will prefer to all the goods of the earth.

91—Like the Holy Family at Nazareth, the Fraternities of the Little Sisters of Jesus will live essentially by the work of their hands. They will possess neither dowries, nor revenue in money, nor anything which should dispense them from living in the arduous poverty of humble working people earning laboriously their daily bread from day to day, uncertain for the morrow, but in trusting abandonment to their Father's Love.

92—Those Fraternities which are unable to maintain themselves by their work because they are more particularly devoted to study or to the exercise of fraternal charity or a more exclusive life of prayer and adoration, will be adopted by a working Fraternity which in certain cases may be joined to the adopted Fraternity.

93—All Fraternities may accept and even, in certain extreme cases, solicit gifts in money or kind, but may not build up reserves for further ahead than one year. Any surplus must be sent to the Mother house. The latter may keep some reserve for foundations in course of establishment, but must never possess a capital sum deposited in a bank. Gifts received will be used for making foundations or the exercise of charity. But, as a provision in case of subjects leaving or being sent away, a sum of money strictly reserved for this purpose, will be entrusted to the Ordinary of the Mother house and may not be used without his formal authorisation.

94—The houses and furniture of the Little Sisters should be always in conformity with the poverty and simplicity of the holy house at Nazareth, and also with the customs of the poor of the neighbourhood. Their chapels also will preserve an extreme simplicity which will be no exclusion of beauty. No superfluous piece of furniture or any unnecessary article should be kept in a Fraternity.

95—The habit of the Sisters, while remaining worthy of the brides of Christ, will be humble and poor, retaining great simplicity of form, and made of common material to enable them to bear on their persons the perceptible tokens of the poverty of their well-beloved Brother and Lord, Jesus, and to bear witness to him.

96—Their food will be simple, and prepared in simple fashion approximating as closely as possible to that of the poor in their neighbourhood. But it will be healthy and sufficiently abundant for the Little Sisters to fulfil as well as possible their obligation of work and service to their neighbour.

When travelling, the Little Sisters will accept, out of friendship, in great simplicity and freedom of spirit, whatever others may be pleased to offer them, with the exception of wine and spirits which remain forbidden to them always and everywhere, except in cases of real necessity or when charity really requires their acceptance.

97—The vow of poverty should never act as a restriction on the love that the Little Sisters ought to have for their brethren. Their poverty, which should cause privations and sufferings to them alone, will enable them, on the contrary—by freeing them from all personal anxiety—to help with what they need those whom the Lord Jesus sends to them.

In the virtue of poverty they will seek above all, far less the material sufferings of an external poverty, than the abjection of humiliation and the contempt which it engenders, the abasement and renunciation of the spirit of poverty, endeavouring completely to empty their understanding, their memory, their will and their heart of all that is not the unique Thought, the unique Knowledge and the unique Love of Jesus.

Chapter 19 : *Manual Labour*

No. 172—The special form of the poverty of the Fraternities of Jesus is to live essentially by the work of their hands.

That is why a sufficient number of working Fraternities will be set up to assume responsibility for all Fraternities which are unable to maintain themselves by their own efforts.

173—The working Fraternities, directly they are properly established, should live exclusively on the wages of the Little Sisters who go out to work. The Little Sisters may obtain the help of lay auxiliaries who are never to be treated as subordinates but as members of the same family.

174—Work, both within the Fraternity and outside, will consist—according to the abilities and trade of the individual—in manual or agricultural work, or in religious or local craftwork —as an exception intellectual work—which is not incompatible with their vocation as Little Sisters of Jesus. They will take especial care that their Fraternities do not turn into important enterprises.

175—The Little Sisters will carry out the holy and humble work of their hands with love, as an essential part in their imitation of Christ the Worker. Like him they will be able to respect its great dignity and nobility. They will devote themselves to it with courage but without anxiety, in close union with him, unsparing of their efforts but depending on him alone to ensure success. They will manifest a sense of responsibility in work and give proof of great delicacy of professional conscience.

CHAPTER III

SOME PROBLEMS OF ACTIVE RELIGIOUS IN THE PRACTICE OF POVERTY

By ABBE H. BISSONIER

Following the studies which deal with the fundamental aspects of religious poverty, this chapter claims no more than to mention some, among others, of the practical questions raised for active religious sisters by the vow and virtue of poverty. It requires emphasizing, indeed, that these problems were raised by the sisters themselves through the reverend Mothers, delegates of the various congregations, who kindly replied to the short questionnaire circulated unobtrusively by the organisers of these meetings. The author of the present study acts, then, in most cases merely as a rapporteur whose function it is to classify the answers and prepare a synthesis.

It can be said, it seems, that there are two sorts of problems which appear to emerge from the answers received from the various nursing, educational or parochial teaching Congregations which contributed to the discussion.

There are the problems in the actual practice of the vow of poverty : these appear to differ only in some few respects from the problems encountered by contemplative nuns which are dealt with elsewhere. Then there are the problems connected with the external and effective witness to poverty in the sense in which it is usually understood in the contemporary world. Here we are brought face to face with difficulties the importance of which cannot be concealed.

The particular problems of active religious sisters in connexion with the actual practice of the vow of poverty appear to concern those which are caused by the management of charitable or other works entrusted to them by an authority different from that of their religious superiors.

Thus it is that the superior of a community of parochial teaching sisters or even the organiser of a charitable undertaking may find herself in the position, we are told, of having to manage a parochial fund of which the accounts are not rendered to the religious superior but to the parish priest. He may well object to the intervention of the superiors of the congregation in the administration of a fund which concerns parochial affairs alone, and at the same time have complete confidence in the sister as a person who, by reason of her position, has been given the management of this fund. Hence arises the temptation, it is asserted, for the sister in question to find in this situation a more or less clearly accepted, or desired, means of withdrawal from the control of her superiors and the risk, by no means fanciful, as the major superiors who raised the question assured us, that the spirit of possession, or at least of independence, in the use of property should tend more or less consciously to favour such a state of affairs.

Similar problems may well arise in other forms of activity; as for example with a teaching sister acting as superior of a school or hostel dependent on a parish fund, or with a nursing sister in charge of a clinic or orphanage dependent on a lay association or one, at least, entirely distinct from the congregation to which belongs this superior or sister-in-charge, fully concerned to maintain two spheres of activity entirely separate.

The answer to the difficulty appears, from the legal point of view, to be relatively easy. Even if the sister's vow of poverty as such does not bind in this sphere of activity, she cannot avoid her vow of obedience which is the safeguard of all the other vows. Moreover, theoretically every fund depends on a superior authority which ought not to hold aloof from its administration or on an association which from time to time should supervise its finances. A religious responsible for the administration of a fund avoids one form of supervision only to fall under another.

In the last place I need hardly point out again here that the limits of what falls directly under the vow do not necessarily coincide with those required by the virtue of poverty, without which the vow itself would obviously lose its real meaning.

This last thought brings us to the second of the two aspects of the question which were enunciated at the beginning of this paper. I refer to the problem, not of the actual practice of the vow of poverty in the eyes of God and of legitimate superiors, but of the witness of the virtue, poverty, which must be borne in such a way that it is manifest and efficacious in the eyes of the contemporary world.

Perhaps I may be allowed to enlarge somewhat on this aspect of the question : the first beatitude reminds us that what is of primary importance is to be poor in spirit, and we can infer from this that it is possible to be spiritually poor amid great riches, but the converse—though too frequently forgotten—is equally true. On the other hand, it is clearly understood that the religious vow does not deprive us of the use of the things of this world but requires us merely to make use of them, not as if we owned them, but in dependence on our hierarchical superiors. It is no less true that this presupposes at the outset that renunciation enjoined by the Gospel counsel, 'sell what thou hast and give to the poor,' and a mode of life in which poverty entails not only a spiritual attitude, but also actual and effective expression through an unpretentious way of life. Lastly, it seems that this poverty in spirit, and even this actual poverty, should 'shine before men' as the edifying manifestation of the essential witness to brotherly love. The Gospel and the Acts of the Apostles remind us of this in more than one place, as other contributions to this book have not failed to emphasise.

Now our active religious communities have informed us that at the present day they experience a real difficulty in the contemporary world, and particularly in the world of the workers— whose insecurity has been made clear in another paper—in bearing witness to poverty in such a way that it should ' shine before men' and 'astonish' them sufficiently to stir up within them the salutary scandal of the Gospel. Not only do our religious communities frequently live in conditions which in no wise appear to be poor in the eyes of our contemporaries, but circumstances sometimes lead them to live on a scale that the majority of families has nowadays been obliged to give up because it is beyond the means of those who, not long ago, would have been able without difficulty to afford such luxury. 'Whenever a mansion is for sale it is bought and inhabited by a religious community,' someone recently remarked rather bluntly. At the present time there are a good many mansions for sale in all parts of France.

The sisters themselves are keenly alive to the seriousness of the problem ; indeed it is they who have drawn our attention to it and emphasised its importance.

They quote as examples : nursing sister obliged to live in the high standard of comfort required by hygiene and the increasing perfection of hospital methods. Then there are teaching sisters who are bound to take into account the middle-class milieu from which their boarders frequently come and to offer their pupils surroundings and material conditions which do not jar too blatantly with their usual manner of life. Even parish sisters who can, in fact, be satisfied with a more modest way of life find that it is yet far and away above that of the urban or rural working class and that they stand out in a contrast which, they assure us, is obvious and extremely striking. Thus a rural missionary sister remarked : 'To have running water, and still more gas or electricity to cook with, is in this place so great a luxury that it astonishes all the country people around us'.

The contrast is more distressing still when two institutions are next door neighbours but draw their pupils or inmates from different classes : the case, for example, of a school of house-wifery for working girls under the same roof with a secondary boarding school. In the housewifery school the girls eat off rough tables covered with bits of worn-out American cloth ; in the boarding school there is a pleasant dining hall. At the housewifery school where a course of dietetics is given the food consists almost entirely of potatoes : the food in the boarding school, that the pupils of the housewifery course may observe on its way to the dining hall, is more varied and of better quality. At the housewifery school where a hygiene course is given the heating is provided by a badly drawing stove, and the air-space is insufficient for the numerous pupils, whereas in the boarding school the class rooms are large, and central heating provides a pleasant temperature throughout the establishment. Lastly, the housewifery school gives the impression of a small building with unpainted and almost squalid walls, but at the boarding school, visitors are shown into almost sumptuous reception rooms inherited from the mansion in which the boarding school has been established, leaving the servants' quarters to the housewifery school. That is the sort of thing, we are informed, which is not only unedifying but gives scandal to our contemporaries.

Other instances have been brought to our notice :

In the life of the sisters. The sumptuousness of their quarters : the enormous houses of certain communities—sometimes unfortunately practically empty—in towns in which the inhabitants are sometimes packed eight or ten in one room. Luxury in the service of meals : in certain religious houses, in order not to mix the various categories of boarders or even guests, meals are served in an incredible number of little dining halls wherein a staff of considerable numbers of servants or lay sisters moves about. Lavish and unnecessary expenditure : for example the purchase of high-powered electric bulbs or a glittering showy chandelier at a time of serious economic crisis. The extravagances of certain religious habits : for example trains several yards long at a time of scarcity of clothes, or the coif that required half an hour every day for it to be put on properly. (It is only fair to mention that eventually the train was reduced in length on the bishop's recommendation and the coif, on the major superior's decision, was changed for one which effected a considerable saving of time.)

In the sisters' activities. The tendency of certain nursing congregations to concentrate on nursing homes with comfortable private rooms reserved, apparently, for those in easy circumstances who find the idea of a public hospital repugnant ; the tendency of certain teaching congregations, originally devoted to the teaching of poor children, to open boarding schools reserved to middle class or upper class pupils ; the obvious preference evinced in certain hostels for better-off students in contrast to the treatment of working girls ; the more or less obvious exclusion from certain parochial activities, in town or country, of girls or children belonging to the proletariat or sub-proletariat. Lastly, the 'paternalism'—to use a term which is in some danger of abuse nowadays, but which provides an accurate interpretation of the reactions of our contemporary world—the paternalism, then, of certain sisters who are sincerely devoted to the unfortunate :

old people, chronic invalids, orphans, prostitutes or youthful delinquents, who are made too conscious of their 'place' by a certain attitude of abruptness or severity.

A whole chapter might be added on the relationship of religious with their paid staff : low wages, poor quarters, insufficient food and leisure etc., lack of affection. One cannot help thinking of the case of a lay nurse, who had reached the very limit of despair working in a hospital run by religious who, unaware of her state, left her alone in a room where, on finishing her work, she returned to find the tin bowl for her meal laid out in advance. Then mention might be made of the lay teachers in convent schools, living on the fringe of a community whose lot seems the more enviable as they hear the sounds of the nuns' quite legitimate merry making coming to them from within the strict enclosure, emphasizing for those without their loneliness of heart.

A major superior wrote to us that she had heard this remark from lay people : 'You take the vow of poverty, but we practise it'. It is possibly not very fair and somewhat maladroit, but nevertheless it makes those think who can accept it humbly and seek to understand it.

Possibly not very fair, and somewhat maladroit, I said. It is quite obvious, in fact, that 'people in the world', as we say, have not made a study of the theology of the vows nor of the Canon Law which concerns them and in this respect make mistakes of interpretation which we have to excuse and as patiently as possible to rectify. It is true, too, that they can only observe religious life in the light which we are able and willing to show it to them, and that is only a very limited and exceedingly imperfect aspect of the thing as a whole.

Thus it is that mothers of a family are sometimes wrong in taxing a nun with her peace of mind and apparent security. They are unable to see all the self-renunciation that this external peace conceals, nor can they know the detachment of heart and burning love of God which, associated with it, is the whole reason for its existence.

The pupils of some boarding schools are not seldom wrong in seeing the sisters of the teaching congregation who educate them, as great ladies with lay-sisters like so many servants whose function is to wait on them. These pupils cannot be aware of the many humiliations by which these exterior honours are offset, nor can they share the private life of the community in which there is far greater fraternal charity and equality in the relationship between the choir and lay-sisters.

The sick are sometimes wrong to take scandal at the comfort of a so-called nursing home de luxe run by nursing sisters whose prices per day are, in fact, less than those of the hospital across the street.

Lastly, girls who are considering the religious life are wrong to take into it with them their own notion of poverty based on a somewhat inexperienced generosity full of internal contradictions. [1]

---

[1] The following remarks on the subject were written by one of the superiors who took part in the inquiry : '*What is the modern girl's ideal of poverty ?*' Girls of to-day with such an ideal, desire a real and authentic poverty which will make them like the masses. They do not withdraw into an attitude of egoism which would prevent their seeing the afflictions of their brothers—questions of social justice find them extremely receptive—and if they enter religious life they come to it with the desire of living a life of actual poverty. Obviously this desire needs to be deepened for occasionally it is more external than interior and in its realisation certain aspects creep in which are not unconnected with the modern decrease in the spirit of sacrifice.

This ideal is too exclusive and contains certain dangers : the tendency to over severe judgement of those who do not see things from the same point of view ; a certain harshness in dealing with others (hard on herself, the girl demands much from others). This love of poverty pushed too far can cause a neglect of, and even sometimes contempt of, other points in the spiritual life. Religious poverty is misunderstood because its spirit has not been fathomed ; there is no realisation, from the very beginning, that dependence is often more painful than privation.

A girl who becomes a postulant, imbued with these ideas, is somewhat disappointed at not finding greater austerity ; she requires a little time to achieve that balance which should exist between all the virtues and to gain an understanding of the fact that in the religious life the supreme sacrifice required is that of one's own will through obedience.

The ideal of poverty among the young is :
    need of absolute renunciation ;
    real freedom from material contingencies ;
    spirit of mutual help, of community.

But—

this ideal, though easily imagined, is inconsistent with what can be actually achieved ;

it is a conception of poverty, arising from fellowship with 'the others' rather than from imitation of Christ ;

it is founded on an attraction for effective, rather than affective, poverty, oblivious of the Sermon on the Mount and 'Blessed are the poor in spirit' ;

it is based on a desire to live by work rather than on charity ;

However subjective, partial and unenlightened these objections and estimates may appear it is no less true that we have a duty to make allowance for and answer them, if not immediately by a sudden and possibly imprudent change of method, at least as a long term policy ; such an answer must take into account the objector's point of view and the truths, however one-sided, thus expressed.

In conclusion I offer a few elements of a solution most of which again have been provided by the religious superiors themselves, thus allowing me to put them before the reader with greater confidence, and submit them for consideration leaving to his judgement whatever corrections may appear.

In the first place come the principles which are applicable at all times. It will be sufficient to mention some of them.

The meaning and exact bearing of the vow and virtue of religious poverty must be made known and accurately defined— it is not necessarily insecurity nor is it destitution.

It should be remembered that poverty does not mean dirtiness any more than hygiene means luxury. The possession of sanitary equipment which provides proper bathing facilities and enables frequent washing of clothes should cause scandal

---

it is an absolute poverty, of somewhat spectacular aspect, aiming rather at exterior than interior renunciation.

The dominant feature of the modern girl's reaction seems to be in the direction of great and real poverty with insecurity, with transient rather than established living conditions, and an habitual feeling of want, even for necessities.

This seems to correspond with several spiritual tendencies of the modern girl :

1. *Need of the absolute.* Either we are poor or we are not. If we are poor we possess nothing ; we want for everything, we embrace the insecurity of the poorest (earning a living from day to day, treatment at a public hospital in case of illness, etc.).

2. *Horror of bourgeois conformism* : There is a dread of the conventional, of convents housed in great mansions, well polished and well maintained, which give the impression of wanting for nothing. Work should be utilitarian and aim at production.

3. *Liking a risk,* for the unforeseen, for managing somehow, for ingenuity of initiative which tackles problems as they come and has no desire to reckon with the various aspects of prudence : foresight, past experience, objective understanding of the present, knowledge of reality, of the actual case in hand, reasonable precaution for the future.

4. *Straightforwardness and generosity* : the fear of finding in the religious life easier conditions than in the world, all the more clearly expressed nowadays when all classes of society experience material difficulties.

to no one : in this respect the English-speaking countries can
offer us a salutary example.

It should be remembered that poverty does not mean ugliness.
Houses and, in these houses, in the first place ' the house of the
Lord ', can be beautiful and simple just as they can be in bad
taste and costly. When will noviciates provide some guidance
on taste, particularly in the matter of religious pictures ?

It should also be remembered that poverty does not mean
inconvenience, and that to gain a day or a few hours is a way
of economising. Simplification or work by mechanical means,
rapid communications, by motor car, aeroplane and telephone,
modern technical equipment, all of which save fatigue as well
as time, are sometimes part of poverty properly understood.

Education of the public or of the sisters themselves on all
these points, is by no means always easy to accomplish, and
there is a real danger of going from one extreme to the other.

A clear distinction should not only exist, but be made clear
to others, between the premises and material equipment intended
for the use of the boarders or lay staff, and what is intended for
the use of the sisters themselves. It is by no means rare, and
there should be no fear in letting it be known, for religious in
one of the mansions mentioned above to install their boarders in
the main buildings and to keep the servants' quarters for
themselves, when they do not use the stables roughly transformed for this purpose. Perhaps the general public ought to
know a bit more about this sort of thing. But then there is the
matter of the 'enclosure'. Is it entirely out of the question, at
least in some cases, for certain 'witnesses', of the female sex,
to be allowed to penetrate within the enclosure and thus be in a
position to inform others that the sisters of this fine nursing
home sleep in the most unostentatious of dormitories, and that
the teaching sisters who own that large mansion and estate live,
themselves, in premises which, for all that they are clean and
healthy, are none the less rudimentary.

On the other hand, there is some need to take the modern
world into account with its conditions and the way it sees
things, with its exacting requirements, in so far as these are
legitimate and, we must admit, in so far as they are the sign of a
certain progress in the world of the Gospel message among the

pick of industrial and agricultural workers, as well as of the middle classes.

Then, too, we ought possibly to pay greater attention to the situation of the workers and the distress in the world to-day. May those of the general public who frequent our parlours forbear to hide from us those who do not desire or do not dare to frequent them, and, at a further remove behind them, those who cannot, who possibly will never, be able to come to us because some trouble, that is in truth an attack on the dignity of a spiritual creature, has reduced them to a level below human state and no longer leaves them either the time or the desire to live.

Perhaps we should go a step further and as a consequence of this increased awareness of the state of the modern world, bring ourselves in all generosity to consent to actual sacrifices which will enable us to live with our disinherited brethren of the twentieth century in closer community of destiny. In this connexion the following points may be suggested with prudence:

The acceptance of less imposing quarters and the allocation of at least a part of our large houses to families that are ill-housed, without deceiving ourselves about the loss of quiet that will obviously ensue.

A simpler habit in certain cases, necessitating less material and less expense for its repair.[1]

In addition, a simpler way of life (I am still quoting, it should be remembered) with the economies that such a course would entail. Less should be spent on travelling ; journeys should be made third class and, unless really necessary, without a companion. Medical treatment should be undergone at the doctor's surgery, or in a hospital or sanatorium in company with the poor, whenever a subject can endure the promiscuity of the public wards in such a way that she is capable of bearing faithful witness to her vocation. The case of a superior general may be quoted : she underwent treatment for a particularly unpleasant complaint in the public ward of the nearest hospital. And there have been nuns who have been patients at sanatoria

[1] Cf. The allocution of Pius XII to the congress of teaching sisters held in Rome in September, 1951.

among patients of all social classes, contriving to exert there an extremely salutary influence.[1]

Lastly it is well, perhaps, to emphasise particularly the need to practise, in respect of the staff of religious establishments and charitable undertakings, not only a considerate charity capable on occasion of reaching heroic level but even, and primarily, strict justice. The spirit of revindication abroad at the present time should not provoke in us such a reaction as to lead us to overlook the fact that many a claim is justified, and more especially that we have no right whatever to impose on others the ideal of renunciation and self-denial to which we ourselves have been called.

Active religious sisters, poor themselves and bearing witness to poverty, remind us, in conclusion, that they still have the privilege of acting as instructors in poverty among others ; among girls in boarding schools or hostels, patients in nursing homes, parishioners of all ages and conditions who come in contact with charitable works.

The following are the suggestions made by these correspondents :

A certain sobriety in the decoration and appearance of convents, provided, we should add at once, that they are neither cold nor ugly nor impersonal.

A certain simplicity, even a certain austerity, of life, but bearing in mind always that boarders, patients or parishioners are not nuns and have not to adopt their ways, even for a few days or hours.

A prudent mixing of social classes, provided care is taken to join to it the necessary education ;

A more profound yet simpler notion of culture avoiding affectation ; it is to be hoped that this will not act to the detriment of artistic culture in which considerable progress is desirable ;

An 'education in money' consisting in learning to possess it, to save it but also to give it. In that connexion it may be sufficient to add : an education in the meaning of ownership in general, of the spirit of sharing, of having things in common

---

[1] There is no need to insist on the duty incumbent on the sister's community to keep in touch with her and uphold her in her time of isolation and trial.

and of brotherly co-operation, without which Christians of to-day and to-morrow will be incapable of confronting the new economic and social problems raised by the evolution of the world.

There then, in substance, is what the spokesmen of the congregations of active sisters have said or written. As may be seen, they have not confined themselves to consideration of the question—that in itself would have been sufficient proof of honesty and courage—but they have furnished the elements of an answer, both daring and prudent, on the basis of which each religious family should be able to examine, in the light of its constitutions and in accordance with its own spirit, what can be done to furnish an effective answer to the crying needs of the world to-day, without in any way compromising the enduring heritage of the past. I shall be glad indeed if, by collecting these suggestions together in an effort to classify them and produce a synthesis, I have been able to contribute to a solution of these problems.

CHAPTER IV

SUPERIORS AND BURSARS

By DOM JULES FOHL, monk of Clairvaux

The ever-recurring economic question, a problem nowadays because always a problem, is closely connected in reality with the temptation of concupiscence. Consequently, in the world outside the cloister, its repercussions are felt through the constant technical and social experiments which tend to obtain for man the enjoyment of the things of this earth.

The paradoxical nature of the Christian solution consists in a direct approach to the problem under its human aspect of avarice, proffering, in opposition to the instinct of possession, the discipline of a general rule of interior detachment and an invitation to an actual and supererogatory renunciation. It was the Church's function to develop a system of property, achieving in the institution of 'religious poverty' a state of effective renunciation, combined with a claim to 'right of use', which could be advanced under a system of collective economy.

In this ingenious juridical construction the evangelical ideal reconciles, in harmony with the orthodox conception of divine Providence, the rightful management of economic assets and private property with human dignity and responsibility. Its canonical elements of 'use' and 'common life' command recognition by the conscience, as a real medium of virtue, i.e. a just measure, accurately determined in accordance with the nature of things and the sanction of supreme authority. Their observance by religious devolves on superiors as a duty of their office ; and if, in this respect, problems arise, there is a ready-made doctrinal solution in existence which is ordinarily taught in noviciates.

The same does not apply to fixing the golden mean in the exercise of the right of use, i.e. of usufruct, determined according to need and granted to religious in respect of the property of others, represented by revenue, and entrusted to the management and distribution of superiors. In fact, the recognition of a personal need includes a certain margin for subjective and social elements, matters of opinion and accepted convention, which by definition are variable factors. Some so-called needs, common to religious in the past and to their contemporaries, have disappeared with them whereas ; our ideas of what is fitting, of hygiene and other varieties of conformity to modern standards, have sanctioned what our forbears would have denounced as superfluous or fanciful. Yet there is nothing arbitrary or capricious here, for it pertains to a legal system to evolve and base the effective regulating authority of a rule on close and vital contact with the life of the subjects who should feel themselves as beneficiaries of the law.

Now, in his contact with life the Christian encounters the universal problem of the relationship of the Gospel to the world. As regards temporalities, this contact finds expression, for religious as well, in exchanges of goods and services. But the religious state cannot be content to accept the good offices of the world in receptive passivity, however blameless in themselves and purely technical they may be. The positive practice of evangelical poverty must operate as a divine virtue of salvation, and appear as the manifestation of an exemplary form of economic and human life.

On this level is placed the active participation of superiors in formulating a constructive jurisprudence of the right of use by religious. In carrying out this task they have the help of the sound tradition of their Order, often recorded in venerable directions and illustrated by classic examples. Sometimes superior authority settles disputed questions.[1] But the majority of solutions, and the best ones, will be found only by those who have the courage to evolve them, since not every case has been foreseen and some of those solved in customaries may be out of date. To avoid being rash, such courage requires a realistic view of exterior circumstances and a certain responsibility in face of the spiritual alternatives that arise as a consequence of modern problems.

[1] Thus the Holy Father was able to decide in favour of the use of bicycles by religious sisters (17 September, 1951) and the S. Congregation of Religious provided the heads of Orders and Congregations with authorised principles concerning the use of tobacco (10 January, 1951).

The characteristics of the contemporary economic system can be reduced to three.

It is based on monetary exchange.

It implies an intense circulation of goods.

It is based on egalitarian and communitarian rather than on hierarchic and individualist social concepts.

This has certain consequences in the temporal administration of religious communities. They are as follows : considerable and increasingly frequent cash transactions ; the general use of verbal and signed agreements binding the Order ; the substitution for seasonal and bulk purchases of buying from day to day ; the replacement by public services, taxes and scale charges, of many domestic tasks and allowances in kind ; the diminution of practical common sense founded on the handling of things and a direct appreciation of their utility or quality, for the benefit of a standardised sharing out and the translation of reality into abstract figures—in short, the preponderance of financial considerations and transactions.

For every custodian of money this system implies the indubitable facilities which caused Ecclesiastes to say 'All things obey money' (10, 19), and it is this which lends new attraction to the ancient temptation to avarice. The ascetic teaching of the Gospel will ever apply its classic remedies, but their efficaciousness will depend on their coming to grips with the fundamental facts of the situation ; and this is related to a sense of proportion which is part of the prudence necessary in the choice and government of superiors.

An examination of the problems raised would seem necessarily to define more accurately the extent of superiors' concern with this economic reality under the following heads :

1. The superiors are themselves religious.
2. They administer a heritage common to the whole Order.
3. They are responsible for an evangelical and social form of life and perfection.

As professed religious, superiors remain subject to all the canonical consequences, and benefit by all spiritual effects, of the vow of poverty common to religious as a body, in accordance with all the well-tried principles of common life, particularly

with regard to food, clothing, furniture and things for their
personal use (C. 593, 594). To these must be added a special
obligation of edification and instruction by their example.

There should be no difficulty, of course, in allowing superiors,
especially major superiors, the means of discharging their
office and of being creditable representatives of their Order.
But there will be some hesitation in linking the prestige of
authority with the use of a habit of special material reserved to
the holders of office, or in fearing a relaxation in obedience as a
consequence of the active participation in housework of a
superior in a small convent ; and encouragement, until the final
victory is won, must be given to superiors whom a certain
refinement, or human motives, would restrain from sharing the
ordinary fare of the community in the refectory. On occasion,
nuns have money in their pockets, particularly when they go
out in the town ; obviously superiors will sometimes be in like
case ; but this legitimate necessity should not be allowed to
degenerate by prescription into the privilege of a private
allowance. As for allowing superiors to accept or bestow presents,
on special occasions, consisting of sums of money for free
disposal, it is contrary to the very nature of the vow of poverty,
for money cannot be an object for personal use (C. 594 § 2)
like a book or a prie-dieu upholstered with tapestry.

Every administrator is confronted with a double problem ;
one is technical and is a matter of competence, the other moral
and concerns fidelity in regard to the owner.

Under the modern economic system a religious administrator
can hardly be considered fitted for his office without intelligent
and practical training, varying according to the importance of
the position, in book-keeping, together with an elementary
acquaintance with contracts and probates, with taxation and
professional and social legislation. Culpable negligence on this
score would amount, in some degree, to a breach of trust ; it is
only a proprietor who can allow himself to incur risks without
harming the interests of others.

The problem of fidelity is bound up with the absorbing
interest of the conduct of business and the accompanying
danger of causing the person in charge of it to acquire the
habit of acting as a proprietor.

This danger is very real, since the continual handling of money serves to emphasize quite clearly a certain antimony between facilities in the use of money and the impediments arising from observation of those formalities intended to safe-guard religious endowments. But religious asceticism, no less than prudence, requires on the part of superiors, as the price paid for technical advantages, the faithful observance of these prescriptions. In spite of their being invested with authority over persons, they do not possess discretionary powers over the endowments of the community of which they are the responsible and removable agents. To exceed the limits of their competence would be an assumption of the functions of ownership and an act of infidelity in regard both to the Order and to divine charity, which is offended by breaches of the vow of poverty. This concern for the souls of those in office will prevent them from taking for a pressing necessity their personal preference for the combination of the offices of superior and bursar, which the Church only allows as a make-shift (C. 516). On the contrary, a religious disposition will be glad, from a sense of duty and virtue, to promote collaboration in this field, and make of it a school of community spirit and a training ground for the responsibilities of office.

On the institutional level, a problem seems to arise nowadays with regard to the functioning of the administrative organs of the community on the one hand, and of the rules of accountancy on the other.

Only too frequently there is doubt about the efficiency of administrative Councils, because often their function is reduced to taking note of a *fait accompli* or to giving approval on trust, for want of personal preparation and previous examination of the documents of the case, to decisions which have become urgent.

Yet reflexion on the temporal administration of religious orders, instead of requiring an examination of conscience[1],

[1] According to an authorised decision of a Roman congregation 'those whose function it is to examine accounts and, after checking, if they merit it, approve them, must be fully persuaded of their very grave obligation in conscience. In the same way those who by their signature or advice participate in temporal administration should realise that, before the Church and in conscience, they assume responsibility for their intervention and its consequences.'

raises a question of method. By reason of its objectives, this administration is involved in general business methods, whereas methods used by religious often remain as they were in other days. So it may be wondered if the purpose of the chest with three keys would not be more easily, and indeed more efficiently achieved, by the requirement of three joint signatures for a document to be binding on an Order.

The problem of the rendering of accounts implies that the other, of keeping them, has been solved. It is to be hoped that the fifty odd questions, relating to temporalities, put to those who draw up the new quinquennial reports,[1] will lead them to reconsider the technical, as well as the ascetical, function of the books of record.

It must be remembered that accountancy must be complete, accurate and genuine. These three aspects each have their own problems.

Complete accounts must include, in addition to the cash account, the whole of the assets and liabilities ; they should also furnish particulars on dealings with a third party from which may result commitments for the Order (e.g. deposits, management of property on behalf of the nuns, etc.) In many cases, the rendering of accounts should include those in kind, and thus make it possible for the accounts to show, in the cost of living, and on the basis of the taxes levied by the provincialate or generalate, the sometimes considerable contribution furnished by gifts. It will be realised that the cash accounts of houses which are run by buying commodities have nothing in common with those which obtain their provisions of fuel or potatoes from the gifts of benefactors. Nor would complete accounts be rendered which were confined to the cash account and household expenses on the plea that remunerative undertakings, real estate or investments were in the name of secular companies. Such companies, in no sense legal fictions, are trustee institutions and really identified with the religious Order by means of an agreement in conscience or good faith, the effect of which is to keep them in entire dependence on the canonical organisation of the Order.

Accuracy in accountancy is a result of the agreement of the

[1] *Elenchus Quaestionum*, 1949, ch. 1, Art IV, questions 87-138.

books and vouchers on the one hand with the real state of the property, and particularly of the liquid assets, on the other. It imposes on the bursar the obligation of checking that orders to pay out money are properly authorised in accordance with the prescriptions of the constitutions, and it empowers her to require a receipt in the presence of witnesses for sums taken by the superiors themselves. Accuracy is also concerned with keeping the accounts of each financial year separate, for otherwise the encroachment of one year on another will swallow up the internal taxes due to provincial or other administrations at a higher level.

A concern for accuracy should increase the efficiency of the administrative functions of the community, by combining them with the constitution of a system of accountancy adapted to the special circumstances of the revenue of the Order and the formulation of annual estimates. The Secular Institutes have thought it prudent to equip themselves with this further guarantee against the risks of an economy based on money, and against the ever-present possibility of religious administrations falling into the spirit of ownership.

The principal quality in rendering of accounts is their genuineness; it is a reflexion of the administrator's fidelity towards the owner. It is a matter of conscience rather than of rules and regulations, and should provoke the desire willingly to explain any matter, with the simplicity of the children of God, required by the authority receiving the accounts. In practice, the classification of items under 'various' is to be avoided so far as possible, and care must be taken that the different headings are clear. If under the constitutions, or by legitimate custom, superiors are authorised to dispose of certain sums, this proper mark of confidence exempts them from the obligation of accounting for their use to others, save to higher authority; it does not bestow on them the prerogative of ownership, of keeping a separate purse from that of the community and of being exempt from the control of account books.

The irresistible object lesson of simplicity and exemplary personal indifference to the supposed material advantages attaching to the rank of superior, together with the fidelity of the good servant esteeming the assistance of her official collaborators and dispensing, in the name of the Father of the family, the goods of the community, by the merits and intentions thus manifested, will have a considerable influence for holy edification and sanctification in the convent. Performance of the duties of state, moreover, provides the office-holders themselves with precious opportunities and authentic indications of spiritual progress ; it will show itself clearly through tenderness of professional conscience, characterised by an increasingly comprehensive and persuasive prudence in the soundness, rightness and appropriateness of their decisions.

But the present situation in most countries affects the function of leadership, which is a superior's, when the appearance and confrontation of new ideologies requires that established customs be reviewed, and institutions and settled teaching thought out afresh.

In their position of spiritual guides, superiors are sometimes confronted with the question of determining whether the development of a common interest in what is a common heritage is desirable in religion. It is acknowledged that the books of account are the subject of official secrecy and, on the other hand, it is a fact that economic evolution has made of them the only certain evidence concerning the exact position of estates and property. It would seem that family spirit, rather than a fear of leakage of confidential information, would suggest its occasional communication ; if this is done by means of a summary, which is both circumstantial and authentic, it will act as a means of quickening the evangelical spirit of religious poverty. In fact, if the concession of the *use* of something ought to correspond with the subjective element of the *need* of the religious, it should none the less integrate him with the general economic and social reality. And if voluntary renunciation is a means of setting free the spiritual love of God from the obstacle of temporal anxieties, it is so only on condition of not being weakened by reduction to mere niggardly parsimony or parasitical extravagance. The fact remains, also, that if administrators of religious property render their accounts to the authorities designated by the laws of the Church, the results of their administration are none the less not without effect on the confidence that they should inspire in their subjects.

Communications of this kind should not be confined to disclosure of general information concerning the internal use of the resources of the community. They can fulfil an ascetic function in the development of virtues essential to the Christian order, but whose practice and merit are accessible to religious only by intention and by means of works of mercy subsidised in the name and on behalf of the community. It may well be believed that such participation will lose nothing of its value if, through the action of superiors, it comes to be effected consciously.

A problem nowadays, by which not only the Church is affected, raises the whole question of private property—its legitimacy, its organisation, its social function. In connexion with the temporal possessions of religious it may crop up as a reproach, a scruple, perhaps even as a feeling of guilt about 'capitalism'.

On the institutional level efforts at a solution of this problem are taking place. It is the duty of religious administrators to contrive at least that the discipline of their Order possesses a certain flexibility of adaptation to the evolution of the general system of property.[1] But their task as spiritual guides is less problematical; it consists in forming a sense of collective responsibility based on the Gospel and in harmony with its pastoral applications in the Church. Independently of changes in the economic system that the prudence of men or force of circumstances may dictate, it is important to emphasise, amid all the claims and objections current to-day, the true character of the religious patrimony as the possession of the Church.

Primarily, and despite appearances resulting from the absence of an appropriate legal status, the temporalities of religious are not so much private property as possessions for public purposes in the Church, just as their moral personality is public. It follows then, that these temporalities should be neither defined, possessed, administered nor used as a joint possession, that is, a form of ownership proper to a body of private owners. Positive education of religious communities along these lines would disclose, in the use of religious property, unsuspected and

---

[1] The apostolic Constitution *Sponsa Christi* contains suggestive and clear directions on the subject of the place of remunerative work in the life of nuns.

valuable resources for an apostolate of the common life, and to the credit of the ideal of that life inspired by the Gospel.

The temporalities of the Church, as property for public use, retain their justification among those forms of the concentration of wealth which are nowadays held in favour and tend to become the monopoly of public authorities or large groups on a professional or trade-union basis. They alone, perhaps, will be adequately effective on the scale of present day communitarian organisation. Considered from the point of view of a tradition going back to apostolic times, the 'patrimony of the poor' and its spontaneous re-establishment, under forms borrowed from all sorts of economic systems, and in spite of extortion and continual plundering, proves a constant factor in the advent of the Kingdom of God in time. By the very purpose for which it is intended, this patrimony is the condition of the independence of its beneficiaries who are, on a last analysis, human persons incorporated in the Church.

Since the origin and the purpose of property, subject to the ecclesiastical law of religious poverty, is to be found in the Gospel, it ought to contribute to the support of the state of perfection and to benefit by the assiduous care bestowed on sacred things. On the basis of existing realities and under the enlightened direction of superiors, there should develop a common conscience of the poor in spirit capable, even in these days, of bringing forth the hundredfold of the good grain of the Gospel.

CHAPTER V

MODERN TECHNICAL DEVELOPMENTS[1]

By J. BONDUELLE, O.P.

All sound evolution of the structure of the religious state would seem to be governed by teleological principles. In this connexion, St Thomas's traditional teaching cannot be too strongly emphasised : the primary end of the religious state is the perfection of Christian life in accordance with the fullest sense of the first commandment and of the second which is like unto the first. Those Orders which are usually known as contemplative have no other end; all the other religious families add to this primary end, combined with it and motivated by it, a secondary end which is always a spiritual or corporal work of mercy. The special characteristic of contemplative Orders is to have no other end than that common to all Orders.

It is important to observe that it is indeed a question of the end in view. The balance of a special religious state is fundamentally dependent on the way in which, on a last analysis, its secondary end has its place assigned within the primary end without in any way diminishing its prerogatives. In all that is governed by the secondary end the primary must have pride of place ; the nursing sister who applies a dressing, in her very act of mercy, is bound to tend to the love of God just as absolutely and just as single-mindedly as a contemplative nun during her times of mental prayer. Yet such a sister's work is certainly a real end ; a work of mercy is the secondary end of the religious state whether it be of preacher, teacher or nurse, and to minimise the importance of the work of mercy would amount to destruction of the whole originality of an Order and to upsetting its balance. If there is a question which arises, instead of the nature, as an end in itself, of the first and second commandments on the one hand or of the work of mercy on the other (and the

[1] A report made by the author to the Congress of the States of Perfection held in Rome, 26 November - 8 December, 1950.

reality of one or the other), it is rather the distinction between the primary and secondary end. In a particular religious state in which examination shows the relative positions of the two ends in their joint and established order, it is always in combination that these two ends operate. The primary end acts only as an integral part of the secondary, which, in its turn, acts only in and by its union with the former.

Although these two great guiding principles may seem far removed from practical issues, they are in fact intimately concerned with them, for it is only in the direct light of these principles that the reasonable and practical use of those devices required by modern progress can be contemplated, whether for greater ease and perfection in work, or convenience in daily life as the title of the present chapter indicates[1]. Consequently our reflexions on the subject will differ according as we are considering a religious order with a single end (perfection of Christian life, typified by the monastic Order) or an Order with a composite end.

I. THE RELIGIOUS ORDER WITH SINGLE END

By a single end we mean the perfection of Christian life by the pursuit of charity. Usually this kind of Order practises strict retirement from the world. The monastic Order provides a typical example, and in one sense it is true, also, of the Mendicant second Orders (Carmelites, Poor Clares, etc.). It has often been said that this is the purest form of religious life, and to some extent that is true. Nowhere else is the relative nature of the things of this world and the use that is made of them experienced more keenly. Religious poverty, which is a voluntary poverty, is a violent assertion of the absolute nature of God ; there is a distinct refusal to put any created thing whatever on a par with him, everything is sacrificed for his sake. But this absolute character of the gift of poverty must be combined with a relative approach in the inevitable use of certain objects without which it is impossible to lead a human life (and in this poverty

[1] The following was the official title of this report : *Relatio quae intercedit inter vitam religiosam et paupertatem ac mortificationem relate ad commodum personale, ad laboris facilitatem, ad adjumenta hodierna ad faciliorem vitam reddendam.*

differs from chastity which, for the religious, can only be absolute, and even from obedience which, in the case of a formal precept, also knows nothing of half measures). This is the paradox peculiar to Christian poverty which is accentuated very sharply in religious poverty : in its religious character it is absolute ; in the use of indispensable goods following the special traditions of each religious family and the needs of the moment, it admits many slight differences of interpretation.

Of their nature modern technical developments do not affect the monastic Order nor those religious families with a single end. It matters little to them in which social or economic region the earthly food of mankind is sought. Generally speaking they are indifferent whether their bread is baked in an oven heated by wood after being kneaded by their own hands, or whether the whole operation is carried out by electricity. Then, too— though from a point of view which is entirely unconnected with the end proper to these Orders—it is expedient that in the Church there should be some who, by their backward methods in temporal matters, bear witness to the spiritual nature of the Kingdom of God. The Reformed Cistercians who have retained their medieval time-table, and in some places, rather out-of-date equipment, still have a function to perform in the Church. It might be said, perhaps, that they perform one by their very backwardness. Those who visit them are moved by the eternal values symbolised by their indifference to transient things. For all that their libraries retain their equipment from a past age, and the want of a card index of the latest model retards their intellectual work, none of this hinders their eager pursuit of evangelical perfection. If this backwardness increases the mortification of their lives, it pertains to the superiors to see that it does not exceed human strength nor the limits of super-natural prudence.

On the other hand there is no reason why such Orders should not move with the times, nor why new orders should not arise in our day which are solely contemplative and yet which adopt towards modern technical developments an attitude of frank acceptance. Monastic libraries or those in the houses of contemplatives could well be established in accordance with the latest models of metallic equipment; domestic work could be mechanised to the full (machines for washing-up, electric vacuum cleaners, etc.), and such a course would provide the double advantage of making possible within the same religious house of a certain (or even a complete) unification of the grades of religious (abolishing the distinction, unknown in the Rule of St Benedict, between monks and lay brothers), and of setting free from some of the heavier work energy that might be employed in activities of a more spiritual nature. In this way, too, another distribution of work is made possible : formerly the lay brothers were employed only on manual tasks; in the future, with all members of the community having access to a more balanced form of life, manual work and intellectual work can be arranged according to the aptitudes of the individual or according to the principle, advocated by the more enlightened contemporary sociologists, of an alternation of activities. Only the way in which the domestic work of the monastery is organised need be re-adapted. But would such a development not compromise poverty and mortification without which there is no religious life ?

So far as poverty is concerned it is difficult to see why abbeys, which in bygone days were allowed by the Church to own vast estates, should not be able, under a different economic system, to possess the necessary equipment to live in an age which is largely technical. The Holy See which is constantly to the fore in the use of scientific discoveries (radio, television, etc.) has here shown the way. There is nothing in the nature of the religious state which is opposed to the collective ownership of even complicated and costly equipment (monotype and litho-graphic printing plant, for example) or of a research laboratory with the intricate apparatus required by modern scientific methods. If science had developed six or seven centuries earlier, abbeys, instead of being centres of culture by the transcription and preservation of manuscripts, would have been so by the establishment of chemical or biological laboratories. It is true that this kind of work requires nowadays considerable capital, and that it is at least doubtful whether an increasingly collec-tivised science, whose research centres presuppose the posses-sion of official grants derived from the revenue of modern states, could entrust abbeys or monasteries with important work of this kind. At least it should be said that it is not contrary to the perspective of the religious state.

In this matter of the collective ownership by abbeys or monasteries, care must be taken to avoid scandal on the part of the public which is itself dependent on a state of civilisation, economic or social organisation, civil legislation and all that these in combination have imparted to the general mental make-up of a people. Particular care must be taken to avoid giving scandal to the poor. Under a system of property which is continually in a state of flux should not churchmen look with especial favour on those who have few possessions and appear, in consequence, in a better position to live the mystery of the first beatitude ? In addition, the present position of religious Orders—which desire, on the one hand, to be in the forefront of scientific research and modern technical progress and, on the other, to lead their evangelical life in full union of poverty with the poorest of our contemporaries—leads to a tension between these two aspects of their life which can be united only by great spiritual fervour and a strict regard for poverty in the use of equipment. Particular care is necessary on this last point since a large amount of capital and expensive equipment will have to be handled. With regard to the position of each religious within such an Order equipped with expensive plant, he should continually make sure that with it all he is the least proprietary of men. The use that he is called on to make of valuable property can and should remain the use of a poor man, and a frugal use with continual reference to the sole end of Christian perfection. By comparison all goods granted by the Lord to an Order will always appear as the full measure of the Gospel, and the religious, dependent upon his Superiors and upon the Lord—who is the master of all possessions—will be ready, like that holy man Job, to bless the Lord on the day when some accident of history should happen to upset the excellently balanced system which has been perfected.

From the point of view of mortification, which is an indispensable factor in all religious life, it cannot be denied that the present development of technical methods, a certain standard of life and progress in the direction of increased comfort, all raise exceedingly delicate problems. Will the old traditional asceticism, based on fasting and abstinence, vigils and labour, disappear ? Considerable discrimination is necessary on this point, for although the basic principles of morality and the foundations of Christian penance remain the same, their actual practice must of necessity develop according to circumstances. Nutrition on a rural standard, which was formerly universal and on which the principal medieval monastic observances were based, has disappeared in many parts to give place to a food standard which, though perhaps more artificial, is also more stimulating. The physique of modern people shows clear signs of this. Careful study of the medical hygiene of the question would certainly be necessary in order to give prudent guidance on a contemporary and urban form of corporal asceticism. Is there a certain margin in voluntary austerities which, formerly corporal, will find their place in future rather in the ascetical practices of common life or in a more careful obedience ? The experience of really spiritual persons, under the control of the Church, can furnish the only adequate elements for a valid judgement.

How will the religious institutions of the second half of the twentieth century develop ? The Church will certainly look primarily to the spiritual qualifications of founders, the edification inherent in their plans, the reactions of Christian people, and will judge of their fidelity to the Gospel in the light of her own experience. It seems necessary that in the discipline of the Church there should be both considerable caution in accepting these new developments in asceticism and great latitude shown in the face of the efforts of really spiritual persons. But it cannot be said too often : Orders with a single end of themselves require no special form of asceticism, for they are an expression of the genius of their founders, and of their own tradition. The doctrine of the religious state can be expressed in many ways.

A venture like that of the Little Brothers of Jesus (the followers of Fr de Foucauld) is significant from this point of view. Their particular purpose is to live the Gospel of Nazareth without any apostolic aim but with the sole concern for a contemplative life in the midst of the people, sharing their life. The traditional asceticism of the cloister with its fasts and vigils necessarily gives way to a school of morality which is much nearer that of ordinary Christians (and in one sense much harder still). Like the other workers they use the machines belonging to the undertakings which give them employment. They have no fine libraries in their houses, but make use of those of the natural communities (municipalities, etc.) in which they live. There is no reason why the evangelical counsels should not be lived to the full according to these very novel rules which may well provide one of the keys to the future of the religious state.

The poverty and mortification of religious, therefore, are being subjected to considerable readjustments in the present evolution of civilisation. Not, of course, in their principles, but in their applications. It may be hoped, indeed, that in face of this adjustment of customs the principles involved will be the better asserted in all their urgency, their spirit and their absolute nature. Many Constitutions on the subject of poverty, for example, seem to be worded inadequately. Frequently they contain a few too hasty paragraphs headed 'Vow and virtue of poverty', generally very short and insufficiently thought out. The poverty of religious, which falls under the vow, is a certain condition of deprivation or limitation and dependence in use which bears witness to the absolute nature of God; it is a chosen sacrifice and, finally, the cause of many and various virtues, from the moral to the theological. Efforts must certainly be made to inspire many Orders with a certain spirit of religious poverty so that, without danger, they may contemplate undertaking the necessary evolution in a contemporary sense.

II. ORDERS WITH A COMPOSITE END

Most of the foregoing reflexions are also valid for those Orders which follow the primary end common to every religious state but are motivated by contingent secondary ends. The absolute nature of the sacrifice of poverty is identical in both cases. Identical, too, is the fundamental determination to work for the perfection of Christian life with the necessary rule of mortification. But the addition of secondary ends may affect the arrangement of means to be employed. Neither the extent of the use of the goods of the earth nor the ascetical rules will be the same. The primary end of the religious state leaves a considerable undetermined margin concerning the actual system of observances regarding poverty and mortification. It is the function of the secondary ends (works of mercy for example) to determine the practical applications. They will differ necessarily according as these secondary ends concern a work of preaching or doctrinal teaching, education or re-education, hospital or rehabilitation work, house to house visiting, social investigation or parochial work. The absolute value of poverty remains the same, but in actual practice the poverty of religious will differ widely in its application following its adaptation to various ends. Why should not the Agricultural school of some congregation use agricultural machinery (combine harvesters, etc.), or their poultry yard be equipped with electric brooders ? It may well be thought that it is an essential requirement of all scholastic undertakings (teaching at all grades) to possess equipment corresponding with the actual level of modern educational technology whether professional training or any other branch is concerned. An Order has no right to lag behind in technical development. To be behind the times would, in this instance, be blameworthy, and even morally so, in those reponsible ; in any case it is among the causes leading to a decline of recruitment, it diminishes that good opinion which is a valuable asset among those associated with the Order, and it may even cause a partial withdrawal of the confidence of the Church. It is one of the points on which Orders tend to become out of date. What, in Orders with a sole end, is something quite contingent (whether they are medieval or belong entirely to their own century matters little in regard to their end) is in this case a necessity imposed by the specific work and its position in a progressive world. The possession of libraries suitable for effective research and original work in theology or philosophy, the equipment of these libraries with the most efficient system of cataloguing, the most convenient form of furniture, etc., is an obligation for those Orders with a doctrinal end. And it is this end which governs the degree of the exercise of poverty. A thousand and one ways are left to them of making use as poor people of equipment that may be quite expensive in itself. In any case the problem for the Order is not the fact of possessing the best possible equipment for its purpose, but of maintaining among the religious the authentic spirit of poverty with regard to this equipment which is not their personal possession but, through their Order, belongs to the Church herself. The standard of life of the individual may be very poor in an Order which, in all that concerns its vocation, allows itself whatever is of service. It is the superiors' duty to pay careful attention and to make sure that in actual daily life and all its details the margin of want (*inopia*) in furniture and in the small objects for personal use remains in accordance with a rule of true poverty.

In fact, it is at this point that the real difficulties begin, either because the work entrusted to one religious may require him to have for his own use objects that are not primarily for the service of communities but of the user and worker, or else because the mechanical equipment of the community favours a certain comfort which is at first sight disastrous to religious life.

For a demographic investigation a religious may need not only a typewriter but a whole collection of card indexes, and even a complete duplicating outfit which in these days represents a considerable capital sum. He may need premises and even a secular staff to work more or less under his orders. He may require what amounts to a private library if he is at work on a branch in which the community library is deficient ; the efficiency of his work depends on it. He may need a whole information service with its subsidiary departments. There is no ready-made solution to these difficulties which remain, of course, special cases and dependent on the persons concerned, their capabilities and, it is to be hoped, on their fundamental attitude to poverty. It pertains to the superiors to keep the control in their own hands, to make sure, if capital is involved, that the requirements of the civil law are properly complied with (possibly by the formation of businesses more or less under lay control), and especially that the religious engaged on the work labours under no misapprehension regarding the scope of his work and the conditions that he considers necessary for it. It is a matter of the spirit in which he works. The use of valuable property can, and should, remain a poor and dependent use, dependent on the judgement of superiors, poor in all the many ways in which a man can look on himself as possessing nothing and dependent on God alone. Here again it is the spiritual quality of the religious that is at stake far rather than the fact of making use of extensive and costly equipment.

The same requires to be said of the necessary mortification. Once again it is the end in view which enables the necessary distinctions to be drawn. Ought I to allow myself an office easy chair when one with an ordinary straw seat would suffice ? Ought I to allow myself an electric razor when an ordinary safety razor would do as well ? Should I have a telephone on my desk ? All sorts of questions of this kind could be raised. They cannot be answered by a simple affirmative or negative, but require all the prudent distinctions that should be present in the judgement of a religious wherein obedience has the last word. One constituent of any decision is the following : Is it solely for comfort, ease, or pleasure ? In this case the religious spirit inclines to a negative answer. Or will such and such an advantage conduce to a better utilisation of my powers in view of the secondary end of my Order ? In that case the religious spirit inclines to an affirmative answer. Do my answers tend to further my principal obligations as a religious ? They will if I am careful about the matter, if I leave it to my superiors to decide, if I do not give way to ease, comfort, or well being, for their own sake. The limits of prudence will always allow for the fact that in doubtful cases two points of view are in conflict : that of the efficiency called for by the secondary end of the Order and that of the necessary mortification of the religious state. Here, then, are two opposing tendencies, two tensions in different directions, which conduct in accordance with religious profession must reconcile into a synthesis in fidelity to the gifts of the Holy Spirit. As long as these two tendencies remain there is nothing to fear, religious life is unharmed, fidelity is kept, and that in spite of inevitable approximations. What is to be feared, and greatly, is the day when one of these two tendencies is no longer felt for it is then that fidelity will be in jeopardy.

One last remark must be added. The equipment required by the specific work of an Order may well not belong to it, but to some private or public management in whose service the religious are employed. Hospitals with their laboratories and operating theatres and the specialised nursing called for by modern medicine, even when under the direction of influential secular managements, can be run by religious nursing brothers or sisters. It is possible indeed that this employment of sisters is likely to assume greater proportions in modern society which is inclined to nationalise or at least to group in large units all sorts of undertakings or institutions and no longer deals with affairs save in large and comprehensive categories. That is, possibly, a fortunate circumstance ; it allows for a proper use in poverty of extremely costly equipment since it makes such use doubly dependent—the dependence of the workman who does not own the tools he uses, and that of the religious who refers everything to his superior. From this point of view the position of religious Orders varies considerably from one country to another. France nowadays possesses, under the control and authority of the episcopate, federations of religious congregations according to certain wide classifications (federations of nursing sisters, of teaching sisters, of sisters doing parish work). If on this point there were important adaptations to be made in the Constitutions of an Order by reason of such a situation, it may well be thought that a method of comparing notes on these lines would be of assistance in effecting numerous adjustments.

Conclusion

This brings us to one of the conclusions that may be gathered from the present report : the actual position from the point of view of timely adaptations of the religious state may vary considerably according to geographical or sociological regions. Local authorities on occasion can be better judges of detail than a central power entrusted with the common good of a wide and scattered jurisdiction. Has the religious state to be the same everywhere ? In the ninth or eleventh centuries it was very different indeed from what it has become. It is now in labour to adapt itself to a world which is not advancing everywhere at the same rate. The central authority, while upholding rigidly the essential foundation of every form of the religious state, will doubtless prefer to promise a certain flexibility either for adaptations in each congregation or for those that are required by the local, regional or national federations of congregations. What must be restored, principally, is the spirit. Now in each congregation the spirit is dependent on those entrusted with the training of the young religious. To keep a careful watch on the quality of the instructors of the religious state would seem to be the primary duty of the major superiors. Training sessions should ensure that they enjoy wide human contacts and a lofty spiritual culture ; these are essential conditions for any effort at adaptation of present day religious.

CHAPTER VI

CONTEMPLATIVES AND THEIR WORK

By Fr. ELISEE DE LA NATIVITE, O.C.D.

This chapter is concerned with a particular and concrete aspect of religious poverty, namely the poverty of contemplative nuns confronted with the exacting requirements of modern life and brought into close contact with modern society by undertaking remunerative work.[1]

How has this problem arisen ? Between the two world wars, and especially at the time, from 1936 onwards, when the Popular Front was in power, the whole question of the means of subsistence of contemplative communities in modern society became particularly acute. Large fortunes, which can maintain a whole monastery are a thing of the past ; the income from dowries is clearly inadequate and almost extinct in view of the rise in the cost of living. A Cardinal-Archbishop told a community of Carmelites in about 1935 : 'The time will come, in twenty years perhaps, when you will be obliged to take up some work to be able to live, a clinic or dispensary or something in that line.' Many bishops, responsible superiors, or chaplains were asking the same question regarding the future of contemplative nuns.

The second great war hastened events. At the time of the Liberation it was no longer a matter of asking questions or trying experiments, but finding a solution at once for all such

[1] This chapter deals particularly with Carmelites. The problems raised by remunerative work are practically the same for other contemplatives, but the exceptional case of the Poor Clares should be mentioned. As a general rule, faithful to the spirit of St Clare, they refuse all payment for their work. Fr Gustave, O.F.M., has supplied us with the following note on this subject :
'In France there are about sixty houses of Poor Clares with about 1,500 nuns in all (most of them Colettines). There are very rarely less than twenty or more than forty nuns in a convent. An investigation carried out in some forty monasteries showed that the economic problem appears as very simple in them. Work takes up four to five hours a day and is held in honour. But the Poor Clares work "to avoid idleness and to give a good example" (St Francis) and also to show their gratitude to benefactors or to help with the maintenance of sacristies. Paid work is an exception and, generally speaking, it can be said that the French Poor Clares have as their chief and usually adequate means of subsistence the alms collected by their out sisters.'

communities by making use of experience already acquired, or else many of them would have been burdened with debt or overwhelmed with anxiety. Work which provided 25% of the income of a monastery had now to account for 60 to 70%. This need for action did more to provide a solution of the problem and to ensure that directions were received with submission than all the remarks and sermons which, though based on common sense, appeared to be abstract or too revolutionary. For seven years we have been engaged on this task, experimenting, noting successes and failures, comparing methods in order to choose the best. Now the problem is solved to the extent that it can be asserted that contemplative nuns, at least so far as communities of twenty to fifty members are concerned, are not necessarily doomed to what some people term, also in this connexion, 'structural reforms'. Nevertheless it must be made clear to the nuns that a serious effort of adaptation is required of them both in their outlook on the subject of work and in the organisation of this work.

The subject will be studied here from this twofold point of view: (1) Education of the nuns' outlook. (2) Organisation of the work.

Their religious outlook requires education (a) on the idea of the contemplative life (b) regarding supererogatory penances and (c) customs which are a hindrance to work.

The rational organisation of work in contemplative communities will be studied especially under these three heads : (a) quality (b) production (c) markets.

Of course the twin effort of education of outlook and organisation of work should proceed simultaneously ; it is here treated successively for convenience of arrangement.[1]

---

[1] The information here given is based on experience gained by contact with Carmelite monasteries. Fr Marie-Eugène de l'Enfant Jesus, Definitor General O.C.D. and Apostolic Visitor of the French Carmels, and also Fr Louis de Sainte-Thérèse, O.C.D., Provincial of the Avignon-Aquitaine province, have had to deal with the same problems and our conclusions agree so far as the main lines of this study are concerned. Our experience is based on approximately 150 Carmels in France. It should be borne in mind that a Carmel, including the turn-sisters, contains an average of twenty to twenty-five members. What is here laid down could be applied with the necessary slight changes to contemplative communities containing between twenty and thirty nuns. It should also be remembered, in order to understand what follows, that a Carmelite nun's timetable, as fixed by St Teresa of Avila, enables two hours to be given to work in the morning, one hour after the midday recreation and two hours in the afternoon between Vespers and the mental prayer at 5 p.m., without in any way lessening the time given to religious exercises or reading.

I

For several years past we have endeavoured to educate the outlook of contemplative nuns on the subject of work ; our efforts have lately been greatly assisted and facilitated by the recent directions of the Holy See which throw considerable light on this subject ; and at this point these precise directions must be quoted for thereby the work of contemplatives receives as it were, the very highest patent of nobility. These are the words of His Holiness Pope Pius XII in the Constitution *Sponsa Christi*. 'As regards manual or intellectual work all men and women without exception, who devote themselves to the contemplative life, are bound to it not only by the natural law but also by an obligation of penance and satisfaction. Besides, work is generally the means by which the soul is preserved from dangers and is raised up to the heights ; through it, as is proper, we collaborate with divine Providence both in the natural order and in that which surpasses nature whereby works of charity are practised. Work, lastly, is the principal rule and law of the religious life and has been from its beginnings, as is shown by the maxim "Pray and work". Certainly the discipline of religious life has, to a great extent, always been based on the command to work and the methods of organising and carrying it out.

'Nuns' work, seen from the view point of eternity should be of the kind that, in the first place, she who undertakes it does so with a holy intention, thinking often of the presence of God ; she should accept it out of obedience and voluntarily join to it her personal mortification. Work carried out in this way will form a constant exercise in all the virtues and a pledge of that marvellous and effective union between the contemplative and active lives after the example of the family of Nazareth.'[1]

In the general statutes for nuns published at the end of this Constitution the following passage should be noticed :

'Nuns, for their part, are bound in conscience not only to earn their daily bread honourably and in the sweat of their brow, as the Apostles teaches, but also to make themselves, as our times require, daily more fitted for and more skilful at their various tasks.'

[1] Const. *Sponsa Christi*.

I am not sure that the importance of these quotations in their bearing on the contemplative life has been realised, even among priests. They cut short a controversy in which the case for one side was founded on apparently irrefutable arguments. We had to contend with nuns or superiors who insisted on the primacy of the life of union with God which was to be preserved against the outside world, not only by enclosure but by a whole body of regulations or customs intended to safeguard recollection. They were determined that the *pia quies* of nuns should be safeguarded and protected against every contingency, that work should be interrupted by prayer and that it should not be too exacting lest fatigue should hamper the soul in its ascent to God. This outlook is exemplified in the following quotation from the Imitation : 'Never be entirely idle, but read, or write, or pray or meditate or do some work of use to the community. But manual work must be undertaken with prudence and it is not suitable for all' (Bk. I, ch.19). Some superiors, imbued with the mentality hinted at by this passage from a book very properly held in reverence as a code of monastic life, protested against this rationalisation, 'modern methods of standardisation, ghastly terms like production and, in short, against materialism obtruding itself on the loftiest spheres of the spiritual life'.

We were by no means as indifferent to these objections as might have been supposed in the present state of affairs. It cannot be questioned that the contemplative life is fostered to greater advantage in a certain liberty of spirit even with regard to considerations of a material nature. We know that from experience among Carmelites of the male branch wherein during a whole year's noviciate, before the professed embarked on studies of a very absorbing nature, we took care to protect them, during their daily two hours of manual labour, from this preoccupation with production. But when it was a question of nuns and of the whole course of their lives, on the one hand we were urged on by pressing necessity, a real matter of life or death for communities unable to survive if they continued to follow old methods, and on the other there was our own experience of a life also dedicated to continual prayer, to seeking union with God and that in spite of advanced studies and, on occasion, of exacting apostolic work. It was our experience, too, that whatever is willed by God is not an insurmountable obstacle to union with him. At the beginning there may be a certain difficulty of adaptation, on some days anxiety or mental strain incompatible with recollection ; but taken altogether, a true contemplative life is possible despite the absence of that *otium*, that *quies*, which some people consider indispensable. Therefore relying on this experience and supported, now, by the directions of the Holy See we must insist on the fact that work, taking up all the time between the hours of the Office, save for the periods of recreation, and conceived without exaggeration in accordance with modern methods of production, is not incompatible with recollection and union with God.

Another remark of the Holy Father's may be urged in support of this policy of education : it is that work is 'an obligation of penance and satisfaction'. All forms of contemplative life comprise customs of supererogatory penance.

The following is a summary discussion of this question of extra penances among the Carmelites ; it sheds light on the subject also in connexion with other Orders such as the Poor Clares, Cistercians and many branches of Benedictine nuns.

The Teresan reform was not confined to revival of the primitive Carmelite Rule or merely abiding by the Constitutions drawn up by St Teresa of Jesus. Very soon it instituted the custom of extra penances, night watches, hair-shirts, more rigorous fasting. Far from dropping these customs the Fathers and the Sisters in the French seventeenth century added to them, with further inventions inspired by de Rance's reform. When, in the nineteenth century, occurred the restoration of religious life, romanticism involved our Fathers and Sisters in still further feats ; stories are still told of those trunks filled with instruments of penance which were known as the 'tombs of nature'. In fact, 'nature' had to be 'killed', the 'spirit of death' was to be practised. Watching until midnight (with 4.30 a.m. as the time for rising) or during the whole night once a week, were practices held in particular honour. Those who took their sanctification to heart were generally noticeable by their fidelity to these customs. St Teresa of the Child Jesus seems to have been an exception ; in this way also she became the saint of modern times, for the psychological endurance of the present generation can scarcely bear more than what is effectively prescribed by the Carmelite Rule and the Constitutions of St Teresa of Jesus. The problem of work has made it urgently necessary to give up these numerous extra penances. It is impossible to work steadily, to occupy usefully the periods of time between the Offices, with only three or four hours sleep a night, with insufficient calories, and if movement is continually hampered by a hair shirt or iron chains. But work, by obliging the nun to make careful use of her free time, imposes on her also a very real penance. She is obliged to give up those periods of silent, solitary relaxation during which an additional period of reading, composition of spiritual notes, perhaps a long correspondence with her director, enabled her to avoid idleness and to snatch certain consolations from the religious life. How much harder may life be nowadays with no other respite than the community recreation ? That forms, it must be acknowledged, a new penance which, accepted in a spirit of faith and confidence, can with every advantage take the place of the former extra penances. In addition, this penance possesses the advantage of bringing the nuns' life, from the point of view of self-sacrifice, into greater harmony with the self-sacrifice of most people who are nowadays tied to their daily work.

When a community has been convinced of the possibility of uniting a working life with an authentic contemplative life, and of the necessity of accepting this in a spirit of penance, there remains the need to make it give up those customs and practices which are incompatible with real production.

There is no question here, it should be emphasized, of the Rule or Constitutions approved by the Holy See, but of customs common to a group of monasteries or practices peculiar to certain houses. This question of customs crops up at every phase of modern adaptation of the religious life, it is treated here in so far as it concerns work in monasteries.

The quantity of customs that it has been necessary to override and get rid of in order to ensure productive work is considerable. We may be allowed to mention some of them : the multiplication of prayers and invocations, litanies and processions added on to the Office and to the two hours of mental prayer ; keeping as holidays the feasts formerly of obligation in the seventeenth century, such as the Invention of the Cross, the Apostles or St Lawrence ; the practice of decorating the Church on all first class feasts without distinction as on the great festivals of the year with, on each occasion, a profusion of plants and artificial flowers necessitating stands, in accordance with the taste of fifty years ago ; the practice of asking the prioress's permission for every little detail, as novices are usually required to do, involving any number of little notes and useless conversations ; waiting at the prioress's door where, standing in a queue, it is practically impossible to produce genuine work ; in the infirmary, the invention of all sorts of little jobs for the infirmarian which withdraw her from the community even when there is no one seriously ill or there are no patients in the proper sense of the word ; the endless mending of old habits or the affectation of sewing everything by hand on the plea that sewing machines were not admitted in convents in past ages.

This adaptation by suppressing old customs requires also, in a spirit of poverty, the modernisation of plant, in the kitchen for example, the laundry or the nuns' work room. The introduction of modern apparatus is an absolute obsession with some and a continual anxiety to many. But it should be possible to replace unreasoning instinct and sentiment by cold reasoning which may well be embraced in an entirely supernatural spirit. A courageous outlay of £200 might easily be offset in two years by improved production ; a machine which appears to be made only for comfort can, by abolishing useless fatigue, make possible sustained work which, carried out under deleterious conditions, would end by becoming inhuman.

I am not saying that all established customs are to be swept aside without heed or discrimination. A certain adroitness is required whenever old customs or traditions are attacked ; otherwise superiors may act as they please and out of caprice so that in the end the unfortunate result is a community at loggerheads. But with wisdom and patience the suppression or simplification of customs must be undertaken, and certain of them require immediate action if other efforts to increase output are not to be neutralised. Obstinate fidelity to these traditions, solely on the principle that it is always dangerous to change anything at all, can become in reality a veritable breach of poverty.

To furnish a practical solution to this problem nuns must be taught the real nature of monastic obedience ; they must be given the essential notions of Canon and religious law so that they make an intellectual distinction between laws of the Church or the Order and practices prescribed by custom or the habits of daily life. We must insist that their minds must first be informed. With some irony we have mentioned a short list of customs to be rooted out ; it should be added that while humour may be employed on occasion the better to demonstrate what idols are to be cast down, care must be taken not to stop at this point and the surrender of outmoded traditions should be given its rightful place in the scheme of religious perfection and shown as a real collaboration with Providence at work in souls and institutions.

II

We have now to consider another side of the problem, the *organisation of work* and, in the first place, the *quality* of this work.

To begin with the products themselves must be mentioned. If superiors in closer touch with the outside world do not keep a careful eye on the work done, there is some risk that monasteries will produce what is badly done or waste their time in turning out old-fashioned embroidery or vestments of a kind which gave satisfaction thirty or fifty years ago but nowadays, thank God, satisfy a rapidly diminishing religious clientèle. The work must be well carried out, therefore, perfect indeed when it is an artistic object, and what is made, however well done, must not be old-fashioned. Novices are formed by nuns who became religious twenty or thirty years ago ; they have to obey, submit their judgement, disregard their own taste and their knowledge of clients' requirements. Sometimes they are obliged to paint devotional pictures or do embroidery of a kind which they are well aware is entirely outmoded, but they dare say nothing. It behoves superiors to keep in touch with fashion and the prevailing taste, if need be, by consulting their younger subjects. But that is not enough. It is necessary, nowadays, to have one or several specialists who will criticise and correct the workmanship of a convent and be able to secure that the product is not only saleable but that its value corresponds with the time taken to make it.

There is another special point to be mentioned in connexion with the quality of work. Generally speaking, nuns possess a culture, an education which enables them to do work, delicate embroidery for example, which has a higher market value than plainer work (like knitting). It is obvious that a monastery which was satisfied with doing knitting would be a long way from reaching the normal level of income in this way. Of course, this only holds good where some choice is available. Very possibly there is nothing for it but to sell potatoes, stick on labels or address envelopes, but if some effort at learning can secure better paid work, this effort should be made. Some artistic work will make anything from three to four shillings an hour. When possible, advantage should be taken of this. Such calculations may seem to smack of commercialism, but in reality they are a form of the practice of poverty.

When the question of the kind of work has been settled production must be put on a proper footing. It is undoubtedly a ghastly word, but it is necessary to realise what our aim is. We may as well admit the term into our language at the same time as what it signifies into our conduct if we are to safeguard the pure contemplative life.

Production must be secured in the first place by scrupulous respect for the working timetable. We mentioned the education required to obtain the surrender of customs which prevent there being a sufficient number of hours free for work. Once these hours have been provided for, the nuns should be induced, to a certain extent at least, to undergo that form of discipline which consists in beginning on time and working until the end of it. It is as good a way of renunciation as another, and unless it is carried out all that has been mentioned elsewhere in this chapter will be devoid of meaning and lead to but mediocre results. The contemplative, either tempera- mentally or from habit, evinces a certain distrust of too strict a material organisation, of anything that is too mathematically exact. Such an attitude may be justified in purely spiritual matters. There is no objection to St John of the Cross saying that he proposes to give a commentary on several verses, then dwelling at length of the first and finishing abruptly. When material work is in question the strict discipline of which we have spoken is required.

For this purpose and in order at the same time to enjoy the advantage of better knowledge of customers or prices, it is a good idea for the work to be put in charge of a well-qualified nun who can superintend it as a whole. In the first place superiors must admit that, nowadays especially, they cannot know and direct everything themselves alone. On the one hand they have too much to do, on the other modern life is too complicated to enable one woman to have everything at her finger's end. Then the Sisters ought to be at least as submissive as an ordinary factory worker who would never claim to have dealings only with her employer but accepts a foreman as go-between. The creation of a special post so that a nun who is more gifted in this way can supervise the whole question of production and sales is a great help to better production.

Such an organisation, as in modern businesses, implies a period of training. Up till now each monastery has provided its own system, haphazardly, and in accordance with its own limited means. But life is hard, and the continual rise in the cost of living calls for an improvement in the earning capacity of nuns' work. Sometimes, in order to organise successfully, it is necessary for a qualified worker to be brought into the monasteries of the same group so that she can train the young nuns in a trade with which she is familiar ; or else the young nuns can be sent to a monastery which already has such a qualified worker. The S. Congregation has said that it will authorise these exits even where papal enclosure is in force. The federations envisaged by the new Apostolic constitution should allow these improvements to be effected.

There is another question in connexion with organisation. Should all the nuns of a monastery each be required to furnish a certain minimum of work per day or should preference be given to the plan whereby a definite number of nuns specialises in it, leaving to others the various offices of the house, prioress, mistress of novices, bursar, if necessary combining two offices in one, such as sacristan and infirmarian ? Either method must be employed according to the available resources of the monastery. When it is possible specialisation by five or six nuns who work five hours a day on an average of five days a week, for fifty weeks a year, produces a distinctly higher output. With the addition of the work of some of the officers of the house, when they have time free for it, it appears that this is the better method.

Once the quality of the work and the output have been disposed of, the further question of markets arises. It can be said at once that where the directions we have given are followed, the organisation just described has been, or can be, effectively carried out providing the necessary good will is present. The problem of a market for the finished product, at least for a fair proportion of monasteries, remains to be solved. It is a question of a technical factor which should be planned on a national scale and requires something more than advice given by a superior.

A certain number of monasteries have discovered sufficient markets for their work and these appear to be assured for some time to come. They can be left to go on in this way and merely helped so to organise their work that these markets are maintained. But there are other communities which complain that, when they organised themselves in accordance with the principles that have here been explained, they were unable to dispose of the goods they produced. There are many reasons for this : sometimes the situation of the monastery in the country or in a small town, or else the fact that there are several contemplative communities in the neighbourhood ; the kind of work in which a community has specialised is no longer needed in the district, either because new enterprises have been started in the same neighbourhood or because what was practicable when commodities were rationed is no longer so when they are plentiful.

This is what has been done about this problem. To begin with M. Echivard has specialised in finding the necessary markets, and has done this work with all the fervour of a pioneer. Then, too, the Paris diocesan branch of the *Aide aux Prêtres* kindly undertook to help contemplatives and we were able to supply the address of Mother Bergasse, of the Sisters of the Cenacle, who has been of the greatest help to some monasteries. But all this is much less than is required. To obtain adequate results there was needed an organisation on a national scale to find markets in France and elsewhere, stimulate sales, supply raw materials at wholesale prices, and provide specialists qualified to criticise the work and rectify mistakes so as to secure the required standard or a higher output.

Here it may be objected that such a plan raises problems concerning taxation, relations with trade associations or workers' unions. And indeed an organisation such as has been sketched above must comprise legal and other experts who will be able to help the nuns to deal with this new state of affairs. It will also possess the advantage of preventing the monasteries from harming each other's interests by sharing out the work according to the needs of each case. Directly we adopt the ideas and terminology of modern industry we must be prepared for that danger to arise which is signified by the word, and the reality, of competition.

The Committee for the aid of cloistered nuns was set up to deal with the whole series of problems of this nature : it is made up of members of the Hierarchy, regular superiors, specially qualified nuns and lay industrial and legal experts. It has been approved by the assembly of Cardinals and Archbishops for action on a national scale.[1]

It was the establishment of this committee which served as inspiration to the following article of the Instruction of the S. Congregation of Religious, published at the end of the Constitution *Sponsa Christi* :

'Ecclesiastical and religious superiors must seek and obtain for enclosed nuns by every means in their power the remunerative work which they need, by making use, should the occasion arise, and in addition to other methods, of the co-operation of devout men and women and even, with due precaution and prudence, of outside societies founded for this purpose ; they must keep prudent watch on the proper execution and arrangement of the work, and organise carefully the co-ordination of the enterprises and work of the different monasteries so that they

---

[1] See below chapter VII for further particulars on the subject of this committee. Although the details given in this and the following chapter apply exclusively to France, in view of their relevance to conditions that are not by any means confined to that country they have been maintained in this English edition of the book. (Tr.)

help relieve or complement each other and that every form of rivalry is entirely absent.'

In conclusion my final words are an assertion of my confidence in the future of contemplatives. Modern society which has caused the disappearance of so many institutions and threatens the suppression of many others, may impose on them new ways of life but will not abolish them. It has been proved by experience, it seems to us, that *they will survive* provided that their responsible superiors help them to do so, and that efforts like the present conference[1] show them the way. If our experiment in this country turns out successfully we shall blaze a trail for others, especially in Spain and Italy. The Constitution *Sponsa Christi* mentions the pitiful conditions of nuns 'who unfortunately are almost starving, are destitute and in extreme want . . . They lead lives of dreadful difficulty which, for the most part, are too hard to bear.' Those words are not, as some have been tempted to think, merely the rhetorical style of the Roman curia. It is literally true that communities of enclosed nuns in Mediterranean countries suffer from hunger to a degree beyond that required by a penitential life. The solution here offered appears to be the most timely and the most effective. And by the same token we are serving an ideal which is dear to all who lead a religious life, the ideal of poverty.

Of course the contemplative life, sustained in this way by organised work, will demand of its adepts more generous and constant efforts at recollection. But the advantages of this new system in relation to poverty are obvious. Ancient monastic traditions are honoured once again : the young who enter the cloister no longer feel somewhat uncomfortable at a life which is outside the present difficulties of the generality of mankind. Nuns live in greater likeness to the poor of Jesus Christ who to-day are workers relentlessly chained to their labours. And for the same reason they live in greater harmony with the life of the Church who, without failing in her mission of charity, is unable to remain indifferent to the conditions of men whose lives are given up to labour.

[1] At which this chapter was read as a paper. (Tr.)

Chapter VII

THE CLOISTER AND COMMERCE

By J. De Vaux

We shall examine first the data of the problem and then the proposed solutions.

I

Basic principles

Work—and manual work especially—is certainly not incompatible with enclosed religious life. Does the same hold good of remunerative work? Current practice and recent Roman decisions should allay any anxiety on that score. The assistance of laymen and of commercial enterprises outside the cloister has even been considered as an aid to nuns in their work.

Organisation

No change has been made, however, in the requirements of Canon Law forbidding the buying of goods for re-sale in an unchanged state—i.e. engaging in ordinary retail trade. The authorised activities consists, as a rule, of work in common or by teams, directed or assembled by the superior.

The setting up of an independent company provides a right solution to various legal problems, but it involves the intervention of a third party and is somewhat disproportionate to the limited requirements of some communities.

When it is a question merely of workmanship, that is of working up customers own materials, a superior can negotiate with a contractor in the name of the *de facto* company constituted by those who do the work. But in no case should these latter be classed as 'home' or 'craft' workers. It has been recognised by the courts that nuns cannot acquire the proceeds of their work nor enter personally into a contract for work.

Practical considerations

The choice of suitable work is a matter of some delicacy. Products that are unsaleable must be avoided and those sought that are adapted to nuns and enclosed religious life. In most cases if raw materials are not provided the agency of a commercial organisation should be utilised in order to secure factory prices. For most kinds of professional work training ought not to be obtained by self-instruction but should be directed by competent persons. Exchange of instructors should be considered. Even the artistic or practical planning of the work should receive as much careful thought as the training of the staff to carry it out.

Markets should be sought methodically.

Financial aspects

The financial question does not arise for work done on customer's own materials. But in other cases it can become very acute either for the nuns themselves or the organisation which renders them assistance. When no separate company with its own finances has been set up, working capital or capital tied up in raw materials, perhaps to a considerable amount, may prove to be a difficult matter. The possibility should be envisaged of calling upon religious institutions in a position to help with gifts or loans, or upon the general public that may be moved by the precarious situation of the nuns or by their intention of supporting themselves by their work.

One aspect of the financial question is to be found in the amount that may be deducted by taxation from the proceeds of work. Of course whatever tax is due should be the object of special study in order to avoid over-assessment. The fundamental financial problem concerns the conditions of allocation to communities of the proceeds of their work. In the case of a contract for work to be done signed by a superior in the name of the community, the superior receives the amount due for the work in the name of the community. This need have no serious results from a taxation point of view. The case is no different if the whole output of work done is sold to a shopkeeper or business man.

Forms of contract have already been prepared which, by various devices, enable a community to share in the proceeds of an external commercial undertaking with which the nuns co-operate by their work.

II

To secure the realisation of a certain number of the desiderata that have been expressed and of the plans that have been formulated, influential authorities have considered it opportune to set up an organisation that would be able to second the nuns' efforts. Through it influential patrons would make known the nuns' financial requirements, persons competent in the matter would examine their needs, organise market research, professional training and eventually the management of undertakings suited to the requirements of the work of enclosed orders.

General activities

The primary necessity was to set up a central organisation to formulate a scheme and put it in operation.

A central committee was formed under the presidency of Cardinal Feltin, Archbishop of Paris, comprising a certain number of the superiors of the Orders to which enclosed nuns are affiliated. Its function is to be morally responsible for the movement in relation to the episcopate, the religious orders and the laity on whose assistance it relies. It will be kept informed of the activities of the central organisation, and of the planning of the work.

An authorised association under the French law 1st July, 1901, has been established with the title *l'Aide au travail des cloîtres*. An effort has been made to combine on its council— on which the members of the central committee may sit— commercial, industrial, financial and legal experts ; a representative of the nuns is present at its meetings. The general meetings of the Association are presided over by the President of the central committee.

The object of the Association is to look for, and put in touch with each other, those who want work done and those who require it, to help with technical and artistic training and also the organisation of the work by advice and by establishing relations with persons qualified in the various trades, to give guidance on financial and legal matters, and eventually to function as an agency and legal depository in seeking and collecting funds.

The establishment of a commercial company, in the legal sense of the word, has been planned and its articles of association drawn up ; but it appears inopportune at the present moment to proceed further in the matter.

Local action

It would be fanciful, and indeed harmful, to try to centralise the whole movement in one place.

It is indispensable, of course, that research should not be scattered in different places, that the examination of legal, commercial and taxation questions be kept together and a single policy adopted, that government offices should not be approached unnecessarily, that contradictory solutions of fundamental problems should not be adopted locally for reasons of facility or of submission to the unreasonable requirements of government departments, industrialists or business men. But market research, technical training, appeals for financial aid will certainly be better organised and more fruitful if local co-operation is obtained. A national centre may usefully be established for the service of all according to the means at its disposal ; on no account should it have rights of control.

Results achieved

A brisk correspondence has enabled some of the needs and possibilities of enclosed nuns to be discovered. A methodical investigation will be carried out to obtain still better knowledge of all sides of the problem. Orders from traders and industrialists have been received and passed on to those requiring work. The perfecting of certain techniques is being planned. Large contracts have been discussed with industrialists. Model contracts have been drawn up and passed on to superiors. The incidence of taxation has been studied in conferences between legal experts and tax officials.

It is unfortunately quite certain that many religious houses are suffering from financial distress, that some have not the slightest idea what they can do to remedy this, that others seek in vain to make productive some type of work, which they recognise as not incompatible with their vocation, and that certain abilities remain merely potential for the lack of guidance.

With the approval of the Holy See measures have been proposed to remedy this sad state of affairs. From these convents no complaints are heard, but an ardent desire for work and a call for help. The *Aide au travail des cloîtres* offers its collaboration in providing an answer to this appeal.

Chapter VIII

THE NEED FOR ACCOUNTANCY

By Dom Pierre Doyere, monk of Wisques

Any study of religious poverty would be incomplete unless it drew the attention of Superiors to their duty in the management of temporal affairs, of perfecting an adequate system of accountancy. For the object of accountancy is, in fact, to record all administrative transactions, in order to facilitate their recall, make their consequences clear and enable them to be checked.

St Benedict Joseph Labre had no need to worry about book-keeping ; but when the circumstances of religious life involve the management of funds and property, whatever its nature, care must be taken over it by reason of the vow of poverty which requires avoidance of waste and confusion. The keeping of proper accounts is consequently the duty of those who have funds and property in their care.

The humble housewife cannot avoid some form of elementary book-keeping, even if all that it amounts to is a list of purchases after shopping to make sure that the money in her purse is correct. The bursar who kept no books and, for example, made shift with throwing the money into a drawer and storing her purchases in a cellar to be drawn on as required, would certainly sin against poverty. Such negligence is a form of wastefulness even when it goes hand in hand with niggardliness in buying.

The same sort of incomprehension, together with a disarming candour, is to be found in certain methods of managing funds. There is no concern about an unexplained surplus because there exists certainty in conscience of having cheated no one ; nor about a deficit with nothing to show for it, on the ground that since the money is no longer there it must have been spent.

Neither a superior's indifference to figures nor a bursar's diffidence in desiring and finding a better method of accountancy will bear examination. 'To be a waster,' runs a French proverb, 'requires an innate gift, but anyone can become a cook' by training. Such is book-keeping ; we have but to learn it. To pretend that it is all too complicated is no valid excuse. Repugnance to set about learning it is a relic of the prejudice against the commercial mentality and is beside the point. For in the case of a religious community one of the essential reasons for accountancy is to provide a clear picture of the material situation, and **thus** furnish the surest way of avoiding slavery to it.

Experience shows that no one is more tied up in problems of accountancy—just as in legal matters and official records—than those who profess to be entirely unconcerned by them.

Want of time is an excuse that can be no longer admitted. Confusion is at least quite as costly, for by force of circumstances, on one day or other, some item of financial information will be required which properly kept books would enable to be found without trouble and which, in their absence, requires unending, complicated and unreliable research.

The function of a system of book-keeping is to furnish knowledge on the state and progress of affairs, accurately, promptly and clearly. It seems hardly possible to imagine circumstances in which this view would not be of great benefit to a community even in respect of its spiritual aims. But, at the present juncture, the economic position is of such importance that it is a matter of urgency to perfect the system of accountancy as the very means which enables it to be verified and controlled. The problem of remunerative work for nuns, recognised by the Constitution *Sponsa Christi* as a topical question, increases the urgency. All those who have any responsibility in this matter—those in charge of work rooms, bursars, superiors, ecclesiastical authorities and, in the last resort central and mutual-aid organisations—are here concerned.

The primary condition is to believe that there is a problem. Once this conviction is held the rest is easy ; all that remains is the question of technical education, save in those cases where, fortunately, members competent in the matter have come to the community with their training already done in the world. This technical training should be received by at least two persons in the community, the bursar and the superior ; their needs are different however.

All systems of book-keeping starting with the Journal lead,

by way of the Ledger, to the income and expenditure account and the balance sheet. The bursar's technical education should be comprehensive ; she should know how to post the various transactions, understand and follow them and, finally, balance the books and prepare the income and expenditure account. It is sufficient for the superior to learn to interpret the results and the final account.

Of course a religious house has other aims than a commercial undertaking, and does not expect the same qualities in its administrative staff ; but it is obvious that mere amateurish good-will can in no department take the place of all other qualifications. No one nowadays would doubt the necessity of professional training for teaching, nursing or social work. Likewise in the domestic life of the convent, without going to extremes of specialisation, some form of training is needed to be an organist, to cook, to knit, for bee-keeping, to undertake book-binding, to fatten pigs, or anything else. We should make sure that there is proper training in keeping accounts and drawing up the balance sheet.

How is this technical training to be provided ? Courses and text books on book-keeping may be useful. But only in part, since they are intended to prepare young students for an executive position in commerce or industry and it will hardly be necessary to make use of any save the preliminary introductory chapters dealing with principles, purpose, categories and methods on the one hand, and, possibly, a few rules concerning keeping the accounts in good material order. For the application and organisation of the system adapted to the special needs of the community a suitable training must be sought elsewhere.

Perhaps at this stage the best training will be derived from oral teaching on the spot. In other words, either the person in question takes a course in a house where there is a proper system of accountancy or someone may come to explain the new methods as they are introduced. In this way it is possible to proceed with moderation and circumspection and in a religious spirit. Generally it will be better to begin with what is there already and improve and complete it, and by subjecting it to the fundamental rules, transform it into a real system of book-keeping rather than of set purpose to abolish one system in order to inaugurate another one ready-made. The accountancy needs of most religious houses are those of a family rather than of a business management, and thus make for a certain flexibility in technical requirements.

Where there exists a real industry, worked by the religious, it forms a case apart. Then it is practically indispensable to separate the two series of accounts—those of the house and those of the industry, the latter being arranged on a strictly business footing and, preferably, with the assistance of a professional.

Accountancy, rather than a science or an art, is a craft. One of minor importance, no doubt, but the discipline of every craft benefits those who welcome it. In this case it calls for the virtues of justice and prudence and inspires a fondness for order and clarity ; the finest spiritual ideal has nothing to fear from what contributes, all said and done, to a realistic outlook.

CHAPTER IX

PRINCIPLES OF ORGANISATION

By GEORGES TOUTIN

The problem has already been stated clearly; communities must do remunerative work in order to meet those material and economic needs which cannot be disregarded as of entirely no account beside the spiritual life which forms the purpose of the Order.

I shall confine myself, then, solely to the question of work considered from the organiser's point of view. In a Carmel of twenty to twenty-three nuns it is by no means easy to carry out remunerative work on account of the small numbers available to do it. This circumstance renders it necessary to employ far more method in order to save time on ordinary duties (housework etc.). In fact, this is the first point to be settled before seeking locally for tasks which can be done at home and scrutinising them carefully in order to choose that which gives the best return, bearing in mind the possibilities of training offered by modern methods. These can be applied under the conditions set out below.

I have been led therefore to arrange this chapter as follows:
- I. How to save time on ordinary duties.
- II. Choice of work—some points about cost price.
- III. Method of training.
- IV. Organisation of remunerative work.
- V. Conclusions.

I. HOW TO SAVE TIME ON ORDINARY DUTIES

It is to be feared that in a convent where the aim is contemplation the idea of time is apt to be forgotten in the face of other considerations, and that often the method of work adopted has been chosen with economy in mind and with the mistaken notion that time costs nothing. This is a point of view that must be changed in the first place, since every hour that is freed can be productive and bring in X pounds for the community if it is passed in remunerative work. The first stage is, then, 'save time on ordinary duties'. To this end I propose that an analysis be made of the use of time and advise each nun who desires to obtain a notion of the meaning of time to draw up each day a chart of employment on the lines of the model below :

HOURS	7	8	9	10	11	12	1	2	3	4	5	6	7

Sister Y   .............----------------******.........****------------------------..........

Sister T   ..........*****----------------.........**------------------**..........

.... Community Horary (for Office, Meals, Recreation)

********** Free time

-------------- Work time (enter description of work done by each nun)

Analysis of the chart

Analysis of these charts will bring out clearly :
    —actual free time
    —time which is spent on useless trifles
    —time which can be set free immediately for remunerative work.

Next each item of work must be analysed in the light of the answers to these questions :

Is it necessary to do this particular task so often ?

Can it be done more quickly ?

Is time lost by needless coming and going, inadequate equipment, defective methods ?

For some repetitive activities an organiser would draw up an analytic chart of the time, for although it is difficult to discover the loss of time on a fairly long activity, it is easy to analyse it when the activity is broken down into elementary stages, each one of which can be examined in detail. This amounts to getting out a chart for work time on the same lines as that for the whole day.

Would it not be profitable to purchase machinery or equipment that would enable one or several hours a day to be saved ? This applies to a vacuum cleaner, mechanical polisher, washing machine, if they are not in use already.

Motion study, by determining the most efficient and least fatiguing movements, can lead to saving of time.

If in this way it is possible to save a few hours per nun it would be advantageous to confine these household tasks to a few nuns in order to free others completely.

II. CHOICE OF WORK—CALCULATION OF COST PRICE

A choice must be made from the work that is available in the locality of that which is most profitable. This brings us to the matter of the calculation of cost price.

The cost price of a piece of work comprises :
> labour costs together with the obligatory social insurances charges
> cost of material or apparatus
> a proportion of overhead costs.

Labour and material costs are generally easy enough to assign to all piece-work ; it is a different matter with the overhead costs. The method usually employed to apportion them is that of sectional estimates.

Without going into details a section can be defined as a group of men or machines carrying out work of the same kind.

Both productive sections and those that are complementary and unproductive, but of use to a part or the whole of the undertaking, must be considered.

In a convent the following division can be made :
> Productive sections :
>> Gardens
>> Poultry yard
>> Workrooms.
> Complementary sections :
>> Premises used for worship
>> Administrative offices
>> Departments for service of the community (kitchens, linen room, refectory, cells).

The overhead costs are entered in the books of account and should be apportioned in the accounts of the departments by means of coefficients corresponding with the nature of these costs ; for example :

rent costs in proportion to the value of the building or estate

insurance costs in proportion to the value of the building or estate

heating in proportion to the area of the premises

electricity in proportion to the power fitted.

This apportionment enables the relative costs of each department to be determined and for the expenses of production to be compared with the amount produced.

In industry where production is the sole aim the complementary departments are borne by the productive departments which, finally, should bear all expenses, reflecting them in the prices charged.

In the light of these principles, and making allowance for premises, equipment, staff and necessary materials, some sorts of work will appear more profitable than others, and this will be one of the factors when a choice is made.

In making this choice too much attention should not be paid to the difficulties of training for, by the method explained below, many processes can easily be learnt. If an Order is willing to make an effort to carry out remunerative work it appears to me to be possible to organise training, in spite of the difficulties of contact with the outside world.

III. TRAINING METHOD

The method here explained has stood the test of experience in many different fields. It enables the necessary movements or professional knowledge to be rapidly acquired. Without mentioning the engineering or building trades where it was first applied, I have personally studied and applied it to the training of workers in

Basket making ;
Ready-made dress-making ;
Spinning ;
and even Banks.

The principles of this pedagogical method, which are valid only in so far as they can be adapted to the technique to be learnt, are derived from the Cartesian mentality, from practical common sense and study of the needs of the learner (whatever his or her age). It regards the learner not only as a person with two arms and an intelligence but also as with a head and feelings which largely influence the employment of those arms and that intelligence.

I confine myself here to setting out the principles of the method which are :

Analyse the difficulties.

Treat each difficulty separately in an elementary exercise (this can be a simple matter of reasoning, appealing to common sense).

Take one difficulty at a time.

Do not go on to another difficulty until the preceding one has been disposed of or has become automatic (in the case of movements to be learned).

Teaching should be practical.

Base it on concrete first principles accepted by the pupil in order to guide her reasoning.

Teaching should be active (do not merely teach orally, but enable the pupil to discover).

Teaching should be productive.

When I was in a ready-made clothing factory where I had to train machinists for production I proceeded as follows :

  Selected the workers who were to undergo training

  Chose the simplest and most efficient movements.

Built up the method by :

  analysing the difficulties of each one of them treating each
    difficulty separately in an elementary exercise

  training an overseer (during planning of the method)

  training workers in four-week courses.

At the end of their course the workers with rational and efficient movements could make up all the articles of the women's ready-made dress trade, among others jumpers and dresses, which certain workers with several years experience in the workroom could only do imperfectly.

I trained these women for three or four months in a department not on production for them to acquire the rapidity of execution necessary in a department paid by results.

After this training they could earn as much bonus as workers with several years experience while producing goods frequently of a higher quality.

Application of this method

The problem consists in bringing technicians in training into touch with enclosed nuns. It might be done by means of active sisters who, trained as overseers, could teach in the monasteries.

IV. Organisation of remunerative work

The problem of planning the most efficient movements and the machinery required should be solved by the training methods. The lay-out of the workroom is all that remains for the most favourable material conditions to prevail. This planning could be undertaken by experts and introduced by the active sisters.

V. Conclusions

I believe that the principles sketched out above should be of very great assistance in the organisation of remunerative work in monasteries.

The value of time and computation of the cost price of a piece of work are the ideas that, it appears to me, would be the most useful to acquire before considering the possibilities of the pedagogical method explained above.

THE END